A HISTORY OF CHINA IN MAPS

Territories and Administrative Divisions

www.royalcollins.com

A HISTORY OF CHINA IN MAPS

Territories and Administrative Divisions

Li Xiaojie

Chief Editor: Ge Jianxiong

A History of China in Maps: Territories and Administrative Divisions

Li Xiaojie
Chief Editor: Ge Jianxiong
Translated by Zhang Jing

First published in 2023 by Royal Collins Publishing Group Inc.
Groupe Publication Royal Collins Inc.
BKM Royalcollins Publishers Private Limited

Headquarters: 550-555 boul. René-Lévesque O Montréal (Québec) H2Z1B1 Canada
India office: 805 Hemkunt House, 8th Floor, Rajendra Place, New Delhi 110 008

Original Edition © 2011 by Jiangsu People's Publishing House
This English edition is authorized by Jiangsu People's Publishing House.

All rights reserved. Without limiting the rights under copyright reserved above, no part of this publication may be reproduced, stored in or introduced into a retrieval system, or transmitted in any form or by any means (electronic, mechanical, photocopying, recording, or otherwise), without the prior written permission of both the copyright owner and the above publisher of this book.

ISBN: 978-1-4878-0934-8

To find out more about our publications, please visit www.royalcollins.com.

CONTENTS

Foreword   *ix*

CHAPTER ONE

Nine Provinces, Commanderies and Counties—Myths and Realities of Administrative Divisions in the Pre-Qin Period   1
1. The Nine Provinces and Five "Fu" in the Book of *Yu Gong*   *1*
2. Territories in the Shang and Zhou Dynasties   6
3. *Xian* (县, county) and Commanderies in the Spring and Autumn Period   9
4. Territories in the Warring States Period and the Commandery-County System   15

CHAPTER TWO

Unification—Territories and Administrative Divisions in the Qin and Han Dynasties   23
1. Expanding from 36 to 48 Commanderies   23
2. The Feoffment System in the Han Dynasty   28
3. Imperial Expansion in the Era of Emperor Wu   39
4. The Feoffment System and Commandery Changes in Eastern Han   46
5. The 13 Departments of Regional Inspectors and Regional Commissioners   56

6. Establishing Protectorates and the Office of Administrators in the Western Regions — 58

CHAPTER THREE
From the Three Kingdoms to the Eight-Prince Rebellions—Territories and Administrative Divisions in the Three Kingdoms and Western Jin — 65
1. Unifying Northern China — 67
2. Kingdom of Shu-Han Appeases the "Yi" Districts — 69
3. Kingdom of Wu Expanded to the Lingnan Districts — 70
4. Two Special Administrative Systems: Remote Control and Nominal Appointments — 71
5. The Western Jin Dynasty and the 21 Regions of the Yongjia Period — 72

CHAPTER FOUR
China Divided into Two Parts—Territories and Administrative Divisions during the Sixteen Kingdoms, Eastern Jin, and the Northern and Southern Dynasties — 79
1. Chaotic Borders of the Sixteen Kingdoms — 79
2. Colony Prefectures, Commanderies, and Counties — 89
3. Redundant Prefectures and Commanderies — 96
4. The "Six Garrisons" of Northern Wei — 97

CHAPTER FIVE
Territories of the "King of Heaven"—Territories and Administrative Divisions in the Sui, Tang, and the Five Dynasties and Ten Kingdoms Era — 101
1. Administration Reforms and Territorial Expansion in the Sui Dynasty — 101
2. Circuits in the Tang Dynasty — 107
3. Three Types of "Fu" — 111
4. The Prefectural Divisions — 119
5. The Jimi System — 120
6. Ten Prefectural Ministers of the Tianbao Period — 124
7. An-Shi Rebellion and the Shrinkage of Tang Territory — 127
8. The Rise of Fanzhen — 128
9. Chaos of the Five Dynasties and Ten Kingdoms Period — 131

Chapter Six
"Strengthen the Trunk and Weaken the Branches"—Territories and Administrative Divisions in the Northern and Southern Song Dynasties — 139
1. Unification of the Song Dynasty and the Implementation of the Route System — 139
2. The 24 Routes of the Chongning Period — 144
3. Wars between the Song and Liao Dynasties — 149
4. Territories and Administrative Divisions of the Liao, Jin, and Western Xia Dynasties — 152
5. General Yue Fei and His Northern Expeditionary Armies — 161
6. The 16 Routes of the Southern Song Dynasty — 165

Chapter Seven
The Crisscrossing Borders—Territories and Administrative Divisions in the Yuan Dynasty — 167
1. The Largest Territory in History — 167
2. Branch Secretariat System and the 11 Provinces in the Mid-Yuan — 168
3. The Multi-Level Administrative Divisions in Local Areas — 175
4. Pacification and Military Commissions — 179
5. Commission for Buddhist and Tibetan Affairs — 182
6. Bechbaliq, Qara-hoja, Hamili, and Penghu Military Inspectorate — 184

Chapter Eight
The Retreating Territories—Territories and Administrative Divisions in the Ming Dynasty — 189
1. Changes in Territory — 189
2. Regional Military Commissions, Provincial Administration Commissions, and Provincial Surveillance Commissions — 190
3. Two Capitals and 13 Provincial Administration Commissions — 192
4. Grand Coordinators and Their Governing Areas — 199
5. Regional Military Commissions and Garrisons — 202
6. Aboriginal Offices — 211
7. Nine Frontiers of the Great Wall — 214

CHAPTER NINE
The Empire in the Shape of a Mulberry Leaf—Territories and Administrative Divisions in the Qing Dynasty   219
1. Unification of Qing Territories   219
2. The 18 Provinces and Their Subordinate Administrative Divisions   220
3. Transforming Aboriginal Offices into Circulating Offices   225
4. Three Generals in Shengjing (Three Provinces in Northeast China)   228
5. General of Ili (Xinjiang Province)   231
6. Tibet and Qinghai Territories   235
7. Uliastai General   239
8. The Two Districts in Monan Mongolia   240
9. Taiwan Province   240

Bibliography   245
A Brief Chronology of Chinese History   247
Index   249
About the Chief Editor   257
About the Author   259

FOREWORD

The book series, *A History of China in Maps*, is comprised of four volumes: *Territories and Administrative Divisions, Ancient Capitals and Cities, Communications and Transportation,* and *Ethnic Migration.* Each volume tells one specific aspect of Chinese history with illustrated maps.

Many scholars have pointed out that the keys to understanding history are the five "Ws": what, when, where, who, and why. Any historical facts, regardless of who or what, and anything, be it spiritual or material, have to be connected with specific space. In other words, they have to take place either at a certain point, in a line, or on a surface of the earth. That's why the factor "where" is crucial to understanding history. Just as the late Professor Tan Qixiang said, "History is like a drama, and geography is its stage. Without a stage, there would be no drama at all."

Spatial factors have always played a significant role in history. They are not only important research contents but also indispensable elements to understanding history. Limited by time and energy, no one could be omnipresent; even if one could be there in person, one may not be able to master the entire range or features of the space. Therefore, maps are of vital importance. In ancient times, although limited by cartographic technologies and gadgets, scholars already recognized the significance of maps; when conducting historical research, they almost always had maps by their side.

Tu Jing (图经), a primitive form of chorography, combined records with illustrations, mostly in the form of maps. Some other historical classics were also attached to these maps, which later formed the historical atlas genre. As early as the third century, based on books such as *Zuo Zhuan* (左传), Jia Dan compiled an atlas of places for allied gatherings during the Spring and Autumn Period (770–256 BC) (春秋盟会图). Aside from this, Jia Dan also made the *Hai Nei Hua Yi Tu* (海内华夷图, *Map of Hua and National Minorities inside Seas*).

Based on this prototype, *Yu Ji Tu* (禹迹图, *Map of Yu's Sites*) was carved onto stone tablets in AD 1137. Such tablets have often been found in provincial schools, meaning they might have been used as teaching tools. In AD 1905, Yang Shoujing published *Shui Jing Zhu Tu* (水经注图, *Maps for Records of Rivers*). These ancient maps were printed in red and black ink with explanatory notes. It is a masterpiece of the historical atlas.

With the development of satellite remote sensing technology, information technology and the Internet, accurate images are now made possible by GPS and Google Maps. People tend to think that traditional maps have lost their charm and therefore should be replaced. However, this is not true. No matter how accurate they may be, Google Maps cannot replace traditional maps, nor their comprehensive, abstract, and specific geographic elements.

Modern maps are not sufficient to understand history. What we need are historical maps related to that era. As time goes by, the environment changes too. Features of physical and human geography in ancient times may differ from what we have today. Even if only minor changes have occurred in physical geography, features of human geography may have experienced profound change. Some elements may have disappeared completely, while some new elements have emerged. Historical maps have to be made according to the exact historical facts and corresponding geographic status.

In August 2010, a deadly mudslide took place in Zhouqu County, Gansu, China. While broadcasting the news, TV stations also presented maps on screen to inform the audience where exactly the catastrophe happened. The audience came to understand how far Zhouqu was from Lanzhou, the provincial capital of Gansu Province. Without a map, the audience would be unaware. The same goes for understanding history, which should be illustrated with maps. Otherwise, readers without such a background may find it hard to develop a spatial concept of historical events, even if they receive explanatory notes. This is because some geographic names no longer exist, while some topography has been altered considerably.

For example, in Cen Shen's poem, "A Song of Farewell to Field-Clerk Wu Going Home in White Snow," written in the Tang Dynasty, Cen saw Wu off in Luntai, and watched him disappear among the Tianshan Mountains. However, the modern Luntai is hundreds of miles away from the Tianshan Mountains. It only make sense when readers have learned that Luntai in the Tang was in fact located very close to Urumqi in Xinjiang Autonomous Region, and to the north of the Tianshan Mountains.

Another example is the city name of Nanjing. After the fall of the Northern Song Dynasty, Zhao Gou proclaimed himself as Emperor of the Southern Song in Nanjing. Later, under the increasing threat of Jin's armies from the North, he fled to Yangzhou and then crossed the Yangtze River. It might not be evident if the readers mix up Zhao Gou's Nanjing with the modern Nanjing, located to the south of Yangzhou. It would not make sense for Zhao to flee in the wrong direction! Nanjing in the Northern Song Dynasty was Shangqiu in today's Henan Province. From there, it went south and reached Yangzhou along the Bian Canal. Such a route is logical. A historical map would greatly benefit the readers in clarifying such cases.

Historical maps may also help bring about new research. For example, Professor Tan Qixiang once collected all the data he could of archaeological findings and cultural relics in the bordering areas of Hebei and Shandong provinces. Having marked them on maps, he discovered a region in the shape of a sea-shell, empty of any relics before the fourth century. And this region happened to be the lower reaches of the Yellow River. Based on further research on regional topography, Professor Tan was able to confirm the river had changed its course many times in that era, making it impossible for human inhabitation. This has never been recorded in any historical literature; only maps have provided a reliable means for research.

The four authors of *A History of China in Maps* have made breakthroughs in their work. Maps are not used for illustrations only, but as an essential part of the books—leading readers through comprehensive and accurate descriptions of history.

We have chosen four topics closely related to maps: Ancient Capitals and Cities, Territories and Administrative Divisions, Communications and

Transportation, and Ethnic Migration. Each book is full of ancient place names and other geographic elements. Without historical maps, one cannot fully understand history, no matter how many words have been written. If readers like our concept, it is possible that we will continue to write more books in future, illustrated with maps.

Here I would like to give credit to Jiangsu People's Publishing House. I am very grateful to have been chosen as the chief editor for this book series. I would like to specify what I have contributed: together with the writers and editors, I have determined the topics, style and requirements on the usage of maps. I have given feedback to the authors on their content and structure. And finally, I have written this foreword. Thank you!

GE JIANXIONG

CHAPTER ONE

NINE PROVINCES, COMMANDERIES AND COUNTIES

—*Myths and Realities of Administrative Divisions in the Pre-Qin Period*

1. The Nine Provinces and Five "Fu" in the Book of *Yu Gong*

There are many theories as to when ancient Chinese administrative divisions first came into being. A dominant one believes it started in the era of Yu the Great.

So how credible is this claim? Before making a judgment, let's take a look at what the Nine Provinces of China part of *Yu Gong* actually describes.

The book of *Yu Gong* (禹贡, *Tribute to Yu*) recorded that Yu the Great divided the world into nine provinces. They were Jizhou (Ji Province), Yanzhou, Qingzhou, Xuzhou, Yangzhou, Jingzhou, Yuzhou, Liangzhou, and Yongzhou. The geographic boundaries of the Nine Provinces reached as far as the Yan Mountains and Bohai Bay in the North, the Nanling Mountains in the South, the Ocean in the East, and Gansu (Longdong) Plateau in the West.

According to *Yu Gong*, the nine provinces were divided as below:

a. Jizhou (冀州):
The curves of the Yellow River formed its western, southern and eastern borders. If compared to modern geography, it would be located to the east of the Yellow River, between Shanxi and Shaanxi provinces, to the north of the Yellow between Henan and Shanxi, and between the west of Shandong Province and southeast of Hebei Province.

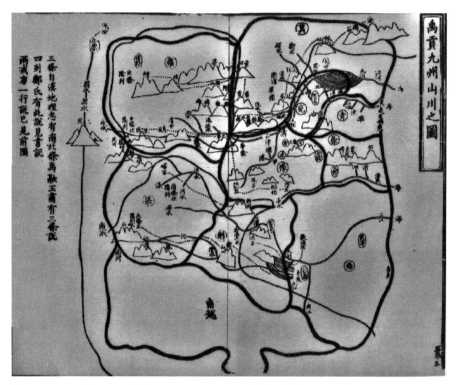

"Mountains and Rivers of the Nine Provinces in the book of 'Yu Gong'" (painted in the Southern Song)

There were several mountains in this region. For example, Hukou (northwest of Ji County in Shanxi and northeast of Yichuan in Shaanxi), the Liang Mountains (Hancheng in Shaanxi), Mount Qi (northeast of Mount Qi in Shaanxi—its ancient name being Pillars of Heaven). Many rivers flowed through this vast land too, for example, the Hengzhang River (the Zhang), the Heng River (Tang), and the Wei River. Jizhou was regarded as the capital province.

b. Yanzhou (兖州):
This province was located between the ancient Ji and Yellow Rivers. Today, it would be on the borders of Hebei, Henan, and Shandong provinces. Here are the Nine Rivers (a lower Yellow River branch with the number "nine" indicating the majority and is not an actual reference), the Yong River (a tributary of the Yellow River), and the Ju River (a branch of the Ji River).

c. Qingzhou (青州):

This province was located between the Bohai Sea and Mount Tai. If compared to modern geography, it would cover the East Liaoning and Shandong peninsulas. Many rivers flowed through it, for example, the Wei, the Zi, and the Wen (nowadays the Great Wen River).

d. Xuzhou (徐州):

This province was located between the Yellow Sea, Mount Tai and the Huai River. Today, it would cover south Shandong, Jiangsu, and north Anhui. There were two mountains, the Meng (nowadays south of the Mengyin in Shandong Province) and the Yu (nowadays northeast Dancheng in Shandong). There were two rivers in the region—the Huai and the Yi.

e. Yangzhou (扬州):

This province was located between the Huai River (to the south) and the East Sea. Today, it would cover Jiangsu, south Anhui, and the east of Jiangxi. There were two lakes, namely Pengli (nowadays Poyang Lake) and Zhenzhe (nowadays Taihu Lake).

f. Jingzhou (荆州):

Located between the Jin and Heng Mountains. Today, it would cover Hunan and Hubei as well as the west of Jiangxi. There were also two mountain ranges—the Jin (Nanzhang in Hubei) and Heng (west of the Mount Heng, Hunan). There were three rivers, namely Jianghan (nowadays the Jialing River), the Tuo, and the Qian (part of the Han River).

g. Yuzhou (豫州):

This province was located between the Jin Mountains and the Yellow River. Today, it would cover Henan and the north of Hubei. The rivers Yi, Luo, Li, and Jian flowed there.

h. Liangzhou (梁州):

This province was located to the south of Mount Hua and east of the Nu River. If compared to modern geography, it would cover south Shaanxi and Sichuan. There were five mountains, namely the Min (Songpan in Sichuan), the Pan (North

Panzong Mountains in Ningqiang, Shaanxi), the Xiqing Mountains (northeast of Tongde, Qinghai), the Cai Mountains (no equivalence today), and the Meng Mountains (west of Chongqing). There were two rivers: the Tuo and the Qian.

i. Yongzhou (雍州):
This province was located to the north of the Qinling Mountains, to the east of the Yellow River, and to the west of the Zhangye River. Today, it would cover the mid and northern part of Shaanxi, Gansu, and the regions to its west. There were five mountains, namely Mount Jin (the North Tiaojin Mountains in northwest Chaoyi, Shaanxi), the Qi Mountains, the Zhongnan Mountains (nowadays Qin Mountains), the Niaoshu Mountains (nowadays southwest of Weiyuan and west of Longxi County in Gansu), and the Sanwei Mountains (nowadays southeast of Dunhuang, Gansu). There were many rivers, for example, the Ruo (nowadays the Zhangye in Gansu), the Wei, the Jing, the Qi, the Ju, and the Feng Rivers.

The names of mountains and rivers mentioned in the book were beyond the knowledge of most people in the era of Yu the Great. It is said that the book of *Yu Gong* could be written in the age of the Warring States Period (476–221 BC), depicting the geography of its own time. The so-called "Nine Provinces" were but a utopian belief by scholars, who dreamed of what the country would look like in future. Therefore, the Nine Provinces by Yu the Great never existed and they were not the earliest administrative divisions in Chinese history.

The book of *Yu Gong* recorded another method of dividing China into different sections, namely the system of Five "Fu" (服).

Seen from the map, the capital would be located in the center, with an extension of five "Fu" in the four directions—North, South, East, and West. "Fu" was a measurement of five hundred *li* (里, one *li* equals 559.8 meters). The hierarchy of Five "Fu" was described as follows:

a. Dian Fu—under direct reign of the capital. Agriculture was its top priority
b. Hou Fu—governed by various Marquises
c. Sui Fu—a buffer area that need to be pacified between the residents and ethnic groups
d. Yao Fu—a marginal area beyond Sui Fu five hundred *li* in all directions
e. Huang Fu—a stretch of barren land beyond Yao Fu five hundred *li* in all directions

五服圖

A map of Five "Fu" in the "Yu Gong" (Ming Dynasty version)

The key difference between the two concepts of Nine Provinces and Five "Fu" is that the former was a forecast of the future, while the latter was a fantasy that looked back on history. Hierarchies did appear in the ages before and after the Western Zhou Period, but there had never been a system of dividing regions according to five hundred *li*.

2. Territories in the Shang and Zhou Dynasties

Researchers nowadays have proven that administrative divisions didn't exist in the legendary age of Yu the Great, nor in the age of the Shang Dynasty and Western Zhou, even though the notion of country had already come into being. The Shang Dynasty ruled in the valley of the Yellow River around 1600–1046 BC. It is said that ancestors of the Qi (契) tribe, once helped Yu the Great to control the floods. Tang was the thirteenth generation of Qi, who ended the Xia and founded the Shang Dynasty around 1600 BC.

According to the *Book of Documents*, there had already been a central and regional division in its original form, with terms such as "Internal Fu" and "External Fu" in its descriptions.[1] This is a system that focuses on the political level, determining its criteria based on the closeness or distance to the Shang king. Additionally, at that time, there was another framework for distinguishing between the Shang king and local authorities. This is the distinction between the "Shang" (kingdom) and the "Four Directions and Four Tu." This hierarchy focuses relatively on the regional level, that is, whether or not the region is under the direct government of the King of the Shang Dynasty. There should be correspondence or overlaps between the "Internal Fu" and the "Shang," the "External Fu" and the "Four Directions" or "Four Tu," but they could not be completely unified. The center of the Shang covered the regions to the north of Henan, south of Hebei, and west of Shandong. The peripheral regions could reach the ocean in the east, western Shaanxi in the west, Sichuan in the southwest, Hunan and Jiangxi in the south, mid-Shanxi in the north, and Liaoning in the northeast.

Researchers also proved that the relationship between the central and regional regimes was akin to inter-country, rather than between counties, with the former

---

1. *Book of Documents*.

controlling the latter to some extent. However, the control from the former should not be regarded as a dominating power nor as centralization. Therefore, it is concluded that administrative divisions didn't yet exist in China, in spite of this mechanism.

The origins of the Zhou Dynasty began with a tribe surnamed Ji (姬), living in the region of Shaanxi and Gansu. As the legend goes, their ancestor, Qi, was an agrarian master and was regarded as the "Lord of Millet." Around 1100 BC, King Wu of Zhou destroyed the forces of Shang. King Zhou of Shang set his palace on fire, dying within. After overthrowing the Shang, King Wu of Zhou started his own dynasty—a period known as Western Zhou (1046–771 BC).

The Zhou Dynasty developed its systems based on the Shang. The King of Zhou was called "Son of Heaven," i.e., the supreme ruler of China. His rule reached central and regional areas, known as "Earth under the Heaven." In other words, the King of Zhou regarded all land within his knowledge as his kingdom.

The regions under direct control by the King of Zhou were called "Zhou Bang" (周邦, State of Zhou), "Zhou," or "Kingdom." The kingdom was often divided into several sections. One was called "Zong Zhou," surrounding twin capital cities Feng and Hao—nowadays Xi'an in Shaanxi. This region also included the Zhouyuan area, where the Zhou people originated and where the capital was located before the overthrow of the Shang Dynasty.

Zhou's previous capital city—before the establishment of the dynasty—was also included in this section. The other was called "Cheng Zhou," around the area of its eastern capital Luoyi, nowadays Luoyang in Henan. Some researchers have proposed that the two sections are actually one.

The area outside "Zhou Bang" was regarded as "Wan Bang" (various states), "Duo Bang," or "Shu Bang," meaning regional regimes. Wan Bang covers a very large area, which is more precisely described in a conversation of King Jing of Zhou in the *Duke Zhao Nineth Year* of *Zuozhuan* (533 BC): "Because of the contribution of Hou Ji in the Xia Dynasty, we had Wei, Tai, Rui, Qi, and Bi as western lands. After King Wu's conquest over Shang, we gained Pugu and Shanyan as eastern lands; we had Ba, Pu, Chu, and Deng as southern lands; and we had Sushen, Yan, and Bo as northern lands." Researchers would usually classify these regional regimes into the following groups:

(1) Group A: Regimes by various Zhuhou (regional rulers)

Dan, Duke of Zhou, was a member of the royal family of the Zhou Dynasty, playing a major role in consolidating the kingdom established by his elder brother, King Wu of Zhou. From this incident, we can learn that the political situation in the early Zhou Dynasty was such that it would have been difficult for the emperor to rule the vast conquered areas directly, so the feudal system was adapted to solve this problem. The so-called feudal system, that is, the feudal state was established by the emperor of the Zhou Dynasty, who gave the land outside the kingdom he lived in to his relatives of the same surname and some meritorious officials of different surnames through a grand ceremony of granting land to the people, therefore establishing vassal states, allowing them to independently manage the land they were given and the people who were attached to the land.

(2) Group B: Canonization of vassal states

This was to turn vassal states into Marquises. For example, it is recorded in the *Chu Shi Jia* of *Records of the Grand Historian* that King Cheng of the Zhou Dynasty rewarded Xiong Yi, the predecessor of Chu, with lands of Zi and Nan rank. Xiong was granted surnamed Mi and lived in Danyang. Although their independence was relatively greater than the previous one, there was still a clear division between the vassals and the ruler of Zhou. The Zhou Dynasty adopted a feudal system, not out of their own desires, but as forced by circumstance. When the dynasty was established, the land was vast and transportation was difficult. It was impossible for the king to rule all the land as domain states. Also, there were potential dangers of rebellions from the conquered. One of the purposes of distributing land to various Marquises was to shield the kingdom from danger through the help of regional rulers. The King of Zhou would then have better control of the periphery or hinterlands. "Wan Bang" would then be under his control, at least officially.

The Marquises were in name ruled by the King of Zhou, and therefore they had to pay pilgrimage and tribute, as well as bear the duty of military drafts. However, the control exerted by the king was very limited. In theory, as soon as the marquises were crowned as the head of their state, their land and people would have nothing to do with the King of Zhou. The marquises had great independence. Within their own fiefs, the vassal in their respective states governed officials according to the central official structure of the Zhou Dynasty.

In addition, these vassal states could subdivide the areas outside their capitals to their own maharajahs, who could continue to subdivide their own lands to their own sons and vassals. In this way, a hierarchy of power was established, with the King of Zhou at the core.

In conclusion, the power of Western Zhou was highly decentralized. Only the kingdom was under direct rule by the King. What happened within the regional states had almost nothing to do with him. There is only a political affiliation between the king of Zhou and the vassals, not an administrative governance relationship. Therefore, there is no central-to-local administrative relationship. Even if we regard it as a central-to-local administrative relationship, this type of relationship is significantly different from the real central-local relationship under the centralization of power in later times. In other words, there was no administrative division of any kind at the local level, as the king of Zhou simply unified the vassals but not governed them. This is because administrative divisions were associated with the centralized state, which in essence divided the people but not the land, and the ruler simply divided the area under his direct control in a hierarchical manner and dispatched officials who could be removed periodically to administer it. Therefore, the familiarized scenery of "It is the king's land and jurisdiction all over the world, and the people living on this land are all the subjects of the king"[2] is only a fictious depiction and does not reflect the real situation of the decentralization of the Western Zhou Dynasty.

In a geographical sense, there was only a difference between the capital and hinterlands: people of the capital governed; while people of the suburb were governed.

3. *Xian* (县, county) and Commanderies in the Spring and Autumn Period

King You of Zhou was the last King of Western Zhou. He deposed Queen Shen and Crown Prince Yijiu, and replaced them with Concubine Baosi as the new queen, and their son the new crown prince. Queen Shen's father, the Marquess of Shen, was furious and sought revenge by attacking King You's palace with the help

---

2. *Book of Songs · Lesser Court Hymns · Decade of Bei Shan.*

of the Quanrong, a minority tribe. King You had lost trust among his nobles and nobody came to his rescue. He was killed together with the new crown prince.

Prince Yijiu was supported by the nobles and became King Ping of Zhou. In the year 770 BC, King Ping moved the capital to Luoyi (Luoyang). This was the beginning of the Eastern Zhou Dynasty. Historians usually divide the Eastern Zhou into two periods—namely the Spring and Autumn Period (770–476 BC), and the Warring States Period (475–221 BC). The former lasted 295 years and the latter 255 years.

During the Spring and Autumn Period, as productivity continued to develop, the differences of social status between those of the capital and of the periphery gradually diminished; the borders between capital and suburb became blurred. In the meantime, a new Commandery-County system was forming, which helped strengthen the king's rule. The emergence of the new system marked the birth of administrative divisions in China.

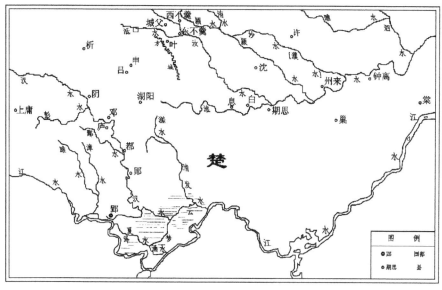

Map of counties in the Kingdom of Chu around 522 BC[3]

---

3. Li Xiaojie, *General History of the Administrative Divisions in China: Pre-Qin Period* (Shanghai: Fudan University Press, 2009), 553.

The *Spring and Autumn Annals* and *Commentary of Zuo* (*Zuo Zhuan*) are the two most famous books documenting history during the Spring and Autumn Period. Both recorded that many countries set up Xian during this time. In 627 BC, the Baidi, a tribe located in the north of Shaanxi Province, crossed the Yellow River and invaded the State of Jin. The troops of Jin resisted and finally defeated the Baidi tribe in Ji (now southeast of Taigu, Shanxi Province). The leading general Xi Que, recommended by vassal Xu Chen, captured the son of the leader of Baidi. The Duke Xiang of Jin rewarded him with the "County of Xianmao." Another example is that in 594 BC, Xun Linfu of Jin led his troops and conquered the Chidi Lu Clan (now northeast of Lucheng, Shanxi Province), and it was regarded as a great achievement for Jin. However, Xun Linfu was almost killed by the Duke Jing of Jin three years earlier because he lost a fight to the state of Chu. Thanks to Shi Zhenzi for talking the Duke Jing of Jin out of dismissing and killing Xun, Xun could make the achievement three years later. The Duke Jing of Jin gave Shi Zhenzi the "County of Guayan" for his intercession.

The earliest Xian set up by Chu recorded in books was called Quan. King Wu of Chu (740–690 BC) defeated the King of Quan and turned it into Xian. A minister was sent from Chu to govern Quan. This was the first of its type during the Spring and Autumn Period. However, the term "Xian" mentioned above was different from the Commandery-County system. The major reasons are: On one hand, Xians were often given by kings to their ministers, and were not under the kings' direct rule. On the other hand, even though some Xians were under the kings' direct rule, its basic organization structure remained unchanged.

Features of a Commandery-County system should include:

a. 100 percent directly ruled by the King;
b. Heads of the counties should not be inherited, but appointed by the King, and the King can replace them whenever he wants;
c. The scope of the counties should be defined after measurement, and not by natural terrain;
d. There has to be basic grassroots organizations.

The emergence of the Commandery-County system took place in 514 BC in the Jin Kingdom. In that year, six governors with different names of the State of Jin, including Han, Zhao, Wei, Zhi, Fan, and Zhongxing, joined together to destroy the Qi and Yanshe clans and then divided the fields of the Qi clan into seven counties and the fields of the Yangshe clan into three counties. They appointed ten people as the governors of ten counties. They were Sima Mimou, the governor of Wu County (now northeast of Jiexiu, Shanxi Province); Jia Xin, the governor of Qi County (now southeast of Qi County, Shanxi Province); Sima Wu, the governor of Pingling County (now northeast of Wenshui, Shanxi Province); Wei Wu, the governor of Gengyang County (now Qingxu County, Shanxi Province); Zhi Xuwu, the governor of Tushui County (now southwest of Yuci, Shanxi Province); Han Gu, the governor of Mashou County (now southeast of Shouyang, Shanxi Province); Meng Bing, the governor of Yu County (now northeast of Yangqu, Shanxi Province); Le Xiao, the governor of Tongdi County (now south of Qin County, Shanxi Province), Zhao Zhao, the governor of Pingyang County (now southwest of Linfen, Shanxi Province), and Liao An, the governor of Yangshi (now southeast of Hongdong, Shanxi Province).

Some of these ten men were picked as governors of counties because of their contributions to the royal family; some were picked because they were sons of elite families, and others were selected because they were wise. So, what is the difference between these ten counties and the ones we mentioned earlier? In other words, why are these ten counties called the counties of prefectures and counties? There are a few details in the historical documentation that can be used as examples to answer this question.

At the time of the above incident, Wei Xianzi was the ruler of Jin, and Wei Wu, the above-mentioned governor of Gengyang, was his concubine son. When Wei Wu became the county governor, Wei Xianzi was worried about people's gossip, so he said to Cheng Zhuan, another governor of Jin, "If I assign Wei Wu as the county governor, will people think that I am ganging up for personal interest and taking advantage of my own power?" When Cheng Zhuan heard this, he replied, "No way! Wei Wu is a man who is very good to the king and the people around him. He thinks of righteousness in the pursuit of interest, and can stay true to his manners and grace." Cheng Zhuan then quoted the story of King Wu of Zhou who, after conquering the Shang Dynasty, crowned a vassal with the same surname, saying that as long as a person is virtuous, the king can appoint him without considering kinship. After hearing these, Wei Xianzi felt much more relieved.

After being appointed as the governor of Qi County, Jia Xin was about to leave for his post. Before he left, he went to see Wei Xianzi. When he met him, Wei Xianzi told him a story. In the past, when Shu Xiang, a governor of Jin, came to the state of Zheng, he did not judge people by their looks. He appreciated a talented yet ugly man named Zong Mie. They soon became acquaintances. Wei Xianzi wanted to use this story to show that he was also a lover of talent. He then said to Jia Xin, "Now you have served the royal family, so I have recommended you to be the county governor. Go ahead, do your best, and don't degrade your merits."

In addition, soon after Wei Wu arrived at Gengyang County as a county governor, he encountered a difficult case that could not be settled. So, he referred the case to the central government, and Wei Xianzi, who was in power, handled it. Wei Xianzi wanted to accept a bribe and settled the case improperly. However, due to Wei Wu's efforts and persuasion, Wei Xianzi finally dismissed the bribe-giver.

In conclusion, the ten counties were no longer fiefdoms. Even though family members from ministers might be prioritized in the appointment of county heads, they must be chosen based on merit. Otherwise, Wei Xianzi would not worry about such rumors when appointing his son. Second, unlike a fiefdom, county heads had to work for and report to the central administration. Furthermore, the ten counties were formed after re-delineation. For example, the estates by Minister Yangshe previously composed of two parts. Yet they became three counties after the map was redrawn. All the above were characteristics of the Commandery-County system.

We have a preliminary understanding of the counties in the Commandery-County system; now, let's look at the prefectures next. Compared with the counties, the records about the prefectures in the Spring and Autumn period are very limited. According to scholars, there is only one reliable and short record in the *Zuo Zhuan*. This record is also recorded in Jin. In 493 BC, Zhao Jian, the ruling governor of Jin at the time, promised in his oath to his soldiers that if they overcame the enemy, the senior generals would be governors of the counties, and the junior governors would be governors of the prefectures. However, the details of the prefectures are not very clear. It is only generally known that prefectures were initially set up in the border areas of the vassal states. Prefectures were named differently from the counties in the prosperous areas, but the distinction between them was not clear. During the early times, the distinction between the counties and the prefectures was not always clear, and there was no subordinate relationship between them. As for the subordination of prefectures to counties, it was not until the Warring States period that it was introduced and clearly implemented.

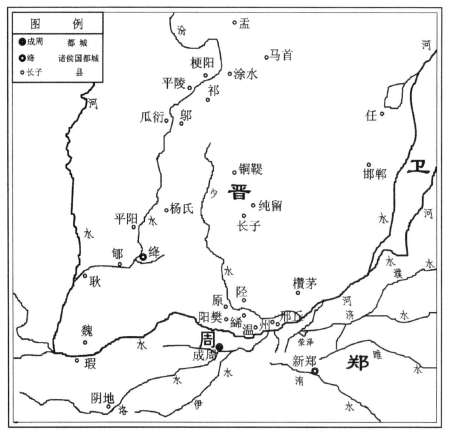

Map of counties in the State of Jin around 500 BC[4]

---

4. Li Xiaojie, *General History of the Administrative Divisions in China: Pre-Qin Period* (Shanghai: Fudan University Press, 2009), 552.

4. Territories in the Warring States Period and the Commandery-County System

During the Warring States Period, ministers and grand masters rose to power, succeeding marquises. Seven vassal states were among the strongest: Qin, Qi, Chu, Han, Zhao, Wei, and Yan—known as the "Seven Warring States."

The following is a brief introduction to the seven states:

The State of Qin first established its capital in Yong (nowadays southwest of Fengxiang, Shaanxi) and later moved to Jinyang and Liyang (northwest of Lintong, Shaanxi). In 350 BC, it finally settled for Xianyang. Its territory covered the western tip of Henan, most of Shaanxi, east Gansu, and a large part of Sichuan.

The State of Qi's capital was Linzi (northeast of Zibo, Shandong). Its territory covered a large part of Shandong and southeast Hebei.

The State of Wei first set its capital in Anyi (northwest Xia County, Shanxi). In 361 BC, it settled for Daliang (nowadays Kaifeng, Henan). Its territory covered southwest Shanxi, east Henan, and a small part of Shaanxi and Anhui.

The State of Han first set its capital in Pingyang (southwest Linfen, Shanxi). Later it moved to Yiyang (west of Yiyang, Henan) and Yangzhuo (Yuzhou, Henan). In 375 BC, it settled for Xinzheng. Its territory covered the mid and western part of Henan, and a small part of Shanxi and Shaanxi.

The State of Zhao first set its capital in Jinyang (southwest of Taiyuan, Shanxi) and later moved to Zhongmou (west of Hebi, Henan). In 386 BC, it settled for Handan. Its territory covered the mid and northern part of Shanxi, southwest Hebei, the Hetao area of Inner Mongolia, and a part of Henan and Shandong.

The State of Yan set its capital in Ji (Beijing). Its territory covered the eastern and northern part of Hebei, south of Liaoning and a part of Inner Mongolia.

The State of Chu set its capital in Ying (northwest of Jiangling District, Jinzhou, Hubei). In 278 BC, it moved its capital under Qin's strike to Chen (Huaiyang, Henan) and later Juyang (nowadays north of Fuyang, Anhui). In 241 BC, it settled in Shouchun (Shou County, Anhui). Its territory covered Hubei, Hunan, a large part of Jiangsu, Anhui, and Zhejiang, as well a part of Shandong, Jiangxi, Shaanxi, and Sichuan.

The vassal states, and the Seven Warring States in particular, reformed their political system and gradually established centralization, while adopting the Commandery-County system in local areas. Lacking historical recordings, one could not tell how the political system transformed into the Commandery-County system during the transition from the Spring and Autumn to the Warring States. The only recordings about commanderies during the Warring States concerned the State of Qin.

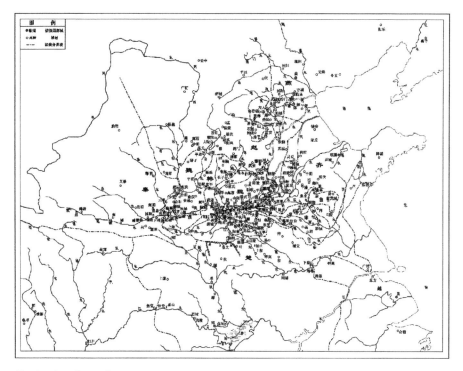

Territories of vassal states, 350 BC[5]

In the early years of the Warring States era, the State of Qin continuously attacked its eastern neighbors and expanded its territory. In 375 BC, the ruling Duke Xian of Qin began to reorganize the community at the lowest level. He ordered the people to be organized into a unit of five families, which was called "Wu," and further organized into a unit of ten families, which was called "Shi." This practice was called "household registration in the unit of five."[6]

---

5. Li Xiaojie, *General History of the Administrative Divisions in China: Pre-Qin Period* (Shanghai: Fudan University Press, 2009), 555.
6. *The Records of the Grand Historian · Basic Annal of the Qin Shi Huang.*

In 350 BC, Duke Xiao hired Shang Yang to carry out numerous reforms as his chief advisor. Shang Yang changed the local political systems by grouping villages into counties. Under his rule, "Each county was governed by a magistrate. There were a total of 41 counties."[7] The district magistrates were appointed by the head of the state for better central administrative control.

It is unknown how other vassal states ruled their counties. However, what is certain is that setting up counties was common practice during the Warring States Period. By the time Qin had exterminated the other states, the number of recorded counties exceeded one hundred. The following is an analysis on the counties' characteristics during this era by comparing their status in the states of Han, Zhao, and Wei.

First of all, the three states usually chose places near rivers or with other geographic advantages to set up their counties. This shows a consistency in geopolitics, a prominent feature of early Chinese history. As we can see above, the counties of the state of Han were located in the upper reaches of the Fen River, and later counties were built in the Shangdang area in the Taihang Mountains Basin; the counties of the state of Zhao were mainly located in the two geographical units divided by the Taihang Mountains (with the Hebei Plain in the east and the Shanxi Plateau in the west). Although detailed information about counties of the state of Wei is not available, with the known location of Wen county, it can be concluded that other counties of the state of Wei were also located along the river. This feature of location continued until the end of the Warring States period, when many counties were set up in the eastern part of Wei, north of the capital city of Daliang and on both sides of the river. The influence of natural factors on the setting of political districts was significant. Since a certain amount of arable land was an important guarantee for the development of a region during the period when agriculture was the mainstay of the economy, the banks of rivers, open plains, and fertile basins all provided suitable sites for cultivation. As the economy grew and the population multiplied, it was logical to take the lead in establishing counties in these areas.

Second, there were many counties in the suburbs of capital cities. This was different from the practice in the Spring and Autumn era, when counties were usually located in the peripherals of the state far away from the capital. In contrast,

---

7. *The Records of the Grand Historian.*

the State of Han set up many counties around its capital Zheng; the State of Zhao did the same around its capital Handan; and the State of Wei around its capital of Daliang. This shows that many counties were set up near prosperous areas. On the other hand, these counties also served the function of satellites around the capital for military security.

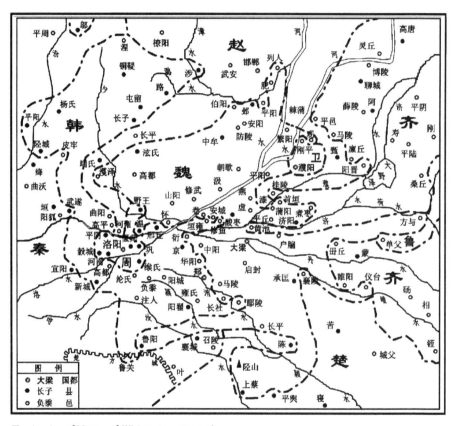

Territories of Han and Wei states, 280 BC[8]

Third, setting up the counties was based on military strategy. For example, the Shangdang District in the State of Han was of great strategic importance. One could tell from a letter written by Feng Yan in the Eastern Han: "The

---

8. Li Xiaojie, *General History of the Administrative Divisions in China: Pre-Qin Period* (Shanghai: Fudan University Press, 2009), 561.

District of Shangdang is like a fortress secured by three mountain passes in the East (Shangdang, Hukou, and Shijin)."[9] With the Taihang Mountains situated to the east of Shangdang, the Zhongtiao Mountains to its south, and the Taiyue Mountains to its west, a valley was formed. With the Hebei plains lying to the east of the valley, Shangdang enjoyed a bird's eye view of the Central Plains. In order to control this district, the State of Han set up several counties here.[10] Shangdang Commandery was established sometime later.

In order to defend his land against nomadic tribes in the North, King Wuling of Zhao set up several commanderies such as Dai, Yanmen, and Yunzhong in his northern territory. The Taiyuan Valley was a prosperous area with military importance; the State of Zhao altogether set up over 30 counties here.

The State of Wei set up such counties as Shaoliang and Heyang to defend itself against invasion from the Qin. Later, Wei set up Xihe and Shang commanderies after the number of counties increased. In conclusion, counties meant not only prosperity, but also strategic importance for defense. Furthermore, the Commandery-County system already existed in the Warring States Period, especially on the borders among states. For example, there were commanderies in Shangdang set up by the State of Zhao and counties in Hexi District by the State of Wei. However, some counties remained independent and may not necessarily held a lower status than commanderies.

During the Warring States period, most of the counties were set up in the border areas to protect against the other vassal states or minority groups outside the country. For example, after the division of Jin by the three states, the western part of the river became Wei's territory, and Wei set up the Shang Prefecture and the Xihe Prefecture in this area to protect against the Qin state in the west. Later, Wei lost these two prefectures and retreated to set up a prefecture in the east of the river, still for the purpose of defending against the Qin's invasion. For example, in the northern part of the state of Zhao, the three prefectures of Yunzhong, Yanmen, and Daijun were established to protect against the Linhu and Loufan minorities. The five prefectures of Shanggu, Yuyang, Youbeiping, Liaoxi, and Liaodong were set up by the state of Yan to protect against the Eastern Hu

---

9. *The History of the Later Han Dynasty · Annal of Feng Yan.*
10. According to *The Strategies of Warring States · The Strategies of Qin*, vol. 1, the State of Han set up 17 counties in Shangdang District.

minority. The two prefectures of Wu and Qianzhong in the state of Chu were also set up to protect against the Baiyue minority and the southwestern Yi.

In addition, the jurisdictive relation between counties and prefectures also slowly emerged. Scholars now speculate that the emergence of this phenomenon was probably due to the following two circumstances.

(1) Group A:
The prefectures were initially located in the border areas of the vassal states, which were relatively barren, but later, due to the continuous economic development of the border areas, the prefectures became prosperous, and in order to facilitate management, several counties were affiliated with the prefectures.

(2) Group B:
In the border areas of vassal states, many counties had already been set up, but due to military needs, prefectures were later set up on top of these counties to facilitate control, thus forming the system of counties under the jurisdiction of prefectures. By the middle of the Warring States period, it was common to find documents about the system of counties under the jurisdiction of prefectures.

All senior officials of counties and commanderies had to be appointed by the heads of states—they could not be inherited. The land within the counties and commanderies were under direct control of the state heads, who would not distribute it as a reward. This arguably marked the moment that the Commandery-County system came into being.

However, it should be noted that the system of prefectures and counties was only widely implemented in the border areas of the vassal states, while in the interior of the vassal states, only counties were established, not prefectures. Moreover, within the vassal states, the enfeoffment of the kinsmen and their governors still existed and was not eliminated by the emergence of the Commandery-County system.

In addition, there was a special case, that is, the State of Qi, one of the Seven Warring States, had a number of counties but never established a prefecture. The state of Qi set up a guarded metropolis on top of the counties, whose role was about the same as that of the prefectures of other states, and Qi divided the whole country into five capitals, such as Linzi, and practiced the system of five capitals.

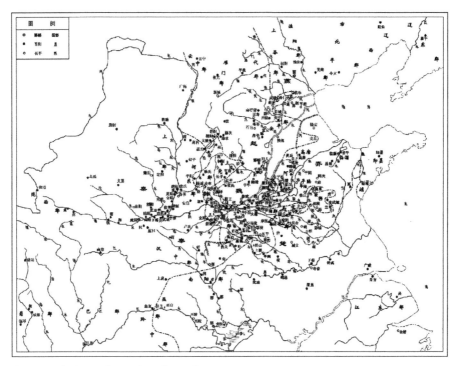

Commanderies and counties of vassal states, 280 BC[11]

At the end of the Warring States period, the state of Qin became stronger and King Ying Zheng started a war to unify the six states in 230 BC and finally completed the unification in 221 BC, establishing the first unified dynasty of the Middle Kingdom in history—the Qin.

---

11. Li Xiaojie, *General History of the Administrative Divisions in China: Pre-Qin Period* (Shanghai: Fudan University Press, 2009), 554.

CHAPTER TWO

UNIFICATION

—Territories and Administrative Divisions in the Qin and Han Dynasties

In 230 BC, Ying Zheng conquered the State of Han. This was the first step in his ambition to unify China. In 228 BC, Qin took Handan, capital of the Zhao State. The King of Zhao was captured and his son fled. Two years later, Qin occupied the State of Yan, and the king had to move east of Liao. In 225 BC, Qin conquered the State of Wei, and two years later captured the King of Chu. In 222 BC, Qin captured the King of Yan and the son of the late King of Zhao. In 221 BC, Qin defeated its final rival—the State of Qi; China was unified for the first time in history. Ying Zheng then established the Qin Dynasty, and he became the Emperor of Qin, known as "Qin Shi Huang."

1. Expanding from 36 to 48 Commanderies

In *The Records of the Grand Historian*, author Sima Qian, wrote: "In 221 BC, after Ying Zheng, the King of Qin had unified China, he summoned all his generals and ministers in capital Xianyang. In this meeting, they discussed how the king should be addressed and how to set up new systems." Regarding the first matter, Sima Qian wrote:

When the King of Qin first took over the world, he summoned the prime minister and the royal historian and said "… With this insignificant self, I raised an army to punish the rebellious, with the protection of the spirits of our ancestors. The kings of the six countries had punished for their sins, and the world had been pacified. Now, if the title was not changed, my accomplishments could not be glorified and passed on to future generations. Let's discuss the imperial title." The prime minister Wang Wan, the imperial governor Feng Jie, the court lieutenant Li Si and others said, "In the past, the territory of the past five emperors spread over thousands of li, including Hou Fu and Yi Fu in the external borders, while the emperor could not govern and regulate the vassals. Now, Your Majesty has raised a righteous army, put an end to the brutal bandits, pacified the world, and divided the population into Commandery-County. It is truly a remarkable triumph that could never be topped even by the Five Emperors. We have discussed with the court academicians and concluded that in ancient times, there was the Emperor of Heaven, the Emperor of Earth, and the Emperor of Tai, and the Emperor of Tai is the most divine. Therefore, we propose, in the name of honor, to call Your Majesty 'Tai Huang.' Your rules should be called 'Zhi' and your order should be called 'Zhao.' Your Majesty should call yourself 'Zhen.'" The King of Qin then said: "Leave 'Tai,' save 'Huang,' and adopt the title 'Di' that has been used for ancient emperors. Therefore, the proper title of the emperor should be 'Huang Di.' Other nomenclatures remain as you proposed." So, the order was given: "It is permissible." Zhuangxiang was posthumously honored as the Emperor. Another order was issued: "I have heard that in ancient times, there were titles but no posthumous names, in middle ancient times, there were titles and posthumous names were given after death based on the deeds and conduct during life. Doing so is like sons discussing their fathers, and subjects discussing their monarchs, it's quite meaningless, I will not adopt this practice. From now on, the system of posthumous names will be abolished. I will be called the First Emperor, and descendants will start from me, called the Second Generation, the Third Generation, and so on, until Ten Thousand Generations, passed down forever, without end."

Ying Zheng was 38 years old when he conquered all the warring kingdoms and unified the country. Dissatisfied with the title "King," he wanted to rule as the first Emperor (Shi Huang) of the Qin Dynasty. All his men agreed.

As for the second matter to be discussed here, it did not go so smoothly, and it even led to a considerable debate. A group of ministers, represented by the prime minister Wang Wan, took the lead in suggesting Emperor Qin Shi Huang. They held that now that Emperor Qin Shi Huang had just unified the six states, they were worried that people in remote states such as Yan, Qi, and Chu would not be pacified if new vassal kings were not appointed. Emperor Qin Shi Huang then submitted this proposal to other ministers for discussion. Almost all the ministers agreed that this was a very good idea and should be implemented. However, the only one who did not think so was Li Si, the court lieutenant, who argued:

> King Wen of Zhou enfeoffed many of his sons and brothers as vassals. There were many of the same surnames. As time went on, the familial relationships became increasingly distant, and they attacked each other as if they were enemies. The vassals fought and attacked each other fiercely, and the Zhou emperor could do nothing to stop it. Now, the whole country is united because of the greatness of Your Majesty and is divided into commandery and county. If Your Majesty rewards all the princes and meritorious families with the taxes collected by the state, it would be very easy to control the people and rule out any thought against your rule, which is the best strategy to stabilize the country. Therefore, it is not appropriate to assign vassals.

Li Si argued that previously King Wen and King Wu of Zhou had distributed their land to princes and relatives of the same surname, but later those marquises turned against each other—even the King of Zhou could do nothing about it. It would suffice to reward princes and generals with tax of the country. There were no disagreements as to ruling the kingdom under the Commandery-County system, which contributed to Qin's prosperity. Distributing land to princes would be improper under those circumstances. After hearing Li Si's words, Qin Shi Huang finally said:

> In the past, all the people in the world suffered from endless wars because of the vassals. Now, I have unified the world relying on the blessing of my ancestors. If I set up vassals right after the world has just settled down, it is tantamount to provoking a war and not seeking peace and tranquility. Isn't it difficult? The court lieutenant agreed.

So, instead of setting up a feudal system, Emperor Qin Shi Huang introduced the Commandery-County system to the whole world, dividing the country into 36 prefectures,[1] each of which had its own Commandery Governor, Commandery Chamberlain, and Imperial Inspector. The officials of these prefectures were appointed directly by the central government and could be replaced regularly. The Commandery Governor was the chief executive of a prefecture and had great power. Apart from that, the Commandery Governor had the right to choose all the officials of a prefecture from the people of the prefecture. The Commandery Governor was allowed to carry out his own way of governing the prefecture, and the central government did not interfere with that. The Commandery Chamberlain was not subordinate to the Commandery Governor but received orders directly from the central government. The superintendent was responsible for monitoring the rule of the prefecture. The Imperial Inspector was subordinate to the imperial chancellor of the central government and was responsible for supervising the local government.

In conclusion, commandery governors, commandery chamberlains, and imperial inspectors worked together to govern commanderies but they did not report to one another. A commandery supervises many counties. If a county had a big population, then the county head would be called "Prefect"; if the population was small, then he would be called "Chief."

In 218 BC, the armies of Qin climbed over the Nanling Mountains to the south to expand their territory. In the meantime, an Imperial Inspector named Shi Lu ordered the construction of a canal connecting River Xiang (in present-day Hunan) to the Li River (present-day Guangxi). The canal, known as "Ling Qu," was completed in 215 BC. The Qin armies took advantage of Ling Qu and conquered Nanyue, an ancient kingdom that covered parts of northern Vietnam and the modern Chinese provinces of Guangdong and Guangxi. Then Qin set up three commanderies in the region, namely, Nanhai (South Sea), Guilin, and Xiang.

Hetao District (the Yellow River Loops)—a region in the upper reaches of the Yellow River—was constantly assaulted by nomadic tribes such as the Xiongnu. In 215 BC, General Meng Tian led an army of 300,000 soldiers north and drove away

---

1. Regarding the names of the thirty-six counties established at the beginning of the Qin unification of the territories, there is still no definitive explanation to this day. For the latest related research, please refer to Xin Deyong, "New Examination of the Thirty-Six Counties of Qin Shihuang," *Wen Shi*, no. 1 and no. 2 (2006).

the Xiongnu people. The following year, Qin set up the Jiuyuan Commandery in the area between the Yin Mountains and east of the Yellow River, governing 34 counties in the region. (Other statements suggest up to 44 counties.)

In the meantime, Qin enlisted laborers to build the Great Wall of China by connecting the walls built previously by vassal kingdoms of Qin, Zhao, and Yan. When completed, the Great Wall started from Lintao (Min County in Gansu) in the West, stretched through the Yellow River and the Yin Mountains regions, and ended in the east of Liao (northeastern coast of Pyongyang in North Korea). Qin also expanded its territory in the southwest with the Chengdu Plains as the base. It later occupied the upper reaches of Dadu River and the Min River, and regions covering parts of modern Sichuan.

After years of expansion, the Qin Dynasty covered a vast stretch of land, including the Yellow River Loops regions in the North, northeastern Vietnam and Guangdong in the South, the Long Mountains, Western Sichuan and the Yunnan-Guizhou Plateau in the West, and the northern part of the Korean Peninsula in the East. By the end of the Qin era, it had set up 48 commanderies and around 1,000 counties altogether. However, Qin did not set up counties in regions where minority tribes were conquered. Rather, it set up March (道), as a political administrative division on the same level as counties.

At that time, the prefectures of Qin were basically divided by mountains and rivers, and the jurisdiction of the prefectures coincided with the natural geographic areas, mainly in the following ways: first, each prefecture was roughly divided according to a geographic unit. For example, Nei Shi, where the capital was located, occupied the Guanzhong Basin, that is, the Wei River Alluvial Plain, which was the most affluent area at that time. The scale of the Hanzhong Prefecture was also roughly equivalent to that of the Hanzhong Basin, and the area of the Nanyang Prefecture was equivalent to that of the Nanyang Basin. Second, if the natural area was large, it would be divided into two prefectures; for example, Yunzhong and Jiuyuan prefectures, which jointly had jurisdiction over Hetao Alluvial Plain. Also, the Ba and Shu prefectures shared governance of the Sichuan Basin. Third, most of the prefectures would occupy a fertile basin or plain as the core district, and then extended to the surrounding plateau or mountains. The prefectures of Beidi, Shangjun, Shangdang, Taiyuan, Hedong, Daijun, Yanmen, etc., all adapted this layout. Each commandery must ensure that it has a sufficient amount of cultivated land in order to provide a solid foundation for agricultural production. On this basis, administrative management can be effectively implemented.

The full implementation of the Commandery-County system in the Qin Dynasty marked the formation of a centralized state, meaning that China therefore became a centralized state with imperial power. Later generations have praised this practice of Emperor Qin Shi Huang and listed "the abolition of the enfeoffment system and vassals" and "abolition of the principalities and establishment of Commandery-County system" as some of the most important events in Chinese history. Although the peasant revolution led by Chen Sheng and Wu Guang put an end to the fifteen years rule of the Qin Dynasty, and the Qin Dynasty did not last for generations as Emperor Qin Shi Huang had wished, the centralized autocratic system of the Qin Dynasty and its establishment of the administrative system in the form of Commandery-County system was not abolished. Instead, it was promoted and advocated for more than two thousand years.

2. The Feoffment System in the Han Dynasty

Although the Commandery-County system was advanced for its time, it was dimmed by the cruel reign of the Qin Empire. Protests rose in various regions. In 209 BC, two low rank army officers named Chen Sheng and Wu Guang led around 900 soldiers to revolt against Qin rule in Daze village (southeast Su County in Anhui). The uprising spurred farmers around the country as well as noble families of the previous vassal kingdoms to turn against their Qin rulers.

Xiang Yu and Liu Bang were the most famous among all rebel leaders. In 206 BC, Liu Bang led his army to capture Xianyang, the capital of the Qin Dynasty, and overthrew the rule of the Qin Dynasty. Xiang Yu and his army later entered Xianyang as well. As the chief of the rebel forces, Xiang declared himself the "Hegemon-King of Western Chu." He divided the Qin Empire into 18 vassal kingdoms and placed Liu Bang in the remote Bashu and Hanzhong Region (Sichuan, Chongqing, and South of Shaanxi) with the title, "King of Han." Soon a civil war erupted between Liu and Xiang, known as the "Chu-Han Contention." In 202 BC, Xiang was defeated in the Battle of Gaixia and took his own life. In the same year, Liu established the Han Dynasty—known as "Western Han"; he became known as Emperor Gaozu of Han.

(1) Feoffment to Kings with Different Surnames in Early Han

In the early years of the Han, Emperor Gaozu named seven generals and ministers outside the Liu family as kings and granted them land. These seven non-Liu vassal kings have long held their own forces. Rather than being enfeoffed by Liu Bang, it could be said that this was Liu Bang's recognition of their de facto separatist control.

The following is a brief introduction to the seven kings:

King Zang Tu of Yan: Zang Tu had been granted the position of marquis by Xiang Yu. As his vassal state in the northeast was far from the Han capital, Emperor Gaozu had limited control over him. Therefore, he largely upheld the status quo.

King Xin of Han: Xin was the grandson of King Xiang of Han in the Warring States Period. He contributed greatly to helping Liu Bang establish the Han Dynasty. Therefore, he was granted the title King Xin of Han after he occupied land which used to be the State of Han.

King Zhang Er of Zhao: Zhang had been granted the title of marquis by Xiang Yu of Changshan. Later he joined Liu Bang. Together with Han Xin, he took the land of the State of Zhao. Therefore, he was crowned King of Zhao.

King Han Xin of Chu: Han Xin was a genius military strategist and leader, contributing greatly to the Chu-Han Contention. Liu Bang listened to the advice of his counsel Zhang Liang, and conferred the title of "King of Qi" on Han Xin in 203 BC. Fearing that Han Xin might threaten his throne, Liu Bang changed his title to the "King of Chu" the following year.

King Ying Bu of Huainan: Ying Bu had been appointed marquis by Xiang Yu. Liu Bang persuaded Ying Bu to join him and granted him the title "King of Huainan." He was then asked to fight against Xiang Yu to get his land back.

King Peng Yue of Liang: Peng Yue was one of the rebel leaders against the Qin Dynasty. In the Chu-Han Contention, Peng led over 30,000 people to join Liu Bang. He successfully cut off Xiang Yu's logistics. Liu Bang had promised Peng the land of the former State of Wei on the condition that Xiang Yu was defeated.

King Wu Rui of Changsha: Wu Rui was a former Prefect of Fanyang (northeast of Boyang in Jiangxi). He had been appointed marquis by Xiang Yu. After Xiang was defeated, he became an ally of Liu Bang, who changed his title to "King of Changsha."

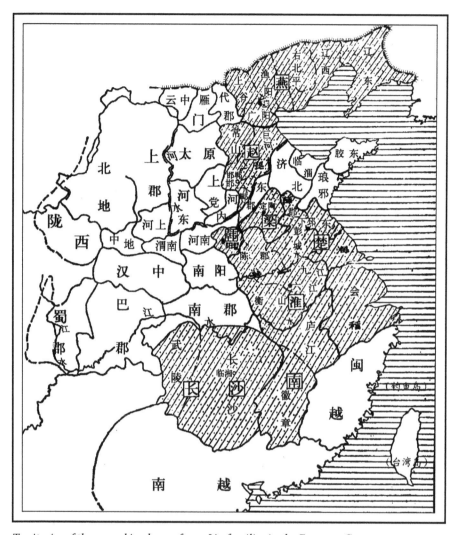

Territories of the seven kingdoms of non-Liu families in the Emperor Gaozu era[2]

The land of the seven kings added up to half the Han Empire. To crown it all, their land was the richest and most prosperous in the East. In comparison, there were only 15 commanderies under direct rule of Emperor Gaozu of Han. The empire was shared by the Emperor and the kings with different surnames

---

2. Zhou Zhenhe, *Geography of Administrative Divisions in Western Han Dynasty* (Beijing: People's Publishing House, 1987), 9.

from the Emperor (see *Territories of the seven kingdoms of non-Liu families in the Emperor Gaozu era*).

Such a political and geographical pattern would certainly displeased Liu Bang. Enfeoffments of these non-Liu vassals was not what he wanted to do. In addition, these vassals had control over armies and did not comply with the dispatches of the central government. In fact, it posed a great threat to Liu Bang's rule. Therefore, from the day of enfeoffment, Liu began to consider how to eliminate these non-Liu vassals one by one, in order to eliminate a concern in his mind.

In the next few years, Emperor Gaozu continued to find faults with the seven kings with different surnames. Eventually all of them were deprived of their titles, except King Wu Rui of Changsha. The reasons why he kept his title were as follows: the Kingdom of Changsha was on the south border of the empire with a scarce population. Wu Rui and his offspring were very careful not to give Emperor Gaozu any excuses to find fault with the family. The kingdom survived until the reign of Emperor Wen, when the King of Changsha had no direct male successors. Emperor Gaozu ordered that kings must only be surnamed Liu; whoever was not should be exterminated.[3]

(2) The Establishment of Kingdoms within the Liu Family
After Emperor Gaozu freed himself of any danger posed from the kings with different surnames, he began to bestow the title (and lands) of "King" within the Liu Family. There were two reasons for this situation: first, Liu Bang believed that one of the main reasons for the short lifespan of the Qin Dynasty, which collapsed quickly after only two generations, was the lack of enfeoffment of vassal states to people of the same surname so that no one would defend the central authority in case of a rebellion. Liu Bang did not want to repeat the mistake of the short-lived Qin Dynasty, so he proceeded to enfeoff people with the same surname, hoping that he could have enough power to support the central government. In addition, the enfeoffed non-Liu vassal kings tended to bargain with Liu about various arrangements and showed insubordination. That was also a reason for Liu to speed up the enfeoffment of vassal kings with the same surname. Second, since the Commandery-County system was merely implemented for a short time during the Qin Dynasty, people did not know well about this system. Many people

---

3. *Records of Han Dynasty · Annals of Wang Ling.*

mistakenly linked the brutal rule of the Qin Dynasty with the implementation of this system, believing that there was a causal link between the two events. Others, though not opposing the implementation of the Commandery-County system, believed that the enfeoffment system was also good and necessary and that both systems could be implemented simultaneously. These views more or less influenced Liu Bang so that he did not abandon the enfeoffment system even though he ruled out vassal kings with different surnames.

However, unlike the enfeoffment of vassals with the same surname of the Western Zhou period, Liu's practice was a mixture of both the enfeoffment system and the Commandery-County system. There were still prefectures called sub-prefectures in vassal states. These sub-prefectures were nominally under the central authority but were actually under the direct jurisdiction of the vassal kings. In addition, the establishment of officials in these vassal states differed from that of the Han prefectures. In terms of the establishment of officials, the vassal states adopted the same way as the Han Dynasty. The central government of the Han Dynasty set up an official called "Taifu" who assisted the vassal kings and also pointed a prime minister who was in charge of all officials. As for the officials ranking below the imperial governor, they would be appointed by the vassal kings themselves. Emperor Gaozu also granted titles and land to a number of marquises, whose land was equal to counties, under direct control of the central government.

The following is a structure of the administrative divisions of the Han Dynasty in its early years.

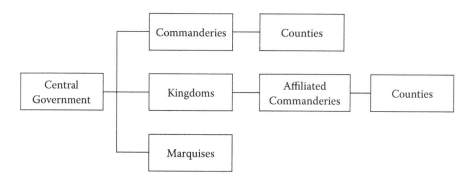

By the twelfth year of Liu's reign (195 BC), Liu was on his deathbed. The substitution of vassal kings with the same surname with one that had different surnames was basically completed. At that time, nine of Liu Bang's siblings of the same surname were vassal kings, and there was only one vassal king of a different surname, the King of Changsha. These vassal states with the same surname were distributed east of the Taihang Mountains, with the larger vassals having six or seven sub-prefectures and the smaller ones having three or four. These sub-prefectures were geographically connected with the state of Changsha, accounting for more than half of the entire territory of the Han Dynasty at that time; while the central Han regime only had direct control of fifteen prefectures, roughly covering the area equivalent of today's Shaanxi Province, southwestern Shanxi Province, northern and central-western Henan Province, most of Hubei Province and Sichuan Province, Ningxia Hui Autonomous Region and Gansu Province. In terms of the covering area, these fifteen prefectures were even smaller than the prefectures in Han Dynasty in the fifth year of Emperor Gao's of the Han Dynasty reign (see *Territories of the ten kingdoms in Emperor Gaozu's later years*).

(3) How Three Emperors of Han Eliminated the Power of Kingdoms

There were many frictions between the kingdoms and the central government. For example, the kings could ask their own officials—lower than commandery governors—to collect taxes and draft free labor. What was more, the kings were competing against the central government for people's loyalty by controlling such resources as salt and iron, and by reducing taxes. In addition, the kings recruited many counsels for ideas against the central government.

After Emperor Gaozu died, Empress Lü came to power. She tried to grant land and titles to her relatives in an effort to curb the power of the kingdoms. She first deposed the King of Liang and the King of Zhao. Then she made the King of Qi and King of Chu cede parts of their land to make room for eight members of her family to become kings. This caused great grievance within the Liu Family.

As soon as Empress Lü died, the Liu family, as well as Emperor Gaozu's previous ministers, got rid of all the kings of the Lü Family and their men. Then Liu Heng became Emperor Wen of Han. The kingdoms also went back to the Liu family. However, the kings were only remote relatives of the Emperor. Many of them had ambitions of becoming the Emperor themselves, posing great danger for Emperor Wen. One of the counsels named Jia Yi put forward the idea that, "The more kingdoms there were, the more powerless they would become." Emperor Wen took the following measures to strengthen his power.

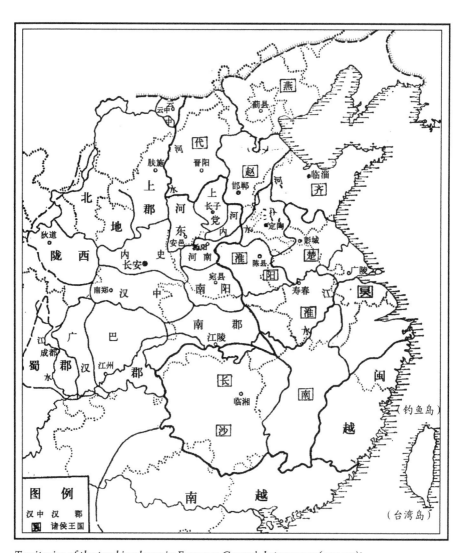

Territories of the ten kingdoms in Emperor Gaozu's later years (194 BC)[4]

---

4. Zhou Zhenhe, *Geography of Administrative Divisions in Western Han Dynasty* (Beijing: People's Publishing House, 1987), 11.

The first thing he did was to reappoint his son from being the King of Huaigyang to the King of Liang. This shift handed geo-political advantage to the Kingdom of Liang, which thrust into the borders of other kingdoms like a knife. The second thing he did was to divide the Kingdom of Qi into seven parts, following the king's death without successors. The third thing he did was to retitle the King of Huainan to King Chengyang, and then he divided the original Kingdom of Huainan into three parts. By shrinking the size of the kingdoms, Emperor Wen successfully limited the power of kings. By the 16th year of his reign, there were 17 kingdoms. And by the later years of his reign, there were 24 commanderies.

Liu Qi, who was the eldest son of the Emperor, became Emperor Jing of Han after his father died. Imperial Counsellor Chao Cuo urged the Emperor to eliminate the kingdoms and retrieve the land for control under the central government. Emperor Jing adopted his proposal and ceded one commandery from the kingdoms of Chu and Zhao each, and six counties from the King of Jiaoxi. This provoked great anger among the kings. When King Pi of Wu received an imperial edict to cede two commanderies from his land, he refused the Emperor's request. As the most senior and powerful of all kings, King Pi called on the other six kings and rebelled. This was known in history as the "Rebellion of the Seven Kingdoms."

King Pi enlisted 200,000 people from his kingdom under the slogan "Kill the Crooked Chao Cuo." Together with the King of Chu, they fought against the King of Liang, who was pro-Emperor. Over ten thousand people were killed. Emperor Jing sent defender-in-chief Zhou Yafu to fight back. In the meantime, he killed Chao Cuo, hoping to stop the rebels. When he learned that Chao was killed in vain and the rebels didn't retreat at all, he was in great remorse and grief. Zhou Yafu, on the other hand, defeated the rebels within three months. The seven kings were either killed or committed suicide.

The power of kings was greatly damaged by the defeat. Emperor Jing shrunk the size of the kingdoms and brought commanderies under control of the central government. As a result, most kingdoms had only one commandery. The kings were also deprived of the right to appoint officials and to levy taxes within their territories. They were no longer in charge of any administration, but lived on a quota of taxes from their kingdoms. Even the quota was determined by the central government. In this way, the status of kingdoms were reduced to the level of commanderies.

Chapter Two

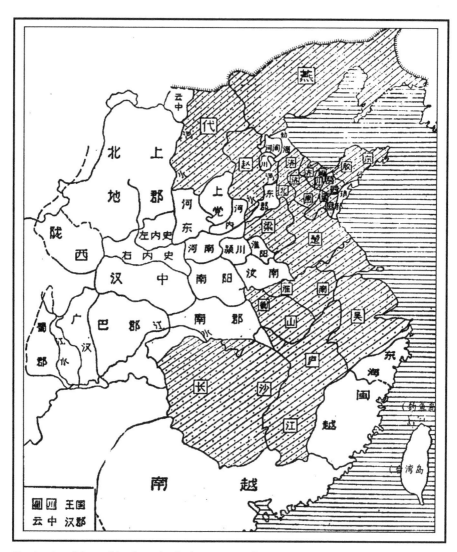

Territories of the 17 kingdoms in the later years of Emperor Wen[5]

---

5. Zhou Zhenhe, *Geography of Administrative Divisions in Western Han Dynasty* (Beijing: People's Publishing House, 1987), 13.

The administrative divisions of the Han Dynasty were then simplified to a two-hierarchy structure as follows:

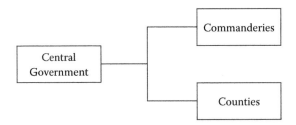

Since the central government took control of the former commanderies, the number increased greatly. In 144 BC, there were 43 commanderies in the empire, co-existing with 25 kingdoms. When Emperor Jing died in 141 BC, his son, Crown Prince Liu Che, became Emperor Wu at the age of 15. Even though the kingdom territory was greatly reduced in Emperor Jing's time, some bigger regions still had numerous counties that extended to thousands of kilometers. In order to eliminate any potential threats, Emperor Wu adopted the proposal by counsel Zhufu Yan to further break up the kingdoms.

In 127 BC, the Emperor publicized an order of "Tui En" (literally meaning extending kindness from kings to their sons). Details of the order were as follows: The feudal lords could grant lands within their territories to their sons based on personal favor. The central government would then establish and confer titles, setting up vassal states. Once the new vassals were established, this area no longer belonged to the original vassal state but had to be ruled by the adjacent prefectures of Han. In this way, the more vassal states were established, the smaller the domain of the vassal kingdoms would become. Therefore, the outcome of the decree of extended kindness was not substantially different from that of the reduction of land, except that the scale was smaller, and it was more acceptable nominally. It seems that the decree of extended kindness aimed to cultivate the willingness of vassal kings, but actually they were forced to adhere to the decree. Since a vassal king could have as many princes as he wanted, and during that time it was natural for vassal kings to have multiple offspring; therefore, there were hundreds of princes in the Western Han Dynasty. And after several generations, the territory of each vassal had been greatly reduced. By the end of the Western Han Dynasty, some vassal states had become the size of only three or four counties.

38 | Chapter Two

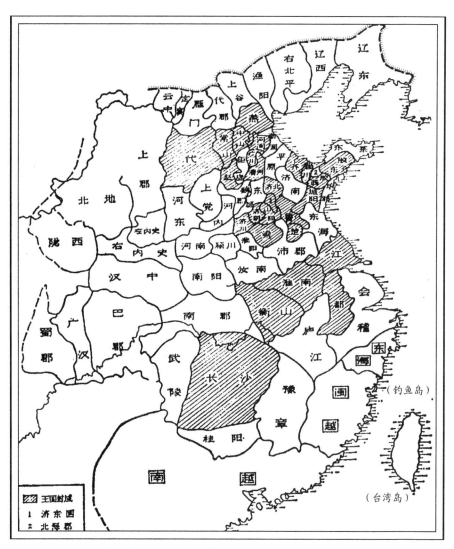

Territories of the 25 kingdoms in the middle of Emperor Jing's reign (151 BC)[6]

---

6. Zhou Zhenhe, *Geography of Administrative Divisions in the Western Han Dynasty* (Beijing: People's Publishing House, 1987), 15.

As a result of the decree of extended kindness ("Tui En"), the strength of the vassal states had been severely weakened and could no longer pose a threat to the central authority. The number of vassal states also dropped from 24 in the early years of Emperor Wu's reign to less than 20 in the final years. Thus, through the efforts of Emperor Wen, Emperor Jing, and Emperor Wu, the threat to the central authority posed by the vassal states of the same surname was finally eliminated.

3. Imperial Expansion in the Era of Emperor Wu

After the "enlightened administration of the Han emperors Wen and Jing," the Han Dynasty recovered and developed economically. By the early years of Emperor Wu, the country had sufficient savings, and the potential threat of secession within the Han Dynasty had been largely eliminated after the rebellion of seven kingdoms were put down. Under this premise, Emperor Wu of the Han Dynasty, with a broute mind, turned to deal with the enemy outside the country and began to expand his territory.

(1) Expansion to the Yi Districts in the Southwest

The "Yi" districts in the southwest roughly equal the area of present-day western Sichuan, south Gansu, west Guizhou, Yunnan, and some Southeast Asian countries. Ancient kingdoms like Yelang, Dian, and Qiong were situated by the Wu and Jinsha Rivers.

During the reign of Liu Che of the Han Dynasty (134–129 BC), Sima Xiangru wrote to Emperor Wu of the Han Dynasty that Commandery-County system could be built in Qiong (now roughly Xichang, Sichuan Province) and Ze (now roughly Yangyuan, Sichuan Province). Therefore, Emperor Wu sent Sima Xiangru to the Xiyi to assign a Chief Commandant and set up more than ten counties in the south of Qionglai Mountain under the jurisdiction of Shu Prefecture. Later on, although the Han court mobilized a lot of manpower to build routes, transportation in southwestern Yi remained inconvenient. At the same time, because Emperor Wu was busy with the Xiongnu in the north, he had to temporarily cancel the construction of a dozen counties in the Xiyi. However, from the military point of view, Emperor Wu retained the Qianwei Prefecture with two counties in Nanyi and one Chief Commandant under its jurisdiction in order to deal with the threat from Nanyue.

After the Han Dynasty achieved a decisive victory in the war against the Xiongnu, it once again shifted its focus on expanding into the southwestern Yi regions. In the autumn of the fifth year of Emperor Yuan Ding (112 BC), Emperor Wu asked scholar-official Chiyi to send troops from Qianwei Prefecture to join the rest of the troops to quell the rebellion led by Lü Jia in the Nanyue Kingdom. The ruler of the small city of Julan (now southwest of Huangping, Guizhou Province), who was afraid that the surrounding cities would take advantage of the opportunity to invade his city if his army was asked to accompany Han's troops in its expedition to the Nanyue Kingdom, rose up in rebellion and killed the envoy from the Han government and the Taishou of Qianwei. The Han Dynasty used the eight lieutenants who were supposed to fight against Nanyue to suppress the rebellion and succeed. In the following year, since Nanyue had been successfully conquered, the Han government, therefore, sent the eight lieutenants to pacify the whole area of Nanyi. They destroyed the Tou Lan Kingdom that was blocking the route to the Dian Kingdom and occupied a large area south of the Zangke River to the Lao River (now Hei River). The Han government built up the Zangke Prefecture by combining the Nanyi area and Qianwei Prefecture. Later, the Han Dynasty conquered the Qiong Kingdom and the Ze Kingdom and set up four prefectures in the Nanyi area according to the geographical distribution of each minority. The four prefectures were: Wudu Prefecture, which was established in Baimadi, the western part of Guanghan Prefecture; Wenshan Prefecture, which was established in Ranmang, the northern part of Shu Prefecture (now north of Maowen, Sichuan Province); Shenli Prefecture, which was established in Zedu, the southwestern part of Shu Prefecture; and Yuexi Prefecture, which was established in Qiongdu, south of Shenli Prefecture (see *Territories of the commanderies [part] in the southwest [111–97 BC]*).

In 109 BC, the Emperor forced the King of Dian to surrender by seizing his neighboring towns. The Kingdom of Dian was situated in the modern Dian Lake area in east Yunnan. Yizhou Commandery was set up to rule the region. A few years later, the empire conquered Kunming, and included it in the Yizhou Commandery. By then the entire region of the Yi had become a part of Han territory, which extended to the present-day Gaoligong and Ailao Mountains. The regions followed the Commandery-County system and were under direct control of the central government.

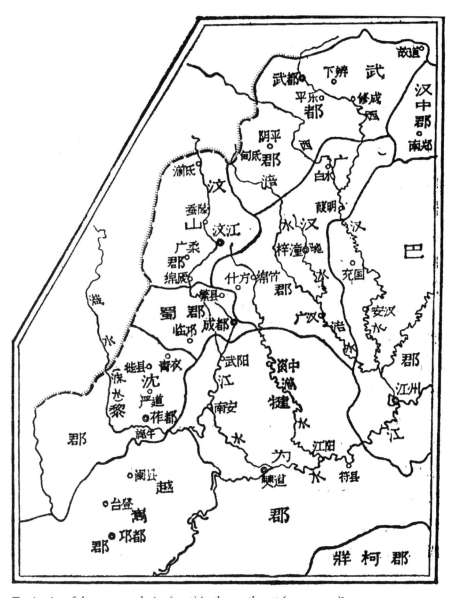

Territories of the commanderies (part) in the southwest (111–97 BC)[7]

---

7. Zhou Zhenhe, *Geography of Administrative Divisions in the Western Han Dynasty* (Beijing: People's Publishing House, 1987), 139.

However, due to the lack of careful consideration at the time of establishment, some prefectures were not suitable for living because of their limited territory and sparse population, so the Shenli Prefecture was deserted at the end of Emperor Wu's reign, and the Wenshan Prefecture was deserted in the third year of Emperor Xuan's reign (67 BC). Both prefectures were merged into the neighboring Shu Prefecture.

(2) Expansion to the Lingnan Districts

As previously mentioned, the Qin Empire had set up Nanhai, Guilin, and Xiang commanderies in the Lingnan districts. When the Qin Dynasty ended, the three commanderies were taken by Zhao Tuo, who named it Nanyue Kingdom. It survived another 100 years or so, because the Han Dynasty was not strong enough in its early years. After economic development became stable, Emperor Wu thought it was time to bring Nanyue under his control.

In the fifth year of Emperor Yuan Ding's reign (112 BC), the prime minister of the Nanyue Kingdom, Lü Jia, started a rebellion, killed the king of Nanyue and the Han ambassador, and set up an army on the border. When Emperor Wu learned of the rebellion, he mobilized the Yue people to join the troops from the south of Yangtze–Huaihe, forming an army of 100,000 people. Emperor Wu divided the force into five groups to put down the rebellion. Fubo General Lu Bode led a group of soldiers from Guiyang (now Chenzhou, Hunan Province) along the Huangshui (now Lianjiang and Beijiang); Louchuan General Yang Pu led a group of troops from Yuzhang (now Jiangxi Province) to Nanyue Kingdom via Hengpu Pass (today's south of Dayu Mountain, Dayu County, Jiangxi Province). Among the other three routes, two of the armies set out from Lingling (now southwest of Quanzhou in Guangxi Province) and Cangwu (now Xunjiang River), and one of them was the army collected at Yelang and marched along the Zangke River (now Beipan River and Hong River). The five armies originally planned to join forces in Panyu, the capital of Nanyue. However, two armies led by Yang Pu and Lu Bode arrived early and completed the task of pacifying the whole kingdom without waiting for the arrival of the other three armies.

Thus, in the sixth year of Yuan Ding, 111 BC, Emperor Wu divided the original lands of the Qin Dynasty—which consisted of Guilin, Nanhai, and Xiangjun—into five commanderies: Nanhai, Cangwu, Hepu, Yulin, and Xiangjun. Two prefectures are located in the south of Xiang Prefecture and in today's Vietnam;

Jiaozhi Prefecture and Jiuzhen Prefecture, which were set up by Zhao Tuo, the former King of Nanyue, were preserved. The Han government established the Rinan Prefecture in the south of these two prefectures, thus extending the southern border of the Han Dynasty to the central region of Vietnam today. In the first year of Emperor Yuan Feng's reign (110 BC), the Han army crossed the sea and seized the island of Hainan, where they set up Daner Prefecture and Zhuya Prefecture. Back then, Emperor Wu had set up ten prefectures in the Lingnan region. However, because the people in present-day Hainan Island constantly rebelled against the brutal rule of the local officials, the Han Dynasty's rule there was never stabilized. Therefore, in 82 BC, Daner Prefecture was incorporated into Zhuya Prefecture; in 46 BC, the people of Shannan County in Zhuya Prefecture rebelled again, and the local government could not sustain itself there. Therefore, Emperor Yuan accepted the proposal of Minister Jia Juan, and finally decided to give up Zhuya Prefecture, too.

(3) Battling the Nomadic Xiongnu Tribes

In the midst of a farmer uprising and nobles at the end of the Qin Dynasty, a nomadic Xiongnu tribe, led by Modu (冒顿单于) in the North, took advantage of the chaos and occupied a vast area of land, including the area previously conquered by Qin general Meng Tian. Xiongnu also ruled parts of the land which used to be the kingdoms of Qin, Zhao, and Yan in the Warring States Period.

By the time Liu Bang defeated Xiang Yu, Xiongnu had become very powerful, posing great threat to Liu. From Emperor Gaozu to the early years of Emperor Wu, the Han Empire could not gain the upper hand in numerous battles against Xiongnu. Therefore, a makeshift strategy was to wed Han princesses to the Xiongnu leaders. However, this could not pacify the nomadic tribes, which continued to invade Han territory on a smaller scale.

As the country became stronger, Emperor Wu set his agenda to fighting back. The first retaliation took place in 129 BC. Two years later, General Wei Qing set out from Yunzhong (present-day Tumotechuan in Inner Mongolia) and conquered the southern part of Hetao District (upper reaches of the Yellow River). Wei later pushed his armies to the west of the Gansu Plateau (Longxi Region). Then, Shuofang Commandery was set up; the Han Empire extended its territory to the Yinshan Mountains.

After taking the southern part of Hetao, the Han shifted their focus to the Gansu (Hexi) Corridor. In 121 BC, the nephew of Wei Qing, General Huo Qubing, twice attacked Xiongnu and entered the Hexi Corridor. Meanwhile, disputes among khans of Xiongnu escalated. Khan Hunye killed Khan Xiutu and led 40,000 of his followers to surrender to the Han. Emperor Wu then set up four commanderies to control the Hexi Corridor and the Huang River. The four commanderies were Jiuquan, Wuwei, Zhangye, and Dunhuang. They opened the pathway to the Western Regions.

(4) Setting up Four Commanderies on the Korean Peninsula
As early as the end of the Warring States period, the state of Yan already began to control North Korea and Zhenfan in the northern part of the Korean Peninsula. After the establishment of the Qin Dynasty, it did not relinquish its control over this area, and the administrative structure left behind by the State of Yan was assigned to Liaodong Prefecture as a foreign subsidiary. In the early years of the Western Han Dynasty, the territory of the Korean Peninsula that once belonged to the Qin was not fully inherited, but was only bounded by the Pei River (now Chongchon River in North Korea). Later, Wei Man of the state of Yan, led thousands of people to cross the Pei River and enter the northern part of the Korean Peninsula, settling in the former area of the Qin defense zone and establishing a regime based on the immigrants of Yan and Qi (now Shandong Peninsula) who had been exiled there. This regime was historically called Wiman Joseon. The area covered the east end of present-day Liaoning Province, western Jilin Province, and the northern part of the Korean Peninsula.

In 128 BC, Emperor Wu sent armies to the Korean Peninsula where Huimo and Korean tribes lived. The leader of Huimo and 280,000 of his people surrendered. Then, Emperor Wu set up Canghai Commandery, covering the eastern coast of the Korean Peninsula. Three years later, counsel Gongsun Hong advised Wu to give up Canghai, since it was too far away. The Emperor adopted his suggestion and cancelled the Commandery.

In 109 BC, Wu sent General Yang Pu and his army to reach the peninsula by sea, and General Xun Zhi by land. The two armies cooperated and forced the Wei Tribe of Korea to surrender in the next year. The Emperor then set up four commanderies on the peninsula: Lelang, Xuantu, Zhenfan, and Lintun, covering the River Han area (see *Territories of the four commanderies on the Korean Peninsula circa 107 BC*).

Unification | 45

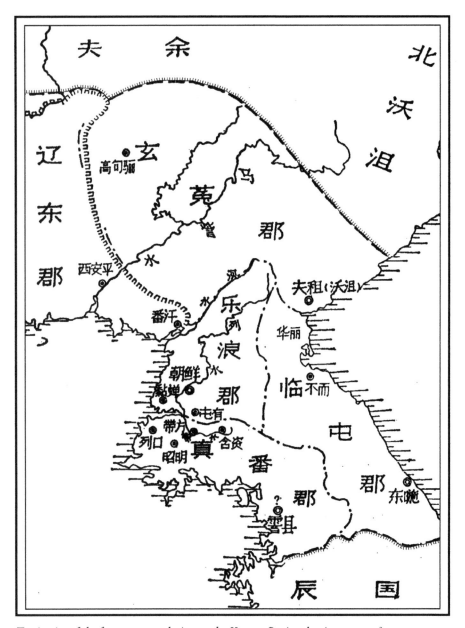

Territories of the four commanderies on the Korean Peninsula circa 107 BC[8]

---

8. Zhou Zhenhe, *Geography of Administrative Divisions in Western Han Dynasty* (Beijing: People's Publishing House, 1987), 208.

In 82 BC, the population of the northern part of the Korean Peninsula was limited, and many parts of it were still undeveloped and controlled by the local people. Therefore, the Han Dynasty abolished the Lintun Prefecture and Zhenfan Prefecture, abandoning part of their jurisdiction and incorporating part of it into the Lelang Prefecture, which was located to the north of the two prefectures. At this time, Xuantu Prefecture also abandoned the eastern part of its territory and was forced to move inward, moving its administration from Wozo on the Korean Peninsula to Goguryeo on the Liaodong Peninsula (now west of Xinbin, Liaoning Province).

As mentioned above, by the time of Emperor Wu, many new Han prefectures had been established as a result of the development of the border areas, and many new prefectures had been divided from the existing ones, so that the number of Han prefectures had reached 91 by 104 BC, and this number was maintained for seven years.

4. The Feoffment System and Commandery Changes in Eastern Han

By the end of the Western Han Dynasty, Wang Mang, a relative of the queen, was in charge of the central government. In AD 5, Wang killed Emperor Ping of Han. In AD 8, Wang proclaimed himself the Emperor—this was the beginning of the Xin Dynasty.

Wang Mang carried out a number of reforms after he ascended the throne. However, his reforms exacerbated the conflicts between the administration and the people. Farmers rebelled against his rule. In AD 23, rebels such as Lülin and Chimei brought about the downfall of the Xin Dynasty. In AD 25, Liu Xiu declared himself as Emperor Guangwu, and his dynasty was known as Eastern Han, because the new capital of Luoyang was located to the east of the original capital of Western Han.

(1) *The Era of Emperor Guangwu*

According to Ban Gu's *Book of Han · Treatise on Geography*, in the second year of Emperor Liu Kan's reign at the end of the Western Han Dynasty, there were 83 Han prefectures and 20 vassal states. Later, three more vassal states, Guangzong,

Guangshi, and Guangchuan, were added, making a total of 106 prefectures and vassal states. After the Xin Dynasty founded by Wang Mang, the vassal states of the Western Han Dynasty were no longer very different from the prefectures of the early Eastern Han Dynasty, and the names of the vassal states remained being the names of the prefectures. Thus, in the early Han Dynasty, the whole country was actually divided into 106 prefectures.

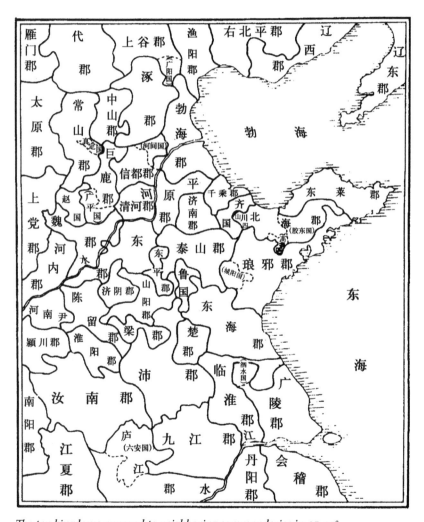

The ten kingdoms annexed to neighboring commanderies in AD 37[9]

---

9. Li Xiaojie, *Geography in the Eastern Han Dynasty* (Jinan: Shandong Education Press, 1999), 5.

In the second year after the complete unification of the country by Emperor Liu Xiu, that is, in AD 37, he began to adjust the existing administrative divisions. Since Emperor Wu's decree of extended kindness, the territory of vassal states in the Western Han Dynasty became smaller and smaller. By the end of the Western Han Dynasty, many vassal states had only a few counties or one county, losing their status as prefecture-level administrative divisions. In the 13th year of Jianwu, most of the ten kingdoms of the Western Han that were annexed had only about four or five counties, so the annexation of these ten kingdoms was inevitable (see *The ten kingdoms annexed to neighboring commanderies in* AD 37).

Six of the ten kingdoms, including Zhending, Hejian, Chengyang, Zichuan, Sishui, and Guangyang, were re-divided into vassal states by Emperor Guangwu before they were merged. The reason is that in the early years of the Eastern Han Dynasty, the emperor needed the support of the Liu clan and the old nobility of the Western Han Dynasty in order to end the chaotic situation as soon as possible. Therefore, from the first to the seventh year of Jianwu, he appointed ten vassal kings out of the clan and the sons of the former kings of the Western Han Dynasty. These ten vassal states are Zhongshan, Lu, Chengyang, Sishui, Zichuan, Zhending, Guangyang (later referred to as Zhao), Taiyuan (later referred to as Qi), Changsha, and Hejian. However, in order to prevent these vassal states from becoming too powerful and forming separatist forces that had been witnessed in the early Western Han Dynasty, Emperor Guangwu took great pains to divide the domain of the vassal kings, except for Taiyuan, so that the other nine states were all enclosed in the territory of the former kingdoms of the Western Han Dynasty. This is because the former kingdoms of the Western Han Dynasty were small and not contiguous with each other, so that these vassal states could not be united geographically, thus making them vain in unifying. Therefore, when the task of these vassal states was completed, Emperor Guangwu could easily downgrade them to marquisates. The above-mentioned six states were included in the ten vassal states that suited the consideration of Emperor Guangwu. After downgrading vassal state of Zhending and others, these vassal states were incorporated into Han Prefecture. Among these, it cannot be said that there was no intention to completely eliminate the residual power of the original vassal kings.

The other four vassal states were Gaomi, Jiaodong, Guangping, and Liuan. Among these four states, except for Liu An, the annexation of the other three states was actually related to the enfeoffment of vassals with different surnames in the early years of the Eastern Han Dynasty. In the process of unification in the early Han Dynasty, Deng Yu, Jia Fu, and Wu Han had made great contributions to Emperor Guangwu, so Deng Yu was made Marquis of Gaomi, Jia Fu was made the Marquis of Jiaodong, and Wu Han was granted the title of the Marquis of Guangping. This phenomenon of having several counties under a marquisate in the early Eastern Han Dynasty was very different from that of the Western Han Dynasty, where a marquis only ruled one county. This arrangement could be said to be an innovation of the Eastern Han Dynasty. The reason for this is that since Emperor Gao Zu, there was an agreement that no king would be made without the Liu clan, and Emperor Guangwu naturally had to follow this regulation. However, Deng Yu and other founding fathers were so meritorious that they deserved to be crowned kings, so Emperor Guangwu adopted a compromise approach by choosing some small territories of the former kingdoms of the Western Han Dynasty as fiefs for meritorious vassals. In this way, these vassal lords could enjoy the status of vassal kings without having the title of vassal kings, thus achieving the dual purpose of rewarding the vassals and strengthening centralized rule. Therefore, from this point of view, the merger of the kingdoms of Gaomi, Jiaodong, and Guangping was already a necessity. As for the merger of Liuan, it was probably due to the small size of the area and the fact that it was located in Hainan, which was not easy for the central government to control in the early years of the Eastern Han Dynasty.

In the early years of the Eastern Han Dynasty, in addition to the merger of ten vassal kingdoms, some Han prefectures in the border areas were also combined, mainly in the northern and northwestern border areas. Between the ten to twenty years of Emperor Jianwu's reign, the northern and northwestern borders were frequently invaded by the Xiongnu and other tribes. Eight prefectures, including Dingxiang, Yunzhong, Wuyuan, Shuofang, Beidi, Yanmen, Dai, and Shanggu, were successively merged, with the people of the former counties moving in. In the 26th year of Jianwu (AD 50), the Xiongnu in the south were pacified and the people of these eight prefectures returned to their homeland. In addition, the northwestern prefecture of Jincheng, which had been invaded by the Qiang, was merged into Longxi Prefecture in the 12th year of Emperor Jianwu but was restored to the jurisdiction of Jincheng Prefecture a year later.

In addition, the Eastern Han Dynasty still inherited the system of vassal lords and kings from the Western Han Dynasty. In the fifteenth year of Emperor Jianwu

(AD 39), Dou Rong, the grand secretary of state, and others submitted a petition for the enfeoffment of royal sons. Emperor Guangwu then first made his ten sons, including Prince Fu, dukes. Two years later, Liu Fu and nine others (Lin Huai, the Duke of Heng, had already died of illness) were promoted to vassal kings. These nine vassal kings were: The nine vassal kings were: King Yang of the Donghai (his title was changed to Yang the Strong in the 19th year of Jianwu), King Fu of Zhongshan (his title was transferred to Pei in the 20th year of Jianwu), King Ying of Chu, King Kang of Jinan, King Xian of Dongping, King Yan of Huainan, King Jing of Shanyang, King Yan of Zuo Yi (his title was transferred to Zhongshan in the 30th year of Jianwu), and King Jing of Langya.

Except for the king of Zhongshan and the king of Donghai, who ruled two prefectures, all the other vassal kings ruled only one prefecture and their territories were scattered and unconnected to each other. This was very different from the situation in the early years of the Western Han Dynasty when the ten kingdoms were enfeoffed by Emperor Gao. Back then, every kingdom has several prefectures, and each one was geographically connected, with the total enfeoffment area accounting for more than half of the territory of the Han Dynasty. This arrangement shows that Emperor Guangwu had learned a lesson from the previous dynasty, granting the vassal kings only nominal titles and providing them with only food and clothing. All in all, there were 12 kingdoms and 81 commanderies in the era of Emperor Guangwu.

(2) The Era of Emperor Ming
After succeeding to the throne, Emperor Ming further set out to consolidate the central government. He was even more cautious than Emperor Guangwu in crowning his sons as vassal kings. One story in the historic document recorded that one time Emperor Ming looked at the map and prepared to crown the princes as vassal kings, considering that they should only enjoy half of the tax in their own prefecture. When Empress Ma saw this, she said to Emperor Ming, "Isn't it too harsh for the princes that we cut the rent of several prefectures?" Upon hearing this, Emperor Ming replied, "My sons will not be the same as the sons of the previous emperor. It is enough for them to live on 20 million yuan of rent and taxation every year."[10] Seven vassal states were established during the

---

10. *Book of the Later Han · Annals of Empresses.*

reign of Emperor Ming, and two of them were separated from the original Han Prefecture, which shows that the size of the vassal states was really small.

Not only was the size of the vassal kingdoms in the Eastern Han Dynasty small, but these vassal kings further distanced themselves from their kingdoms. They did not manage their people within the kingdoms, and sometimes they did not even go to live in the kingdoms they had been given but only stayed in the capital city to enjoy the rents of the kingdoms. At the same time, the central government gradually tightened its control over the vassal kings, especially during the time of Emperor Ming, who was not as close to the vassal kings as he had been in the time of Emperor Guangwu. Naturally, the guard against the vassal kings was also strengthened. The incident of Liu Mu, the Jing King of Beihai was one good example. In the reign of Emperor Guangwu, Liu Mu made a wide range of acquaintances and guests. When the law became stricter under Emperor Ming, he dismissed all his guests in order to protect himself and avoid any trouble. Therefore, he turned his attention to music to spend his time.

Therefore, it can be seen from the example that although the Eastern Han Dynasty was still practicing the parallel system of prefectures and states, in reality, these kingdoms were no different from and could be regarded as Han prefectures.

There were also changes in the setting of Han counties during the Yongping years. Emperor Ming established Yongchang Prefecture in the southwestern region of Ailao. Compared with the Western Han Dynasty, most of the Eastern Han territory had shrunk, except for the southwestern region, which was extended, and this extended area was the Yongchang Prefecture.

Emperor Wu of Western Han had conquered the northern part of Ailao districts and set up two counties to be governed by Yizhou Commandery. Afterward, the status of Ailao districts went downhill. In AD 51, during the reign of Emperor Guangwu, one tribe leader from Ailao districts called Xianli yielded to Eastern Han. And the Emperor granted Xianli to be the leader of Ailao districts. The latter paid annual tribute to Han.

In AD 69, the King of Ailao and his son yielded to Han. Emperor Ming then set up two counties Ailao and Bonan in the area. Later he established Yongchang Commandery by combining the two counties with six counties from Yizhou Commandery.

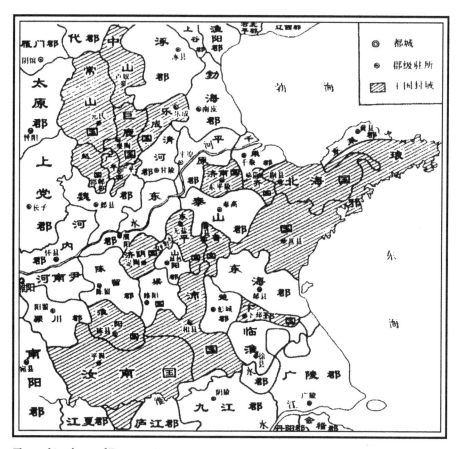

The 17 kingdoms of Eastern Han in AD 73[11]

The Yongchang Prefecture covered a wide arrange of area, including not only most of present-day Yunnan Province but also the eastern part of present-day Myanmar. However, the eight counties under the Yongchang Prefecture were all located in the northeastern part of the prefecture, that is, within the territory of the former Yizhou Prefecture, while no county was built in the area where people of Ailao lived. It can be seen that the king of Ailao still had great power, the Han Dynasty had limited rule over the Ailao area, and the development of the local economy was also extremely limited. The Han Dynasty only levied a light corvee and tax in this area. The establishment of the Yongchang Prefecture had not completely shaken the Jimi system.

---

11. Li Xiaojie, *Geography in the Eastern Han Dynasty* (Jinan: Shandong Education Press, 1999), 7.

Eastern Han inherited the method of Western Han in terms of managing its territories in the Southwest, i.e., the "Yi" districts with minority tribes. The method was to combine pre-existed commanderies with newly established counties, forming a new commandery. One good example was the Yongchang Commandery. This was to let the advanced area help the under-developed regions, while strengthening administration in the area. By AD 72, there were altogether 17 kingdoms and 79 commanderies in Eastern Han (see *The 17 kingdoms of Eastern Han in* AD *73*).

(3) The Era of Emperor An
Emperor An created a system of "Shu-Guo," i.e., dependent states in the border regions of the empire. The status of Shu-Guo equaled that of commanderies.

Such words as "Shu-Bang" (dependent regions) already appeared on weapon inscriptions of the Qin State in the Warring States. In the Han Dynasty, the name "Shu-Bang" was changed to "Shu-Guo," to avoid repetition in awe of Emperor Gaozu's name Liu Bang. During the reign of Emperor Wu of Han, the Xiongnu King Hunxie killed King Xiutu and led 40,000 of his followers to surrender to the Han. Therefore, the Han government set up five commanderies to settle these people. Each Shu-Guo set one governor to manage all the affairs within the Shu-Guo, thus the position of Chief Commandant came into being. Later on, apart from the Xiongnu, more and more minority tribes were attached to the country, such as the Qiang at the time of Emperor Xuan's reign. More and more subordinate states were therefore established. By the time of the Eastern Han Dynasty, many border prefectures had already established subordinate states, and subordinate states became a special administrative division. The names of most of these states contained the names of their prefectures, such as the Shu-Guo of Anding and the Shu-Guo of Zhangye. Some of them were set up under the Chief Commandant of the original prefecture, such as the Chief Commandant of the northern part of Guanghan, which was in charge of several prefectures, while others were only set up within the prefecture and functioned as a county, such as the Chief Commandant of Qiuci in Shang Prefecture. The Chief Commandants of the various Shu-Guo were also decentralized from being ruled by the central government in charge of minority affairs in the Western Han Dynasty to the governors of the prefectures. So the reign of governors of commanderies was only geographically separated from that of the Taishou of the prefectures.

By the time of Emperor An, six important Shu-Guos had become independent commanderies, hence official administrative divisions. The income for Shu-Guo commandants also equaled that of Commandery grand administrators, registering 2,000 *dan*. This was an important achievement for Eastern Han.

The six Shu-Guo were the following:

a. Liaodong Shu-Guo: It was located on the northeastern border of Eastern Han. Such nomadic tribes as Wuheng and Xianbei had yielded to the Han, and the Emperor drew some parts out of Liaodong and Liaoxi commanderies to form this Shu-Guo.
b. Zhangye Shu-Guo: It was located on the northwestern border. It was originally in the mid part of Zhangye Commandery.
c. Zhangye Juyan Shu-Guo: It was located on the northwestern border. It was originally the northern part of Zhangye Commandery. Its name was changed to Xihai Commandery by the end of Eastern Han.
d. Guanghan Shu-Guo: It was located on the southwestern border. It was originally a part of Guanghan Commandery. Its name was changed to Yinping Commandery by the end of Eastern Han.
e. Shujun Shu-Guo: It was located on the southwestern border. It was originally a western part of Shujun Commandery, named Shenli County in Western Han.
f. Jianwei Shu-Guo: Located on the southwestern border, it was the earliest Shu-Guo set up by Eastern Han. It was originally a southern part of Jianwei Commandery. Its name was changed to Zhuti Commandery by the end of Eastern Han.

In addition, the Han prefectures during the reign of Emperor An experienced frequent disruption and chaos. In the fourth year of Emperor Liu Hu (AD 110), due to the invasion of western Qiang, the territory of the Jincheng Prefecture had to be annexed once again, and people had to move to Xiangwu in the Longxi Prefecture (now southeast of Longxi in Gansu Province). In the second year, for the same reason, the Shangjun and Beidi prefectures were moved to Zuofengyi region; the Anding Prefecture was moved to Youfufeng region; and the seat of a local government of the Longxi Prefecture was also moved from Didao (now Lintao in Gansu Province) to Xiangwu. In this way, the Han Dynasty's register was much smaller than before. In AD 118, after the rebellion of the Qiang was put down, the Jincheng Prefecture was moved to its original place again. In AD 124, Longxi Prefecture also returned to Didao from Xiangwu.

(4) The Era of Emperor Shun
In AD 129, Eastern Han retrieved three commanderies in the northwest. They were: Anding, Beidi and Shangjun. However, as nomadic tribes in the northwest continued to attack the bordering commanderies, many territories shrunk. For example, by AD 141, five commanderies had moved their capital cities close to central China. Shangjun Commandery and Beidi Commandery moved to Zuofengyi, Shuofang Commandery moved to Wuyuan Commandery, Anding Commandery moved to Youfufeng, Xihe Commandery moved from Pingding (northwest of Fugu, Shaanxi) to Lishi. In conclusion, the northwestern territory of Eastern Han had shrunk considerably.

By AD 140, there were 85 commanderies and 21 kingdoms. There were also 1,180 counties.[12]

(5) The Era of Emperor Ling
By the outbreak of the Yellow Turban Rebellion in AD 184, the Eastern Han Dynasty had no time to mind their borders. Some border prefectures were either given up completely or partly, and the border generally receded to the line of today's Sanggan River, Lüliang Mountain, Yellow River, and Liupan Mountain. North of this line is owned by the Qiang and Hu, where lived many ethnic groups such as the Xiongnu, the Xianbei, and the Qiang. There were also a certain number of Han people who lived there, and this situation lasted until the end of the Western Jin Dynasty.

From the reign of Emperor Ling and especially during the time of Emperor Xian, the country was in turmoil, and the government was in the hands of powerful officials. The Han government was only an empty title. At that time, many Taishou and regional commissioners set up their own new prefectures, and the establishment and abolition were carried out in rapid succession, making the changes in the counties during this period extremely complicated. By AD 219, the total number of commanderies and kingdoms had increased to 137 (123 of which

---

12. Li Xiaojie, *Geography in the Eastern Han Dynasty* (Jinan: Shandong Education Press, 1999), 10.

were Han prefectures and 14 were kingdoms).

5. The 13 Departments of Regional Inspectors and Regional Commissioners

In the *Book of the Later Han · Biographies of Liu Yan*, it is recorded that in AD 188, the government assigned the senior official of the central government, Nine Ministers, to be the Regional commissioner. Its aim was to calm down the people. From then on, Zhou (state) became an administrative division above the prefecture (state) level. How was the state assigned, and how did it develop into a first-class administrative region? To answer this question, it is necessary to start with the Ministry of the 13 Departments of Regional Inspectors established by Emperor Wu of the Western Han Dynasty.

In terms of administrative divisions, the Han Dynasty basically inherited the Commandery-County system of the Qin (except for the addition of vassal states). However, the prefectures in the Han Dynasty were smaller than those in Qin, the fiefdoms of the vassal states were reduced to form new Han prefectures, and many new prefectures were established in the time of Emperor Wu, so that the total number of prefectures reached 109 by AD 104.

However, there were pros and cons. On one hand, it might reduce the number of administrative personnel. On the other hand, the layers added could make it difficult to implement orders of the Emperor, and to pass grassroots information to the central government. In order to solve this dilemma, Emperor Wu decided to set up a department of of "Ci Shi"—Regional Inspector. They inspected a number of commanderies and kingdoms to see if officials had committed crimes. The rank of regional inspectors was quite low, earning only 600 *dan*, much less than that of a commandery grand administrator, who earned 2,000 *dan*. It was a stroke of genius to create a lower rank officer to inspect officers with higher ranks. In this way, the Department of Ci Shi would not become a first-rank administrative division. Yet at the same time, it streamlined the management of the central government.

In the era of Emperor Wu, there were 13 departments of regional inspectors. They were: Yizhou, Youzhou, Bingzhou, Yanzhou, Yuzhou, Qingzhou, Xuzhou, Jinzhou, Yangzhou, Liangzhou, Yizhou, Jiaozhi, and Shuofang.

In the meantime, the commanderies near the capital would be inspected by the Metropolitan Commander. By the end of Western Han, the name of regional inspectors were changed to regional commissioners as an indication of higher rank. Their income also rose to 2,000 *dan*. However, this didn't last long. When the country returned to normal following the chaos, the name of regional commissioners went back to regional inspectors (in the early years of Eastern Han). And their income went back to 600 *dan*. For most of Eastern Han, the department of Regional Inspectors was not upgraded to an administrative division. This was because the central government wanted to maintain the Commandery-County system.

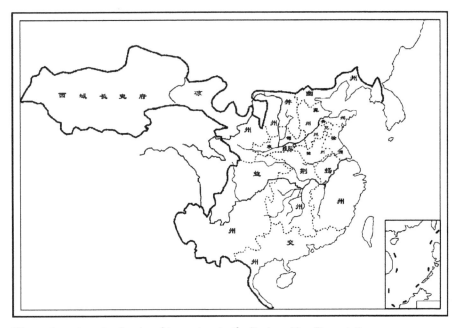

The 13 departments of regional inspectors in the Eastern Han Dynasty[13]

At the end of Eastern Han, the Yellow Turban Rebellion swept across northern China. The central government resorted to turning the department of Regional Inspectors into an administrative division in order to fight back. As depicted in *The Records of Eastern Han*, annals of Liu Yan, the central government sent

---

13. Sketchmap based on Tan Qixiang, *Atlas in Chinese History* (Beijing: SinoMaps Press, 1982).

Chamberlain Liu Yan, a high rank officer, to be Yizhou Regional Commissioner. To make it easier for Liu to summon all forces in quelling the rebels, he was given the power of military, administration, and finance.

Afterward, appointing regional commissioners became common practice. Even a warlord could name himself regional commissioner. The Commandery-County system since the Qin had become a "Region-Commandery-County" system.

In AD 194, Emperor Xian set up a new region called Yongzhou. It was set up by combining four commanderies from the Liangzhou and Hexi regions. Hence, there were 14 regions in total. In AD 213, Regional Commissioner Cao Cao, who already controlled Emperor Xian, decided to follow the concept of the nine provinces depicted in the ancient book of *Yu Gong*. He ordered the regions governed by Colonel Director of the Retainers to be called Yongzhou, Jizhou, and Yuzhou. Liangzhou was to be annexed to the Yongzhou; Youzhou and Bingzhou to be annexed to the Jizhou; and Jiaozhou was to be divided and annexed to the Jingzhou and Yizhou. However, Jiaozhou was already under the control of Sun Quan in the southeast of China. Therefore, the nine provinces ideal was only possible in the regions where Cao Cao had control. In AD 220, Cao Cao's eldest son, Cao Pi, became the Emperor of Wei. He carried out the system of 14 regions. And that was the end of the variations of administrative divisions in the Eastern Han era.

6. Establishing Protectorates and the Office of Administrators in the Western Regions

(1) The Establishment of Protectorates in the Western Regions
The Western Regions in the Han Dynasty covered a region near the west-end of the Hexi Corridor. In the present-day that would be a vast region to the west of Dunhuang in Gansu. Back then, there were over a dozen small kingdoms with different languages in the region. Those kingdoms located to the south of Tianshan were usually urbanized with cities and towns. In contrast, those to the north of Tianshan, were mostly nomadic tribes.

Before the era of Emperor Wu, the kingdoms in the Western Regions were conquered by the nomadic Xiongnu tribe. In 138 BC, Emperor Wu sent Zhang

Qian to the Western Regions, aiming to strike an alliance with the Yuezhi Kingdom (present-day north Afghanistan) against the Xiongnu. It took Zhang Qian and his men 13 years to travel to the Western Regions and back. Unfortunately, an alliance with the Yuezhi Kingdom was not possible. However, the team brought back firsthand information of the Western Regions.

In 119 BC, Zhang Qian was sent there for a second time. This time, Zhang led a delegate of over 300 men well equipped with valuables. They made it to the Wusun Kingdom (present-day Yili and Issyk-Kul Lake in Kyrgyzstan). Four years later, the King of Wusun sent delegates to join Zhang Qian on their journey home. Together they went back to Chang'an, capital of Han. Some of Zhang Qian's assistants were sent to visit other countries in the Western Regions. They reached Dayuan (present-day Fergana Basin on the borders of Uzbekistan, Tajikistan, and Kyrgyzstan), Anxi (present-day Iran), Shendu (present-day India), as well as Yumi (present-day Hetian in Xinjiang). These kingdoms all sent delegates to visit Chang'an. Thus, the Han Empire had better communications with the Western Regions.

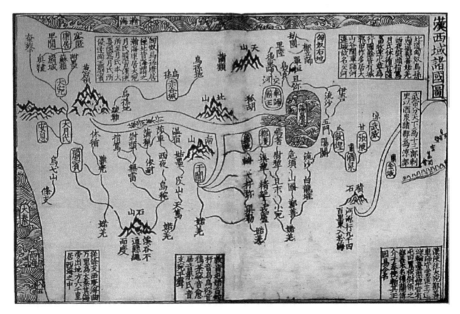

Kingdoms of the Western Regions (printed in the South Song Dynasty, AD 1260–1264)

However, the Xiongnu still controlled many kingdoms, especially those to the north of the Tianshan mountains. Emperor Wu sent armies to fight them. One of the most famous generals was called Li Guangli. He led armies into the Kingdom of Dayuan. Kingdoms in the Western Regions were astounded by Li's achievements and they yielded themselves to the Han.

In 60 BC, Khan Xianxianchan of Xiongnu, who was in charge of the Western Regions, surrendered to Han. Henceforth all regions around Tianshan were under Han control. Emperor Xuan appointed Zheng Ji as the Protector-General of the Western Regions. Zheng had been to the Western Regions many times and had mastered sufficient knowledge of the region. He set up "Mu Fu" (Filed Office) in Wuleicheng (present-day west Luntai in Xinjiang). This was the famous protectorate in the Western Regions, and it marked the beginning of direct control by the central government of the Han here.

In 48 BC, Wu and Ji colonels were set up in Cheshi (present-day southeast Turpan in Xinjiang). The colonels' main duty was farming and defense, and they had to report to the protectorate in the Western Regions.

The area under the jurisdiction of Protectorates in the Western Regions included the north and south of the Tianshan Mountains, west of the Yumen Pass and Yangguan Pass, and the present-day Lake Balkhash, the Ferghana Basin, and the Pamir Plateau. Protectorates in the Western Regions was a special military administration of the Han Dynasty. The status of the governor of the Western Region Bureau was similar to that of the Taishou of the Han Prefecture. But there were no counties under the Protectorates in the Western Regions, and it was a military guardianship of about 50 small states. On behalf of the Han Dynasty, the Protectorates in the Western Regions were in charge of foreign relations and the military operations of these small states, mediating disputes within and outside the country, maintaining the stability of the Western Region, and preventing the Xiongnu from invading. For instance, after the Xiongnu Chieftain Zhizhi fled to the Kangju state, he repeatedly mobilized troops to invade the Wusun, even venturing deep into the city of Chigu, where he burned, killed, and plundered the Wusun people. The Wusun, being unable to match the military power of the Xiongnu, could only tolerate this and did not dare to live or graze near Chigu city anymore. Not only that, but Chieftain Zhizhi also extorted wealth from other Western Region countries such as Dayuan. In response to this situation, Gan Yanshou, who was then the Protector-General of the Western

Regions, and the Deputy School Lieutenant Chen Tang, among others, believed that if measures were not taken promptly to change this situation, it wouldn't be long before the cities and countries of the Western Regions would be in peril. As a result, they convened the armies of the various Western Regions countries under the presumed order of the central government of the Han Dynasty, and, together with the agricultural forces of the Wuji School Lieutenant of the Han Dynasty, they collectively set out to attack the Xiongnu Chieftain Zhizhi. After a fierce battle, the Han forces killed Chieftain Zhizhi and decisively defeated the Xiongnu army, ultimately stabilizing the situation in the Western Regions.

In conclusion, protectorates in the Western Regions were a part of Western Han territory. At the end of the dynasty, when Wang Mang took the throne, the Xiongnu regained their control over the Western Regions. The contacts between the Han and the kingdoms was cut off. Hence, the protectorates were also abolished.

(2) The Establishment of Eastern Han's Office of the Administrator in the Western Regions

After Liu Xiu had established the Eastern Han Dynasty, those small kingdoms in the Western Regions came to Emperor Guangwu of Han and asked for protection against the Xiongnu, because they could no longer stand the heavy tax levies. However, Emperor Guangwu refused their requests. His priorities were to solidify his reign, rather than setting up protectorates in the Western Regions.

By the time of Emperor Ming, the Han Dynasty had the strength to fight the Xiongnu. It launched a war against them. In the 16th year of the Yongping era (AD 73), Emperor Ming dispatched the Grand Coachman, Ji Rong, from Gaoque (now northeast of Hangjin Houqi in Inner Mongolia), the Carriage Chief Commandant, Dou Gu, from Jiuquan (now Jiuquan in Gansu), the Horse Chief Commandant, Geng Bing, from Juyan (now southeast of Ejin Banner in Inner Mongolia), and the Cavalry Chief Commandant, Lai Miao, from Pingcheng (now northeast of Datong in Shanxi). They divided their forces into four routes to launch a northern expedition against the Xiongnu. General Dou Gu defeated King Huyan of the Xiongnu in Tianshan Mountain, captured the city of Yiwulu (now west of Hami, Xinjiang Uygur Autonomous Region), and set up garrisons. At the same time, Dou Gu sent Ban Chao as an envoy to the west. With only 36 people, Ban Chao was able to use the influence of the Han Dynasty in the western region and his own courage to consolidate the states of Shule (present-day Kashgar area in Xinjiang), Shanshan (present-day Ruoqiang area in Xinjiang Uygur Autonomous Region), and Yutian (present-day Hotan area in Xinjiang Uygur Autonomous Region), opening the way to the western region for the Han Dynasty.

In the seventeenth year of Yongping, the Han Dynasty re-established the Protectorates in the Western Regions and the Wuji Commandant, with Chen Mu as the governor and Geng Gong and Guan Rong as the commandants. Geng Gong stationed in Jinpu city, a part of the later kingdom of the Cheshi, and Guan Chong stationed in Liuzhong city, a part of the former kingdom of the Cheshi (present-day Shanshan, Xinjiang Uygur Autonomous Region), each stationing several hundred people. After that, the Eastern Han and the Xiongnu started to fight over the western region.

In AD 90, General Dou Xian sent his army to fight the Northern Xiongnu and again seized the land of Yiwulu. The situation in the western region changed in favor of the Han as the main force of the Xiongnu moved farther west. In the third year of Yong Yuan, Qiuci, Gumo (now west of Wensu, Xinjiang Uygur Autonomous Region), and Wensu (now Wushi, Xinjiang Uygur Autonomous Region) surrendered. Therefore, Emperor He re-established the Protectorates in the Western Regions, and appointed Ban Chao to be stationed in Taqian city in Qiuci. Ban Chao remained as Protector-General of the Western Regions. In addition, Emperor He appointed Xu Gan as the administrator stationed in Shule. At the same time, the Wuji Commandant was reset, leading five hundred people guarding the front line of Gao Changbi (now Gaochang Ancient City in the southeast of Turpan, Xinjiang Uygur Autonomous Region). The chief of the Wu Bu was also set so as to defend the rear side of the Cheshi.

In AD 106, some kingdoms in the Western Regions betrayed the Han Empire. In the next year, they constantly attacked Han's protectorates, which forced the Han's central government to remove the administrative divisions. The Western Regions were once again under the control of the Xiongnu.

In AD 123, Emperor An of Han appointed Ban Yong, son of Ban Chao, as the Officer of the Administrators in the Western Regions. Ban Yong deployed 500 people in Liuzhong. Since then, Eastern Han had never set up any protectorates in the Western Regions. With the help from other troops, Ban Yong defeated the Xiongnu in a few years and the Han regained its position in the Western Regions. In AD 131, the central government of Han set up a position of Cavalry Commandant in Yiwu to be in charge of farming. Later, Eastern Han weakened its control over the Western Regions, and its northwestern territories retreated to the south side of western Mt. Tianshan.

CHAPTER THREE

FROM THE THREE KINGDOMS TO THE EIGHT-PRINCE REBELLIONS

—Territories and Administrative Divisions in the Three Kingdoms and Western Jin

In the first year of the Zhongping era under Emperor Ling of the Eastern Han Dynasty (AD 184), the Yellow Turban Rebellion led by Zhang Jiao, a man from Julu (now southwest of Pingxiang, Hebei Province), broke out. Although the main force of the uprising army lasted only one year and was suppressed by the ruler, it completely shook the ruling foundation of the Eastern Han Dynasty, and the whole country declined ever since.

In the process of suppressing the uprising, Regional Commissioner, the governors of the states took the opportunity to expand their power and to take over land. The main reason for the situation was that these states ruled over large areas, with an average of seven or eight prefectures under one state. In addition, these states had the material base to be the dominant force over one side, especially after provinces were transformed from supervisory districts to administrative districts. Therefore, it was much easier for division and separation to emerge.

In AD 189, Regional Commissioner Dong Zhuo of Bingzhou invaded the Han capital of Luoyang. He deposed Emperor Shao and poisoned the Emperor's mother. Afterward, Dong Zhuo named a member of the Liu Family as Emperor Xian. Critically, Dong declared himself as counsel-in-chief, controlling the entire central government. This provoked great adversaries throughout the Commandery. Rebellions broke out everywhere. In AD 192, Dong was killed.

Since then, the separatist landscape of the world was set clear: Liu Yan had occupied Yizhou (now Sichuan Province); Yuan Shao had captured the three states of Ji, Qing, and Bing (now south-central Hebei Province, northeastern Shandong Province, and Shanxi Province); Liu Biao had controlled Jingzhou (now Hunan and Hubei Province); Cao Cao had occupied the two states of Yan and Yu (now southwestern Shandong and Henan Province); Gongsun Zan had occupied Youzhou (now northern Hebei Province); Tao Qian occupied Xuzhou (now south of Shandong Province and north of Jiangsu Province); Yuan Shu occupied Yangzhou (now between the lower reaches of the Yangtze River and the lower reaches of the Huaihe River); Sun Ce occupied the east of the Yangtze River (now southeast of the Yangtze River); Han Sui and Ma Teng settled in Liangzhou (now Gansu Province); and Gongsun Du settled in Liaodong.

That year, Regional Commissioner Cao Cao greatly strengthened his military forces by enlisting 300,000 people from the Yellow Turban Army. Afterward, he occupied Xuzhou by defeating Regional Commissioner Tao Qian. Then, Cao Cao abducted Emperor Xian from Chang'an to Xu (east Xuchang in Henan). The purpose was to control the other princes and regional commissioners in the name of Emperor Xian.

Cao Cao wiped out two other major military forces, namely Yuan Shu and Lü Bu. In AD 200, Cao defeated his greatest northern opponent, Yuan Shao, in the Battle of Guandu (south Zhongmou in Henan). Cao's plan to unify China was obstructed when his forces lost to the joint armies of Sun Quan and Liu Bei in the Battle of Chibi in AD 208. From then on, the three forces shared the territories of China. Sun Quan was based in the southeast, ruling the land to the south of the Yangtze, while Liu Bei occupied southwest China, blocking the forces of Cao Cao with steep mountains.

In AD 220, Cao Pi, the eldest son of Cao Cao, deposed Emperor Xian of Han and declared himself the Emperor of Wei with Luoyang as the capital. One year later, Liu Bei declared himself as the Emperor of Han in Chengdu, known as "Shu Han." In AD 222, Sun Quan declared himself as the King of Wu in Jianye (present-day Nanjing). Then, in AD 229, Sun became the Emperor of Wu. Hence, China entered the Three Kingdoms era.

In terms of administrative divisions, all three kingdoms adopted the Prefecture-Commandery-County system from the Eastern Han Dynasty.

1. Unifying Northern China

After Cao Cao was defeated, he turned his priorities to the Guanzhong and Guanxi Regions. Eventually he unified the northern part of China, after defeating military forces such as the Han Sui, Ma Chao, and Zhang Lu.

Among the three Kingdoms, Wei occupied the greatest part of China, Wu ranked second, and Shu-Han was the smallest. Wei had 12 regions. They were: Sizhou, Jizhou, Bingzhou, Yuzhou, Yanzhou, Qingzhou, Xuzhou, Youzhou, Liangzhou, and northern Jingzhou and Yangzhou. In present-day China, that would be the provinces of Liaoning, Hebei, Henan, Shandong, Shanxi, Gansu, and a large part of Jiangsu, Anhui, Hubei, and Shaanxi (see *Territories of the Three Kingdoms*).

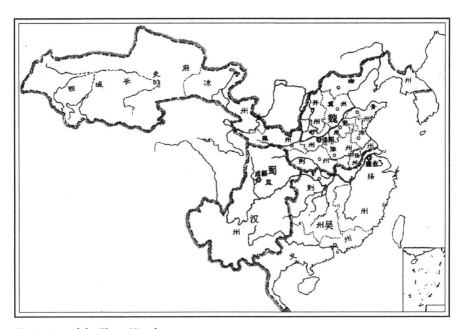

Territories of the Three Kingdoms[1]

---

1. Sketchmap based on Tan Qixiang, *Atlas in Chinese History* (Beijing: SinoMaps Press, 1982).

Emperor Wen of Wei continued the Feoffment System. In AD 223, he granted many members of his family marquis land and titles. The emperor learned the lessons of Western Han, so he didn't grant the marquises any administrative power. They lived on the tax levies of their commanderies and could pass on their titles to heirs. However, they didn't have any power to seriously threaten the central government. Among the administrative divisions of the Wei state of the Three Kingdoms, the administrative districts established on the Korean Peninsula are worth mentioning. During the Eastern Han Dynasty, Xuantu Prefecture was completely merged into Liaodong Prefecture, and Lelang Prefecture abandoned its area in the east of Daling. During the reign of Emperor Xian, Gongsun Du was in charge of Liaodong, Xuantu, and Lelang prefectures. In the middle of Jian'an at the end of the Han Dynasty, Gongsun Kang, son of Gongsun Du, divided the wasteland south of Tunyou County in Lelang Prefecture and established the Daifang Prefecture on the Korean Peninsula. Later the Japanese and Koreans on the peninsula came under the jurisdiction of the Daifang Prefecture. After the destruction of the Gongsun clan by the Wei state, the four prefectures of Liaodong, Xuantu, Lelang, and Daifang were set under the jurisdiction of the Wei state. The Lelang Prefecture, which was located on the Korean Peninsula, governed the area south of the present-day Cheongcheon River, Langlin Mountain, and south of Weixing. The Daifang Prefecture was located in the south of the Lelang Prefecture and governed the area of the present-day South Yellow Sea and North Yellow Sea.

Emperor Wen paid special attention to the Western Regions. In the early years of his reign, he reset the positions of Wu and Ji colonels and the Office of Administrators. The former was headed by the regional inspector of Liangzhou, with its seat in Gaochang. The latter's seat was placed in Haitou (present-day relics of Loulan in Luobupo, Xinjiang). Emperor Wen also granted titles and seals to the kings of commanderies in the Western Regions. For example, Yiduoza, King of Cheshi, was named "Palace Attendant of Wei" and given seals. The emperor ruled fewer kingdoms in the Western Regions than the Han dynasties, however, the major countries, such as Qiuzi, Kangju, Wusun, Shule, Yezhi, Shanshan, and Cheshi were under his control. Likewise, those kingdoms paid annual tribute to Wei.

2. Kingdom of Shu-Han Appeases the "Yi" Districts

After the Battle of Chibi, Liu Bei, who was the weakest at the time, took advantage of the opportunity to seize Hubei. Liu had Zhuge Liang and Guan Yu guarded Jingzhou while he led his troops westward into Ba and Shu, capturing Yizhou (now Yunnan and southern Shaanxi Province, east of Kangding in Sichuan and west of Guizhou Province).

After Liu Bei entered Yizhou, he began to take measures to control the surrounding minority regions. The most important of these measures was his management of the South China region. When Liu Bei made three visits to Zhuge Liang's cottage, Zhuge Liang advised him in the "Longzhong Plan" that he should defend the Jing state and Yi state, guard fortresses, unite ethnic minorities in the west, appease the people in the Yiyue area in the south, ally with Sun Quan externally, and repair regulations and laws internally.[2] In this context, the Yiyue area refers to the tribes in Nanzhong. Nanzhong was the area south of the Dadu River in Sichuan and the area around Yunnan and Guizhou, which was named because it was in the south of Ba and Shu. Nanzhong was originally a place where southwestern Yi lived. After Liu Bei set the capital in Chengdu, he set up Lai Jiang Chief Commandant (Zhiwei County, present-day Qujing, Yunnan Province) to rule the Nanzhong region.

In AD 223, not long after Liu Bei died, one of the generals in Yizhou Prefecture, Yong Kai, betrayed the Shu-Han Kingdom and surrendered to Wu. Simultaneously, he solicited minority tribes, led by Meng Huo, to fight against Shu-Han. Zhu Bao, the Taishou of Zangke Prefecture, and Gao Ding, the king of Yuexi Kingdom, also responded to Yong Kai.

In response to the rebellion in Nanzhong, in the third year of Jianxing (AD 225), Zhuge Liang led troops in three separate campaigns to suppress it. At that time, Yong Kai had been killed by Gao Ding. Zhuge Liang led one division of troops, slew Gao Ding, crossed the Lu River (present-day Jinsha River), and engaged in battle with Meng Huo. Zhuge Liang captured Meng Huo seven times, and each time he released him. Ultimately, this strategy made Meng Huo sincerely submit. After Zhuge Liang suppressed all rebellions in four prefectures of the Nanzhong District, he renamed Yizhou as Jianning Prefecture. Later, he set up the Yunnan

---

2. *Records of the Three Kingdoms · Book of Shu · Biography of Zhuge Liang.*

Region by combining parts of the Jianning and Yuexi prefectures. Additionally, it was stipulated that all local officials below the governor of these prefectures would be local chiefs, in order to achieve a better governance effect. In this way, the Han people and local minority groups began to live peacefully together.

3. Kingdom of Wu Expanded to the Lingnan Districts

Before the Battle of Chibi, the Kingdom of Wu had already set up such prefectures as Kuaiji, Wu, Danyang, Yuzhang and Lujiang. After the battle, it expanded to the Lingnan districts. Among the three regions of Eastern Han (Jinzhou, Yangzhou and Jiaozhou), Wu had complete control of Jiaozhou, while sharing the first two with Wei—the Yangtze River was the dividing line. The area of Wu would cover the following provinces in modern times: Zhejiang, Jiangxi, Hunan, Fujian, Guangdong, Guangxi, Jiangsu, Anhui, Hubei, a part of Guizhou and a northern part of Vietnam.

In the fifth year of Huangwu (AD 226), because Jiaozhou was located in the remote Lingnan area, Sun Quan divided part of Jiaozhou and established Guangzhou, which was soon abolished. In the seventh year of Yong'an (AD 264), the State of Wu again divided the land of Jiaozhou to set up Guangzhou (equivalent to most of today's Guangdong Province and Guangxi Province) and this time Guangzhou was preserved. Therefore, the State of Wu contained Jingzhou, Yangzhou, Jiaozhou and Guangzhou.

In order to develop agriculture, the area to the west of Wuxi in the Wu Prefecture (Shanghai, East of Zhejiang, and the area to the south of Yangtze in Jiangsu), was set up as an agriculture commander, with the seat in Piling (Changzhou, Jiangsu). The Commander was originally a military position. However, in this special case, it had become an administrative division. Later in Western Jin, Piling Agriculture Commandery was renamed as Piling Prefecture, covering modern Changzhou, Zhenjiang, Wuxi, Wujin, Jiangyin, and Danyang in Jiangsu Province. It officially became an administrative division.

Apart from the Agriculture Commandery, within the jurisdiction of Danyang Prefecture, the Wu also set the Agriculture Commandery (now north of Jurong, Jiangsu Province), the Hushu Agriculture Commandery (now Hushu town in Jiangning, Jiangsu Province), the Liyang Agriculture Commandery (now Liyang,

Jiangsu Province), and other Agriculture Commanderies that had the same jurisdiction with the county. These Agriculture Commanderies were changed into counties in the early years of the Western Jin Dynasty.

4. Two Special Administrative Systems: Remote Control and Nominal Appointments

In the era of the Qin and Han dynasties, regional inspectors and Taishou had actual governing areas, and they were administrative divisions. The princes of the Han Dynasty also had real divisions. However, in the Three Kingdoms era, there were systems of remote control and nominal appointments, which made some administrative divisions exist only in the imagination. Therefore, the administrative divisions could also be a mere nominal title.

The differences between the remote control and nominal appointments were as follows: "The act of nominally governing territories outside of one's actual control (i.e., where the home government cannot exercise administrative power) by establishing local officials such as regional inspectors, prefecture administrators, etc., and symbolically exercising rule over the area, is known as "remote control." On the other hand, granting land that is in fact not under one's control as a fief to princes and lords of one's own country is known as "nominal appointment."[3] That is to say, "remote control" involves the appointment of governors and prefects in provinces and prefectures that are not under one's actual control, while "nominal appointment" means that the enfeoffed princes and kings only have an honorary title, with their enfeoffed territory located within another country. This system is a particular product of a fragmented period. At that time, the three kingdoms of Wei, Shu, and Wu each held a part of the territory. Each hoped that one day they could defeat the other two opponents and unify the country under their rule. Therefore, when this ambition was not or could not be realized, they had to resort to the methods of "remote control" and "nominal appointment" to satisfy themselves psychologically. Here is an example.

---

3. Gu Jiegang and Shi Nianhai, *The Evolution of China's Boundaries* (Shanghai: Commercial Press, 1938), 137.

According to historical records, Huang Quan once was the regional inspector of Yizhou in Wei Kingdom and Tian Yu was the governor of Pingzhou. Yizhou was an important area of Shu Kingdom when Huang Quan was the governor of Yizhou. Pingzhou was still under the control of the Gongsun clan when Tian Yu was appointed the governor of Pingzhou.

The practice of "remote control" and "nominal appointment" was especially prevalent in the Wu Kingdom and the Shu Kingdom. In AD 229, Wu and Shu planned to divide the world. The Shu Kingdom took over Jizhou, Yanzhou, Bingzhou, and Liangzhou. The Wu Kingdom ruled over Yuzhou, Qingzhou, Xuzhou, and Youzhou. The two kingdoms set their own governors and sheriffs. However, these regions were actually territories of the Wei state at the time, and it was impossible for the states of Wu and Shu to realistically establish governors or Regional commissioners there; it was just nominal "remote control." In addition, the states of Wu and Shu also virtually enfeoffed several vassal kings, such as King Liu Yong of Lu, King Liu Li of Liang, King Liu Chen of Beidi in Shu, and King Sun He of Nanyang, King Sun Ba of Lu, and King Sun Fen of Qi in Wu. These territories were all within the boundaries of Wei, and were not actually occupied by the states of Wu and Shu.

After the unification of the Wei, Shu, and Wu states by the Western Jin Dynasty, the political basis for the establishment of the "remote control" and "nominal appointment" system no longer existed, so this system disappeared. Later, during the Southern and Northern Dynasties period, this system was revived for a time, but the scale of its remote rule and feoffment was far less prosperous than during the Three Kingdoms period.

5. The Western Jin Dynasty and the 21 Regions of the Yongjia Period

In AD 263, the Kingdom of Wei conquered Chengdu, capital city of Shu-Han. Emperor Liu Shan surrendered to Wei. Two years later, Sima Yan forced Emperor Yuan of Wei to resign. Sima Yan then declared himself the Emperor of Jin, known as Western Jin. In AD 280, Jin defeated the Kingdom of Wu, ending the Three Kingdoms; China was unified again.

(1) The Feoffment System of Western Jin

In terms of administrative divisions, the Western Jin regime continued the three-tier system of Prefecture-Commandery-County adopted during the Three Kingdoms.

However, the unification of the Western Jin was extremely brief. Starting from the first year of Taikang (AD 280) when Jin Wu Emperor Sima Yan destroyed Wu, to the outbreak of the "War of the Eight Princes" in the first year of Yongning (AD 301) during Emperor Hui's reign, there were only twenty-one years in total. The short life of the Western Jin Dynasty was certainly due to a variety of reasons, but it is inseparable from the measure of enfeoffment of the royal family in the early years of Western Jin.

After the establishment of Western Jin, in order to avoid repeating the loss of power of the Wei royal family and the powerlessness of the feudal princes, and to ensure the long-term stability of the dynasty, Jin Wu Emperor Sima Yan, soon after ascending to the throne, ordered the enfeoffment of twenty-seven members of the royal family as kings, using prefectures as their realms. Among these twenty-seven people, none were his sons. Apart from three who were his brothers, the other twenty-four were descendants of his grandfather Sima Yi, that is, Sima Yan's great-uncles, uncles, and cousins, hence they were referred to as "royal princes" or "princes of the blood." This practice was markedly different from the established rule of the Western Han that only sons and brothers of the emperor could be ennobled as kings of the same surname. This was mainly determined by the unique circumstances of the early Western Jin.

At that time, Emperor Wu of Jin had no son to be crowned king. In order to unite the royal family to defend the imperial power, Emperor Wu took a step back to crown people from the clan kings. Unlike most founding emperors, Sima Yan's ascension to the throne was already largely preordained. The transition from Wei to the Sima clan had largely been accomplished by his grandfather, Sima Yi, and by figures from his father's generation, such as Sima Zhao and Sima Shi. Many descendants of Sima Yi had exerted considerable effort for this cause. To express his gratitude for their contributions, Sima Yan felt compelled to confer the title of king upon these uncles and cousins.

However, because these royal kings were not close enough to the emperor, it was extremely difficult to achieve the effect of supporting the royal family.

Therefore, the practice of crowning the clan people in the early years of the Western Jin Dynasty was naturally a misguided move. However, its consequences were not so bad. Because at that time, the vassal king's domain was not large, only the size of a prefecture. These kings did not control the local power, and the local rent was also very limited; therefore these kings could not possess financial resources and would not have posed much of a threat to the central government. The big mistake made by Emperor Wu was to appoint the clan kings to be the commander-in-chiefs and guard some important Zhou. This was originally a pacification practice. Since the enfeoffment in the first year of Emperor Wu, the clan kings were able to prevent the development of other clans. But as time went on, the conflict between them and the imperial power became more and more obvious. Faced with the growing power of the clan kings, Emperor Wu came up with two ways to deal with it: one was to separate the power of the clan kings by crowning royal sons; the other was to order the clan kings who were staying in the capital to live in their respective states, so as to keep them away from the center of power. However, the clan kings were reluctant to go to their own states because of the excellent living conditions in the capital. In order to alleviate the discontent of these clan kings, Emperor Wu adopted a series of pacification measures, such as increasing the rewards, setting up armies and governmental institutions within the fiefs. However, these measures provided the clan kings with a good opportunity to take over the military and political power. They gradually became political forces that could compete with the central imperial power.

During the Western Jin Dynasty, there were about twenty states, and important states had governors who acted as the military heads, some of whom had several states under their jurisdiction and were very powerful. In order to deal with these clan kings who held both military and civil power and at the same time coveted the emperor's throne, there was only one effective way, that is, to improve the status of the royal kings by making them more powerful and able to compete with the clan kings. To this end, Emperor Wu took two specific measures: one was to send these royal princes to their respective fiefdoms, each serving as a provincial governor, which helped diminish the power of the royal princes. The second was to break the longstanding rule since the mid-Western Han Dynasty that only one county could be conferred as a fiefdom. This expansion of the royal fiefdoms allowed the princely states to govern two to three, and even up to four counties. This was a phenomenon not seen since the reign of Emperor Jing of the

Western Han Dynasty, and it starkly contrasted with the current situation where royal princes were only governing a single county.

The original intention of Emperor Wu was to form a powerful alliance of royal kings against the clan kings, so as to defend the central imperial power. However, what Emperor Wu did not anticipate was that the princes he had high hopes for were also dreaming that they would one day become emperors themselves. Therefore, the measures Emperor Wu took did not achieve the desired effect. On the contrary, after his death, the conflict of interest between the two groups, the royal kings and the clan kings, intensified and finally, during the problematic reign of Emperor Hui, a major internal struggle broke out within the Sima family. At that time, King Sima Liang of Runan, King Sima Wei of Chu, King Sima Lun of Zhao, King Sima Jong of Qi, King Sima Yi of Changsha, King Sima Ying of Chengdu, King Sima Yong of Hefei, and King Sima Yue of Donghai fought against each other and staged the Rebellion by the Eight Kings for 16 years.

The eight major players in this conflict were:

a. Sima Liang, son of Sima Yi, titled Prince of Runan;
b. Sima Wei, son of Emperor Wu, titled Prince of Chu;
c. Sima Lun, son of Sima Yi, titled Prince of Zhao;
d. Sima Jiong, nephew of Emperor Wu, titled Prince of Qi;
e. Sima Ying, son of Emperor Wu, titled Prince of Chengdu;
f. Sima Ai, son of Emperor Wu, titled Prince of Changsha;
g. Sima Yong, distant cousin of Emperor Wu, titled Prince of Hejian;
h. Sima Yue, distant cousin of Emperor Wu, titled Prince of Donghai.

This internal war within the ruling group caused great damage to the country and its people. The corrupt rule of the Western Jin Dynasty led to conflicts and warfare between different ethnic groups. Eventually, most of the royal kings and the clan kings faded away in history together with the Western Jin Dynasty, leaving only one clan king, Sima Rui, to establish a remote regime in Jiangdong to continue the royal line of the Jin family, while the vast north was plunged into the chaos and turmoil of sixteen kingdoms of five ethnic groups.

The two attempts of enfeoffing vassal kings in the Western Han Dynasty and the Western Jin Dynasty showed that the changes in the scope of administrative divisions (including the special administrative divisions of vassal states) could be used as a political method. In order to strengthen the imperial power, the Western Han Dynasty gradually reduced the territory of every vassal state, whereas the Western Jin Dynasty adopted the method of expanding the territory of the kingdom in order to increase local power. Unfortunately, both of these two methods triggered civil strife, and neither of them achieved the desired effect. This showed that in an era when the Commandery-County system was in place, reverting to the old practice of conferring land to feudal princes was no longer in step with the times. As a result, lessons were learned from the Han and Jin dynasties, and after the Sui Dynasty, this system disappeared forever. What remained were only symbolic titular conferrals to the imperial sons, without actually granting them land.

(2) 21 Regions of the Yongjia Period

During the Western Jin Dynasty, the state was the highest level of administrative division. In the first year of Emperor Wu of Jin, Sima Yan seized power from the Wei Kingdom in AD 265 and occupied fourteen states, including Sili, Yan, Yu, Ji, Qing, Xu, You, Bing, Yong, Liang, Jing, Yang, Yi, and Liang. Five years later, Emperor Wu set up Qinzhou by combining the northwest part of Yongzhou and the other two states. After another two years, Ningzhou was established by cutting off the Yizhou in the southwest. In AD 276, a part of the northeastern part of Youzhou was set aside as Pingzhou. Thus, the total number of regions in Western Jin was 17.

In AD 280, the Western Jin Dynasty finally destroyed the Wu Kingdom south of the Yangtze River and obtained the four states of Yang, Jing, Jiao, and Guang. Yangzhou and Jingzhou were merged into one state. There were 19 states, 171 prefectures, and 1,232 counties (see *The 19 Zhous of Western Jin*).

In the nineteen states during the Taikang period, the areas governed by Jingzhou and Yangzhou were too vast. They had jurisdiction over most commanderies and counties, making governance quite inconvenient. In AD 291, Emperor Hui of Jin set up Jiangzhou Region by combining parts of Jingzhou and Yangzhou. In AD 307, Emperor Huai of Jin set up Xiangzhou Region by combining parts of Jingzhou and Jiangzhou. The area was to the south of Dongting Lake and to the north of the Wuling Mountains. Today, it is Hunan Province. Until then, there were 21 regions in Western Jin. As the years governed by Emperor Huai were called Yongjia Years, therefore the administrative divisions were also known as the "21 Regions of the Yongjia Period."

The set up of the 21 Regions of the Yongjia Period combined the ideal divisions in *Yu Gong* and the realities from Han dynasties to the Period of Three Kingdoms. The size of regions were more or less the same and the even divisions had their merits. However, Western Jin did not last very long before it was overthrown by minority tribes.

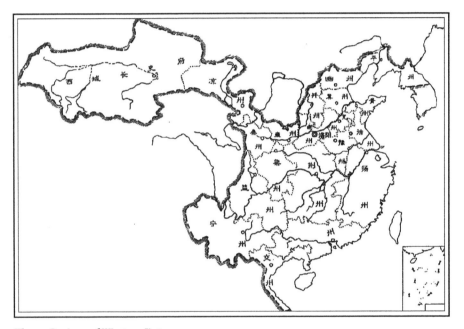

The 19 Regions of Western Jin[4]

---

4. Sketchmap based on Tan Qixiang, *Atlas in Chinese History* (Beijing: SinoMaps Press, 1982).

1

CHAPTER FOUR

CHINA DIVIDED INTO TWO PARTS

—Territories and Administrative Divisions during the Sixteen Kingdoms, Eastern Jin, and the Northern and Southern Dynasties

In AD 316, the Xiongnu conquered Chang'an, capital of Western Jin. Emperor Min surrendered and his empire fell.

Since Eastern Han, many northern nomadic tribes moved to the Yellow River regions. Those tribes included the Xiongnu, Xianbei, Qiang, Zhi, Jie, Lushuihu, and Dingling. Their population thrived throughout these years. Meanwhile, they accumulated political and military strength while living with Han people in the same regions. On the one hand, they wanted to abolish the heavy burdens of tax imposed on them. On the other hand, they seized every opportunity to obtain power and wealth, hoping one day to control a region or the entire country.

The Rebellions of the Eight Princes at the end of Western Jin was a golden opportunity. Thus, several kingdoms in the Yellow River regions, Liao River regions, and Sichuan Valley were set up. China was then divided into several parts until the Northern Wei reunited the country. In history, this period was known as the Five Nomadic Tribes and Sixteen Kingdoms.

1. Chaotic Borders of the Sixteen Kingdoms

In order to put on a show of strength, the Sixteen Kingdoms often divided their regions into smaller ones. And the kings often named their regions after places in other parts of China. Thus, the administrative divisions became chaotic. The following is a brief description of the Sixteen Kingdoms:

(1) *Han and the Former Zhao*

In AD 304, Liu Yuan, the King of the Xiongnu, rose in revolt in Lishi (now Lishi, Shanxi Province) in the name of helping Sima Ying, the King of Chengdu. Liu Yuan soon moved to Zuoguo (now north of Lishi County) and claimed to be the King of Han. In AD 308, Liu Yuan moved the capital to Puzi (now Xi County, Shanxi Province), and in October Liu Yuan upgraded his title to Emperor of Han. The next year, the capital was moved to Pingyang (now southwest of Linfen City, Shanxi Province). In AD 311, the Han invaded Luoyang and captured Emperor Huai of Jin. In AD 316, the army marched to Chang'an and captured Emperor Min of Jin, ending the reign of Jin. Around AD 317, the territory of the Han extended north to Yin Mountain, today's Sanggan River, Yan Mountain, south to the Huai River, Qinling, and west to the Yellow River, Longdong. Liu Yuan established Yongzhou in Pingyang (southwest of today's Linfen, Shanxi Province), and he also set up Youzhou in Lishi (today's Lishi, Shanxi Province).

In AD 318, Emperor Liu Can was killed by Jin Zhun, a powerful minister. Liu Yao, a Han general who had already conquered Guanzhong, declared himself emperor in Chang'an and joined Jie people Shi Le, another Han general who had conquered Guanzhong, in a rebellion. In the following year, Liu Yao changed the name of his state from Han to Zhao and set the capital in Chang'an. It was known in history as the Former Zhao.

The territories of the Former Zhao covered an area from Luoyang in the east, to the upper reaches of the Yellow River in the west. Its northern border reached the Northern Wei Plateau and its southern border reached southeast Shanxi. The Former Zhao also set up some nominal states in its territory, including Qinzhou and Liangzhou in Shanggui (now Tianshui, Gansu Province), Shuozhou in Gaoping (now Guyuan, Gansu Province), Youzhou in Beidi (now Yao County, Shaanxi Province), and Yizhou in Qiuchi (now Wudu, Gansu Province). The Former Zhao claimed to cover 7 regions and 34 prefectures. Then the Former Zhao was defeated by the army led by Shi Le and retreated to the Guanzhong area. In AD 328, Shi Le defeated and captured Liu Yao. One year later, Shi Le's general, Shi Sheng, conquered major parts of Former Zhao and put it to an end.

(2) The Later Zhao and Ran Wei
In AD 319, shortly after Liu Yao declared himself the King of Zhao, Shi Le also declared himself as the King of Zhao—known as the "Later Zhao." Shi Le set up his capital in Xiangguo (present-day Xingtai, Hebei Province). In AD 330, Shi Le upgraded his title to the Emperor of Zhao. Five years later, Shi Hu ascended to the throne and moved the capital to Ye (present-day Linzhang, Hebei Province). After Later Zhao wiped out Former Zhao, its territories reached their zenith, stretching eastward to the sea, westward to today's Hetao region in Inner Mongolia, crossing the Huai and Han Rivers to the south, and reaching today's northeastern Hebei and northern Shanxi to the north. Within this expansive area, Later Zhao established twelve stat—Si, Luo, Yu, Yan, Ji, Qing, You, Ying, Bing, Shuo, Yong, and Qin—controlling approximately one hundred counties.

In AD 349, Emperor Shi Hu died. His adopted grandson, Shi Min, killed the new Emperor and massacred all the Jie and Hu peoples within the territory. In the next year, Shi Min reverted back to his original surname of Ran and declared himself King of Wei. In history, his kingdom was called Ran Wei. At that time, many regions in his territory declared independence. Therefore, the king only controlled a small part of Later Zhao. In AD 352, Ran Wei was replaced by the Former Yan.

(3) The Former Yan
At the end of the Western Jin Dynasty, Murong Gui, the leader of the Murong tribe of Xianbei, occupied the present-day Daling River Basin. Murong Huang, the son of Murong Gui, expanded the territory of the tribe, taking over the Liaodong Peninsula and reaching the Luan River Basin in the east. In AD 337, Murong Huang declared himself the King of Yan, with his capital at Changli County (present-day Yixian, Liaoning Province), and later moved the capital to Longcheng (present-day Chaoyang, Liaoning Province), historically known as Former Yan. He first set up his capital in Changli County (Yi County in Liaoning), and then moved to Longcheng (Chaoyang). It is known as the "Former Yan."

After Former Yan eliminated Ran Wei, it moved its capital to Ji City (modern-day Beijing), and shortly thereafter, relocated to Ye. The greatest extent of Former Yan's territory reached the Liaodong Peninsula in the east, today's Sanggan River, Yan Mountains, and areas around Chifeng, Inner Mongolia in the north, the

Huai River in the south, and parts of northern Shanxi and the east of the Qin River Basin in the west. Within this domain, Former Yan established nine state: Ping, You, Zhong, Luo, Yu, Yan, Qing, Ji, and Bing, which collectively governed seventy-four prefectures. In AD 370, Former Yan fell to Former Qin.

(4) The Former Liang

In AD 301, Zhang Gui was appointed by Emperor Hui of Western Jin as the regional inspector of Liangzhou, covering the Hexi area. After the Western Jin ended, Zhang clan continued to occupy Liangzhou. It is known as the "Former Liang."

Former Liang, with its capital at Guzang (today's Wuwei, Gansu Province), primarily covered the Hexi Corridor. Its territory extended from the Yellow River in the east to Yumenguan (the western boundary of today's Gansu Province) in the west, from the Qilian Mountains in the south to Juyanze (located in today's Ejin Banner, Inner Mongolia Autonomous Region) in the north. It established six stat: Liang, He, Sha, Ding, Shang, and Qin, which together governed thirty-two prefectures. In the later period of Former Liang, it also controlled the Western Regions, where it installed an administrator. In AD 376, it was eliminated by Former Qin.

(5) Cheng Han

In AD 298, during the eighth year of Emperor Hui of Jin's reign (Yuankang era), there were consecutive years of famine in Guanzhong. Li Te, a leader of the Di people who originally lived in Badi and moved to Longdong and Guanzhong at the end of the Eastern Han Dynasty, led the displaced people into Sichuan. By AD 301, the first year of Emperor Hui of Jin's reign (Yongning era), Luo Shang, the regional inspector of Yizhou, ordered the displaced people to return home by July. The displaced people's request to depart after the autumn harvest was not granted. Therefore, in October of that year, the displaced people chose Li Te and others as their leaders and rose in revolt in Mianzhu (north of today's Deyang, Sichuan Province) and attacked Chengdu. Three years later, Li Xiong declared himself as the King of Chengdu. Two years later, he upgraded his title to the Emperor of Dacheng. In AD 338, Li Shou changed the name to Han, known as "Cheng Han."

The territory of Cheng Han included most of present-day Sichuan, except for the western part of the western Sichuan Plateau and the western part of the Hanzhong Basin. In this area, there were originally three states, namely Liang, Yi and Ning. After Li Xiong became emperor, he split Liangzhou to set up Jingzhou in Ba Prefecture (now Chongqing); Split Ningzhou and set up Hanzhou in Xinggu Prefecture (north of Yanshan, Yunnan). During the reign of Li Shou, he split Ningzhou and set up Anzhou in Zangke Prefecture. Therefore, there are six states and 31 prefectures in total. Huan Wen, the general of the Eastern Jin Dynasty, attacked and destroyed Cheng Han in AD 346.

(6) The Former Qin
After Shi Hu's death, the Di tribe's chief, Fu Hong, led his people to fight the Later Zhao. In AD 350, Fu Jian, son of Fu Hong, conquered Guanzhong District and the capital city of Chang'an. The following year, Fu Jian declared himself the King of Da Qin, known as the "Former Qin."

In AD 357, Fu Jian took over the country, pacified the Guanzhong region, then destroyed the Former Liang, the Former Yan and Dai. In AD 373 he seized the Liangzhou and Yizhou of the Eastern Jin Dynasty and occupied the Sichuan Basin. In AD 382, Fu Jian sent Lü Guang to the west. Two years later, Lü Guang took control of the entire western region and set up the Western Region Lieutenant in Qiuci (now Ku, Xinjiang Uygur Autonomous Region). Before the Battle of Fei River in AD 383, the Former Qin had completely unified the north, covering the Huai River in the south, the Yangtze River west of present-day Wanzhou in Chongqing, the Mongolian Plateau in the north, the eastern part of the Turpan Basin in Xinjiang, the Qilian Mountains, the Huang River Basin, the Minshan Mountains, the eastern part of the Sichuan Plateau, and the Liaodong Peninsula in the east. Its territory was the largest among the Sixteen Kingdoms, including Si, Yong, Luo, Qin, South Qin, Yu, East Yu, Bing, Ji, You, Ping, Liang, He, Liang, Yi, Ning, Yan, South Yan, Qing, and North Xu twenty states. After the defeat at the Battle of Feishui, the Former Qin collapsed, and the Later Yan, Later Qin, Yan, Western Qin, and Later Liang declared independence. In AD 385, Fu Jian was captured and killed by the Later Qin. The remnants of the Former Qin managed to hold out in the western part of Guanzhong and the Longdong region for a while. By AD 394, they were defeated by the Later Qin.

(7) The Later Qin

In AD 384, Yao Chang, the leader of the Qiang people, rose up in the Weibei region and declared himself the King of Qin for ten thousand years. This period was referred to as the Later Qin.

In AD 386, Yao Chang upgraded his title to Emperor. The title of his reign was Da Qin. After the destruction of the Former Qin, the territory of Later Qin was roughly the size of the northwestern part of the Former Qin, covering Hetao, north of the Qinling Mountains in Shaanxi, southwest of Shanxi, most of Ningxia and east of Tianshui in Gansu. The Later Qin had eight states and fifty prefectures. In AD 403, the Nan Liang and Bei Liang attacked Hou Liang, which later surrendered to the Later Qin. However, the territory of Hou Liang was soon divided up by other regimes and Later Qin only got part of the territory of the Hou Liang. Later in AD 407, the north of the Weibei Plateau was occupied by Helianbobo whereas the Later Qin seize most of the south of the Yellow River (now Henan Province). In AD 417, Liu Yu of the Eastern Jin Dynasty led the army to the northern, marching to Chang'an. Yao Hong, then ruler of the Later Qin, surrendered, marking the end of the Later Qin Dynasty.

(8) The Later Yan

In the last years of the Former Yan, Murong Chui, a member of the Yan clan, tired of being suspected, and surrendered to the Former Qin. He was trusted by Fu Jian. After the defeat of Fu Jian, Murong Chui made himself king of Yan in AD 384, which was referred to as Later Yan. Two years later, he became emperor and set his capital at Zhongshan (now Dingzhou, Hebei).

After recovering the old territories in Liaodong, the Later Yan destroyed the Western Yan in AD 394 and took possession of the area of present-day Shandong in the same year. In the following year, the eastern, western and northern parts of the territory of the Former Yan were largely restored. However, the southern border of the Later Yan only extended to the southern border of Shandong and the area from Luoyang to Shangqiu in southern Henan. The Later Yan had nine states and fifty-five prefectures. In AD 397, the Northern Wei army conquered Zhongshan and the lord of Later Yan was forced to move his capital to Ye. The next year, Murong De founded the Southern Yan. The area of today's Shandong no longer belonged to Later Yan and it had to move its capital back to Long. What's more, its territory was reduced to that of the early days of the Former Yan.

The eastern part of its territory had been taken over by Goguryeo and only the area west of the Liao River to the lower reaches of the Luan River was saved. In AD 407, the Later Yan was replaced by the Northern Yan.

(9) The Southern Yan
In AD 398, most of the territories of the Later Yan were seized by the Northern Wei. Murong De, brother of the Emperor of Later Yan, declared himself King of Yan with his base in Huatai (now the ancient city in the east of Hua County in Henan Province). This period was known as "Southern Yan." Afterward, the Southern Yan developed south-east and captured the two states of Qing and Yan, controlling most of the area in present-day Shandong. The following year it set its capital in Guanggu (now northwest of Qingzhou City in Shandong Province).

At its peak, the territory reached the sea in the east, and western Shandong in the west. Its northern border reached the Yellow River and its southern border reached northern Jiangsu. It claimed to have five states and twelve prefectures, whereas it had only two states plus the northern part of Xuzhou. In AD 410, Liu Yu of the Eastern Jin Dynasty led the army and marched northward, capturing the capital Guanggu and ending the reign of the Southern Yan.

(10) The Northern Yan
In AD 407, General Feng Ba and his people killed the Later Yan Emperor, and made Murong Yun their king. Murong Yu reverted to his original surname of Gao, known as the "Northern Yan." Two years later, Gao Yun was killed. Feng Ba became his successor and made Longcheng (present-day Chaoyang) the capital.

The Northern Yan's territory covered present-day eastern Hebei and the western regions of Liaoning. Although it claimed to have five regions and 12 commanderies, it used to be Pingzhou and the northeastern part of Youzhou in the Western Jin era. In AD 436, the Northern Yan was ended by the Northern Wei.

(11) The Western Qin
In AD 385, Qifu Guoren, a Xianbei chief in the Longxi Region, declared himself in Yuanchuan (present-day northeast Yuzhong, Gansu) as the Grand Khan, known as the "Western Qin." In AD 388, his brother ascended the throne after his death and moved the capital to Jincheng (northwest Lanzhou, Gansu).

The Western Qin Dynasty had a narrow territory. Although there were 12 prefectures, it only covered the area between Lanzhou and Longxi in Gansu Province today. After defeating Yang Ding, leader of the Di people, the Western Qin Dynasty occupied the area of Wudu and Cheng County in Gannan at the present day. In AD 400, the Western Qin was destroyed by the Later Qin Dynasty and was downgraded to a vassal state. In AD 409, the Western Qin took advantage of the decline of the Later Qin Dynasty; Qifu Qiangui declared himself the King of Qin again. In AD 414 the Western Qin Dynasty was destroyed by Southern Liang, which moved the capital to Fu Han (now southwest of Linxia County, Gansu Province), occupying the eastern belt of Qinghai Lake in Qinghai Province.

At its peak, Western Qin covered Longxi District in Gansu and eastern Qinghai. In AD 430, the Kingdom of Tuyuhun conquered Western Qin. The following year, the Western Qin administration surrendered to Xia.

(12) The Later Liang
In AD 384, Lü Guang, a general of the former Qin Dynasty, returned to Liangzhou after conquering the Western Regions. After hearing that Fu Jian was defeated in Feishui, he lived in Guzang and called himself Liang Regional Commissioner and Duke of Jiuquan in AD 386. This dynasty was referred to as the Later Liang.

The territory of the Later Liang covered the area from the west of Hexi Corridor to the whole western region, including one state, that is, Liangzhou, and twenty to thirty prefectures. Since AD 397, as the Southern Liang, Northern Liang and Western Liang had been established one after the other, the territory of the Later Liang had become smaller and smaller. Under the attack of Southern Liang and Northern Liang, Later Liang was destroyed by Later Qin in AD 403.

(13) The Southern Liang
In AD 397, Tufa Wugu, the leader of a branch of the Xianbei in Hexi, declared himself the Grand Chanyu and the King of Xiping. He seized control of places such as Jincheng, an event historically referred to as the establishment of Southern Liang. This period was referred to as the Southern Liang.

Two years later, the Southern Liang moved its capital to Ledu (now Ledu, Qinghai Province), occupying the eastern part of Qinghai in the present day, and then moved to Xiping (now Xining, Qinghai Province) in the same year. It moved its capital back to Ledu again in AD 402. In AD 406, Guzang was seized by the

Southern Liang from the Northern Liang and its territory expanded to the east Hexi Corridor. In AD 410, the Southern Liang were defeated by the Northern Liang and gave up the territory of the Hexi Corridor. Four years later, it was conquered by the Western Qin.

(14) The Northern Liang
In the same year of the establishment of Southern Liang in AD 397, Juqu Mengxun, leader of the Lushuihu ethnic group in western Hebei Province, rose to power. He assisted Duan Ye, a member of the Xiongnu and the Taishou of Jiankang (now the southern part of Gaotai County in Gansu Province), to be the Duke of Jiankang. The reign was known as the Northern Liang.

In AD 401, Juqu Mengxun killed Duan Ye and declared himself the Duke of Zhangye. He placed his capital in Zhangye and ruled over the central part of the western corridor in Zhangye in AD 410. Two years later, he moved the capital to Guzang. The Western Liang was destroyed in AD 421. Up to then, the scale of the territory of the Northern Laing had reached its peak, covering roughly three states and twenty-three prefectures. In AD 439, The Northern Liang were destroyed by the Northern Wei.

(15) The Western Liang
In AD 400, the King of Northern Liang appointed Li Dun as the Grand Administrator of Dunhuang. Soon, Li Dun declared himself as the Duke of Liang, known as the "Western Liang," with Dunhuang as its capital.

Its territory covered the Western Regions and a part of the Hexi Corridor with Jiuquan as its western border. While it boasted "18 component counties," only two, i.e., Jiuquan and Duhuang left over from the Han dynasties were actually under its control. In AD 405, Western Liang moved its capital to Jiuquan. In AD 420, its king was defeated and killed by Northern Liang. In the next year, the kingdom came to an end.

(16) Xia
In AD 407, Helianbobo, a Xiongnu chieftain, took possession of Dacheng (now southeast of Hangjin in Inner Mongolia) and declared himself the King of Daxia. This dynasty was known as "Xia." In AD 413, Helianbobo built Tongwancheng (now north of Baichengzi in Jingbian County of Shaanxi Province) as its capital.

Chapter Four

Xia occupied the area from Hebei to Longdong and Shaanbei, and continued to attack Weibei, threatening Later Qin. In AD 418, Helian Bobo attacked Guanzhong, the Eastern Jin troops retreated, and Xia's territory expanded to Guanzhong. Xia claimed to have nine provinces: You, Yong, Shuo, Qin, North Qin, Bing, Liang, Yu, and Jing, with twenty-one counties and nineteen cities, but in reality, it only had parts of the provinces of Yong and Qin during the Western Jin period, as well as part of Sizhou. In AD 427, Northern Wei captured Tongwancheng. The remnants of Xia in Guanzhong and Longdong contested with Northern Wei and even managed to annihilate Western Qin in AD 431, but in the end, they could not stand up against the power of Northern Wei. Xia's king, Helian Ding, had no choice but to move west to Hexi, but unfortunately, they were ambushed by the Tuyuhun on the way. Helian Ding was captured, and the Xia kingdom was consequently destroyed.

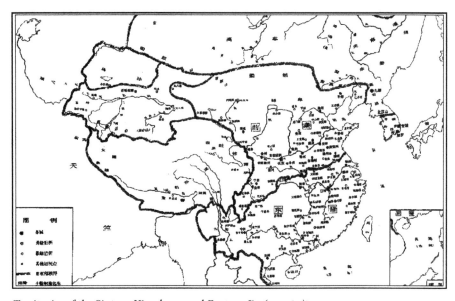

Territories of the Sixteen Kingdoms and Eastern Jin (AD 382)[1]

---

1. Sketchmap based on Tan Qixiang, *Atlas in Chinese History* (Beijing: SinoMaps Press, 1982).

During the Sixteen Kingdoms period, there were also a number of other regimes, such as the one built by the Yang clan of Di ethnic that occupied the area around Qiuchi (now area between Xihe, Hui County, and Wen County in Gansu Province). In addition, the leader of the Zhai clan took Huatai and Liyang (now northeast of Jun County in Henan), the Dingling tribe leader Zhai once used Hua Tai and Liyang (northeast of today's Henan Xun County) as bases and called himself the King of Wei, the Xianbei Murong family established the Western Yan in Zhangzi (southwest of today's Shanxi Zhangzi County), Qiao family established Later Shu in Chengdu, and the Dai regime, which is the predecessor of the Northern Wei and already existed at the end of the Western Jin Dynasty, etc., but traditionally these regimes are not included in the Sixteen Kingdoms.

2. Colony Prefectures, Commanderies, and Counties

Shortly after the Western Jin ended, Sima Rui, the Prince of Langya, declared himself King of Jin in AD 317 in Jiankang (present-day Nanjing). The next year, he declared himself Emperor Yuan of Jin. Since Jiankang was located to the east of Luoyang, Sima Rui's dynasty was known as "Eastern Jin."

At the terminus of Eastern Jin, its administration and military forces fell into the hands of Liu Yu, who was originally a defender-in-chief. In AD 420, Liu Yu deposed Emperor Gong of Jin and named himself Emperor Wu of Song. The Song was the first of the Southern dynasties. The Northern and Southern dynasties lasted for a period between AD 420 and AD 589, following the tumultuous era of the Sixteen Kingdoms.

The other three dynasties in South China after the Song were: Qi, Liang, and Chen. The Northern dynasties first started with the Northern Wei in AD 389. Then, the Northern Wei was divided into the Eastern Wei and Western Wei. Later, the Eastern Wei was replaced by the Northern Qi, while the Western Wei was replaced by the Northern Zhou.

In terms of administrative divisions, Eastern Jin, and the Southern and Northern Dynasties all adopted the Prefecture-Commandery-County system. However, the tumultuous era also affected the scale and forms of the system. Therefore, the administrative divisions in this period had distinct characteristics.

(1) Colony Prefectures and Tu-Duan (土断, localization)

In AD 320, the Emperor Yuan of Eastern Jin set up the first colony county—Huaide County—in the vicinity of Jiankang, the capital of Eastern Jin. This marked the beginning of large-scale colony commanderies and counties. In Huaide, the Emperor relocated the Han Chinese who moved south with him in the war.

Colony commanderies and counties were a prominent feature of the administrative divisions in the Eastern Jin and Southern dynasties. Reasons for their establishment can be traced back to the Western Jin. Back then, northern China was chaotic because of civil wars and nomadic tribe attacks. Most civilians chose to move south due to this.

In AD 317, when Eastern Jin was established by Sima Rui, many nobles, officers, and landowners brought their families, relatives, and servants here for shelter. From AD 307 to AD 453, Han migration south never ceased. This was the first of its kind in Chinese history and was known as the "Migration to the South in the Era of Yongjia."

In total there were four major migrations:

a. The first spike took place when Sima Rui, then-Prince of Langya, moved to Jiangdong District. Over 1,000 families travelled with him. Since then, thousands of people joined from places such as modern Hebei, Shandong, Henan, and Anhui.

b. The second spike occurred in the first few years of Emperor Cheng's reign of Eastern Jin. In AD 326, Su Jun, Minister of Agriculture, and General Zu Yue rebelled against the empire. Shi Le, chief of the Jie tribe, took advantage of the chaos and attacked southern China. This triggered a new round of migration south of the Yangtze. The migrants included civilians from south of the Huai River as well as those who had previously moved there from the north.

c. The third spike took place in Emperor Ai's era (AD 362–365) and continued for another 20 years. There were constant wars in central China. Tens of thousands of people moved from present-day Shaanxi and Gansu to the Han River and Sichuan Valley areas.

d. The fourth major migration took place during the reigns of Emperor Wen (AD 424–453) and Emperor Ming (AD 465–471). The central part of China that had been retrieved by Emperor Wu fell into the hands of nomadic tribes. The northern part of Huai was taken by Northern Wei. Tens of thousands of people moved across Huai to the South.

The Han Chinese mostly migrated to the following regions: Jingzhou, Yangzhou, Liangzhou, and Yizhou. The total migrant population was over 700,000. Another 200,000 people moved to modern Shandong in eastern China. Meanwhile, a great number of people went further south to Fujian, Guangdong and the mountainous region of southern Anhui.

According to statistics, the population that migrated south accounted for over one-eighth of the northern part of Western Jin. Among the residents in the south, one out of every six people originally came from the north. This did not include private armies and peasants who belonged to landowners and nobles.

With such a large number of southern migrants, the ruler of the Eastern Jin Dynasty was naturally faced with the question of how to effectively control and manage these migrants. If the Eastern Jin government could not take an effective measure to settle these immigrants, it was very likely to result in riots and other incidents, which posed a serious threat to the Eastern Jin regime. The Eastern Jin and the Southern Dynasty obviously noticed this problem and adopted two main approaches to appease these immigrants. On the one hand, they allowed the leaders of big clans to take up positions in the central or local government in order to make use of them. On the other hand, as these migrants all migrated collectively in the form of clan and tribal groups, the Eastern Jin and Southern dynasties governments implemented a policy of setting up new state-prefecture-county three-level administrative divisions in the main areas where these migrants settled. They used the names of their original northern residences as the names for these new divisions, in order to control and manage the large number of immigrants. Since these new administrative divisions were all relocated within the already existing southern divisions, they were referred to as Colony Prefectures, Commanderies, and Counties.

There were mainly four reasons for the appearance of Colony Prefectures, Commanderies, and Counties. First, people at the time believed that the migration to the south was only a temporary phenomenon and that the lost lands in the north could be quickly recovered. Therefore, the local administrative institutions were still organized in the form of the old territories, and the original names of the administrative divisions were retained. This nostalgia also expressed a determination to recover the old lands as soon as possible. Second, the orthodox concept was deeply rooted. Although there was a division between the north and the south at that time and each regime claimed to be orthodox, in the eyes of ordinary people, there still existed the traditional concept that "Di and Rong have never become emperors since ancient times."[2] Therefore, the common view at the time was that the Eastern Jin regime, "despite its geographical location in Wu and Yue, was the legitimate successor to the throne."[3] Although the territory of the Eastern Jin regime was incomplete, it was reluctant to admit its lack of power and could only use the nominal status of the relocated provinces, prefectures, and counties to comfort itself. At the same time, it was stipulated that the new provinces, prefectures, and counties established by the Sixteen Kingdoms and Northern dynasties should not be relocated to express the denial of their authority. Third, the migrants held high status and had strong regional and community sentiments. After migrating to the south, the migrants still lived in clusters according to their clans. They regarded the preservation of their original status and the maintenance of their native places as matters of utmost importance. Therefore, they absolutely did not mix with the local indigenous people in their place of migration. In response to this situation, the Eastern Jin and Southern dynasties government had to adopt the method of Colony Prefectures, Commanderies, and Counties in order to manage them separately. Fourth, the Eastern Jin and Southern dynasties government wanted to use the method of Colony Prefectures, Commanderies, and Counties to attract more people from the north to the south to ensure a source of soldiers and labor, and to pacify the migrants who had already moved south, so that they could live and work in peace and contentment, and promote further economic development.

It was for these reasons that Colony Prefectures, Commanderies, and Counties were established in the Eastern Jin and the Southern dynasties. From the Emperor Yuan of the Eastern Jin Dynasty to Kingdoms of Song, Qi, Liang, and Chen in the Southern dynasties, a large number of Colony Prefectures, Commanderies, and Counties were set up, forming a situation in which there were "dozens of Colony Prefectures, hundreds of Colony Commanderies and

---

2. *Book of Jin · Records of Yao Yizhong.*
3. *Records of Wangmeng* attached to the *Book of Jin · Records of Fujian.*

thousands of Colony Counties."[4] At the end of the Eastern Jin Dynasty, after Liu Yu recovered the Qing and Xu states in his northern expedition, he added the word "Bei" [North] to the names of the original states and counties in order to distinguish them from Colony Prefectures, Commanderies, and Counties. After Liu Yu became the emperor and established the Song Dynasty, the word "Bei" was deleted and the word "Nan" [South] was added to the names of Colony Prefectures, Commanderies, and Counties.

In terms of geographical distribution, colony commanderies and counties were mainly set in the lower reaches of the Yangtze River. For example, Xuzhou, Yanzhou, Youzhou, Jizhou, Qingzhou, Bingzhou and their affiliated Commandery-County were established in the vicinity of Jingkou (now Zhenjiang, Jiangsu) and Guangling (now northwest of Yangzhou, Jiangsu). In the vicinity of Wujin County (northwest of Wujin, Jiangsu), over 20 colony prefectures and 60 counties were set up. In addition, Colony Prefectures, Commanderies, and Counties were also very common in the mid and lower reaches of Yangtze River as well as the southern part of the Qinling Mountains in Shaanxi. Therefore, the depiction by Tang Dynasty poet Zhang Ji in his poem "Journey to Yongjia," which states, "Many people from the north fled from the barbarians to the south, and the southerners can still speak the language of Jin today,"[5] is an apt portrayal of this situation.

When these Colony Prefectures, Commanderies, and Counties were initially established, they did not have actual jurisdictions but were a separate administrative system temporarily residing within the inherent administrative divisions of the South. The migrants also enjoyed generous treatment from the government within these areas, including reductions or exemptions from taxes and services. Initially, the goal of establishing these areas was to recover the old lands. However, because the Central Plains could not be recovered for a long time, the natives and migrants lived together, which caused chaos in household registration and made it very inconvenient for the government to manage. At the

---

4. Hong Liangji, "Preface to the Record of the Territorial Extent of the Eastern Jin Dynasty." This article is also included in the "Collection of Literature A," vol. 8 of *The Collection of Juanshige*. Enlarged edition of "The Complete Collection of Hong Beijiang" published in the third year of the Guangxu era in the Qing Dynasty by Hong's Lecture Hall.
5. Zhang Ji, *Zhang Wenchang's Collected Works*, vol. 4, found in the Song Dynasty Sichuan edition of *Continuation of Ancient and Obscure Books*.

same time, the preferential treatment enjoyed by the migrants in these areas also caused the government to lose a significant amount of financial resources. As a result, the Eastern Jin and Southern dynasties' governments decided to reform these Colony Prefectures, Commanderies, and Counties using a method known as "cutting off the land."

The so-called "Tu-Duan" was to localize migrants. Migrants were then registered where they lived and had to pay taxes the same way as locals. As a result, many colony commanderies and counties were canceled. They were then governed by local commanderies, or vice versa. Another solution was to divide parts of the colony commanderies to be governed separately.

From the Emperor Cheng of Eastern Han until AD 560, there were nine Tu-Duans in total. The consequences were as follows: colony commanderies and counties had their own land, and a large number of migrants were quickly localized. After the Sui Dynasty had unified China, borders between the south and north disappeared, and the colonies disappeared as well.

(2) "Shuang-Tou" (双头) Prefectures and Commanderies

It is generally believed that Shuang-Tou prefecture and commandery first appeared in the Eastern Jin Dynasty. In the *Biography of Mao Qu*, which is attached to the *Biography of Mao Bao* in the *Book of Jin*, it described that during the reign of Emperor Xiaowu of the Eastern Jin Dynasty, Mao Qu was the Internal Historian of the Qiao and Liang prefectures. During the reign of Emperor An, he was the Taishou of Yidu and Ningshu prefectures. At the same time, Wen Chumao was the Taishou of Baxi and Zitong prefectures. In addition, Mao Jin, Mao Qu's brother, was the governor of Liang and Qin prefectures, and he was also the Taishou of Lüyang and Wudou prefectures. It was clear that Shuang-Tou prefecture and commandery was already a common phenomenon during the reigns of Emperor Xiaowu and Emperor An.

The reasons why this became a common practice during the Eastern Jin and Southern dynasties were as follows: due to continuous war, the population became scarce and the land barren, or possibly, the land was taken by rival kingdoms. The central government preferred not to combine provinces. As a result, a makeshift solution was to let one regional inspector govern two regions, or one grand administrator govern two commanderies. There were some Shuang-Tou prefectures and commanderies that ruled over only one county. It was really abnormal since there was no need for such two prefectures to exist if they only ruled over one county. An example can be found in one Shuang-Tou prefecture and commandery established in the Northern Wei Dynasty. Xincai and Nanchenliu Prefecture, a Shuang-Tou prefecture and commandery, only ruled over one county, that is, Zhouyang County (now west of Linquan, Anhui Province).

There were three forms of Shuang-Tou prefecture and commandery. First, the overseas states or prefectures were ruled by the actual states or prefectures. For example, in the Eastern Jin and Song dynasties, the two states of Qing and Ji were ruled by Dongyangcheng county (now north of Qingzhou, Shandong). Also, the Dongguan and Langya prefectures were ruled together in Qushan (now Haizhou, Lianyungang, Jiangsu Province) in the Southern dynasties. Second, two overseas states or prefectures were ruled in the same place. For example, Qinghe and Guangchuan prefectures in Song Dynasty were the overseas prefectures belonging to Jizhou state, and these two prefectures were ruled in Pangyang city; and the two overseas states of Qing and Jizhou were ruled in the Yuzhou state. Third, two actual prefectures ruled over the same place. This situation is only found among the Shuang-Tou prefectures and commanderies. For example, in the Song Dynasty, the two prefectures of Runan and Xincai were ruled together in Xuanhu City in Cai County, Runan Prefecture (now Runan, Henan Province).[6]

Most of the Shuang-Tou prefectures and commanderies were located on the northern borders of the Eastern Jin and Southern dynasties. The Northern dynasties copied this. Even today, Shuang-Tou prefectures and commanderies could be found in central Sichuan, south Shaanxi, west Shandong, and the Huai River regions. According to statistics conducted by Hu Axiang, there were nine Shuang-Tou States altogether and 70 Shuang-Tou prefectures.[7] Those administrative divisions experienced frequent changes. For example, the seats were often relocated. Sometimes, two regions would be separated and then reunited again. As soon as the Sui Dynasty unified China, the Shuang-Tou prefecture and commandery disappeared with the abolition of Shuang-Tou prefecture and commandery.

---

6. Hu Axiang, *Territory and Administrative Divisions during the Six Dynasties* (Xi'an: Xi'an Map Publishing House, 2001), 258–259.
7. Hu Axiang, *Territory and Administrative Divisions during the Six Dynasties*, 263.

3. Redundant Prefectures and Commanderies

There were still rules to setting up administrative divisions higher than commanderies at the end of Eastern Han. For example, in the early years of Western Jin, there were 19 regions, 171 commanderies and 1,232 counties. Every region would govern 8 to 9 commanderies on average; every commandery 7 to 8 counties. However, the rules were broken in the Eastern Jin, and the Northern and Southern dynasties.

Reasons for the growth lie in the following aspects: due to continuous wars, there were more decorated generals. Also, there were many generals from rival kingdoms who had surrendered. The central government tended to reward them with titles of regional inspector or grand administrator of commanderies. However, as each administration had limited land, the only possible solution was to divide regions and commanderies into smaller ones and then make room for new regions and commanderies.

However, in the early stage of the Liang Kingdom in the Southern dynasties, the number of prefectures and commanderies had not increased significantly. According to historical records, in AD 502, there were 23 states, 226 prefectures and 1,300 counties in Liang. But less than 50 years later, the number of regions, states and prefectures increased to an unimaginable level. There were 103 regions and 586 commanderies in Liang in AD 546.

The Northern dynasties also set up too many states and prefectures. After the Northern Wei Dynasty unified the north, there were less than 20 regions. But in the later years of Emperor Xiaowen's reign, there were more than 80 regions. After the Northern Wei Dynasty was replaced by the Eastern and Western Wei dynasties, there were more than 110 states and more than 410 prefectures existing. During the Northern and Southern dynasties there were more than 200 regions and nearly 1,000 prefectures. Compared with the Western Jin Dynasty 250 years ago, the number of states and prefectures increased more than ten times. At this time, many states only ruled over one or two prefectures, and many states only governed one to four counties. Some states even did not need to govern any counties, only retaining their names. According to the historical records, there were 65 prefectures in Liangzhou set up by the Southern Qi in Hanzhong region, of which 45 prefectures were located in barren areas or had no residents. In addition, there were also Shuang-Tou prefectures and commanderies where two states jointly govern one prefecture or county respectively. Up until then, the number of redundant states and prefectures reached the peak. In addition, the Northern Dynasty not only established a large number of states and prefectures but also set up a lot of officials, especially the prefecture regional inspectors. There were even three governors in a single region. Due to the increase of prefecture regional inspector, the Taishou gradually lost control in power. This, however, made way for reforms by Emperor Wen of the Sui, who later removed commanderies and set up the State-County system.

4. The "Six Garrisons" of Northern Wei

The Northern Wei was a dynasty set up in central China by the Tuoba Family from the nomadic tribe of Xianbei. It lasted from the 4th to the 6th century. The Northern Wei unified North China with force; therefore, it practiced a system of "Zhen-Shu" (military Garrisons). This was to solidify its reign and quell rebellions. In reality, the central government made adjustments according to different characteristics in different districts. For example, in its southeastern part, an area where its major population was composed of Han Chinese, the "State-Prefecture-County" system was kept complementary to the garrison system. The officers of garrisons and regions shared the same seats, with garrisons in charge of military affairs only. The governor of the garrison, the garrison general, was responsible only for military affairs and not for the administration of local civil affairs. It was a different story when it came to areas where the Xianbei and other minority tribes were the main inhabitants. Here, there are no established prefectures or counties; instead, management is conducted through military garrisons. The roles filled by the garrisons and their underpinning Shu are largely equivalent to those of prefectural Commandery-County. Garrison commanders and Shu leaders—known as garrison chiefs—are akin to prefecture regional inspector and prefectures Taishou, respectively. They are responsible not only for military matters but also for civil governance. Consequently, the military garrisons in this area morphed into local governing institutions where military and political affairs are integrated. Therefore, in the early Northern Wei period, the highest level of local administrative divisions was a combination of prefectures and garrisons.

North Wei northwest military garrisons managed by the garrison people mainly consisted of three kinds of people. One was the majority of the inherent members of the Tuoba tribe; they had been accustomed to the original way of life, not willing to move with the royal family, and still practicing their tribal system. Another part of the people who were forced to migrate here were Han and other minorities. After the capital of the Northern Wei Dynasty was built in Pingcheng, the rulers put the people who were plundered during the war in this area to work in agriculture or nomadic work in order to enrich the human and material resources of the capital and the northern part of Inner Mongolia. Thus, in this area, there was a phenomenon of Tuoba Xianbei people mixed with Han Chinese and other ethnic minorities. Another type of people sent here was criminals. For the above three types of people, the military garrison was the most appropriate way to make them subordinate to the military garrison, and not to set up a separate civil administration.

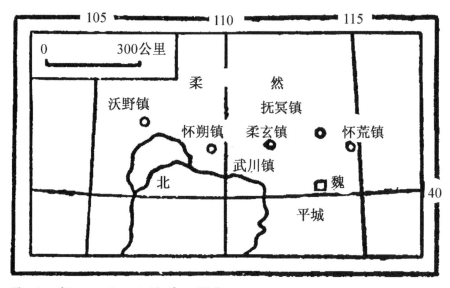

The six military garrisons in Northern Wei[8]

The garrisons were very popular for about 60 years, from AD 422 to AD 484. Later, all the military garrisons in the interior were successively converted into states, becoming purely civilian institutions. Only the northern military garrisons

---

8. *Basic Facts in Chinese History (History and Geography)* (Beijing: China Youth Press, 1981), 43.

were retained in order to defend against the southern invasions of the Rouran, a northern minority, and suppress local resistance. These northern military garrisons, from west to east, were Gaoping (today's Guyuan in Ningxia), Bogulü (on the ancient Yellow River sandbar, southwest of today's Lingwu in Ningxia), Woye (northeast of Wuyuan in Inner Mongolia today), Huaishuo (southwest of Guyang in Inner Mongolia today), Wuchuan (west of Wuchuan County in Inner Mongolia at Tucheng), Fuming (southeast of Siziwangqi in Inner Mongolia at Tuchengzi today), Rouxuan (northeast of Xinghe County in Inner Mongolia at Taiji Temple today), Huaihuang (today's Zhangbei in Hebei), and Fuyi (north of Chicheng in Hebei today). The so-called "Six Garrisons of the Northern Wei" refers to Woye, Huaishuo, Wuchuan, Fuming, Rouxuan, and Huaihuang, which are located in the central region of today's Inner Mongolia (see *The six military garrisons in Northern Wei*).

In the early years of Northern Wei, the six garrisons were close to the capital city of Pingcheng, forming a natural defense. Therefore, the central government attached great importance to them. As soldiers and officers had to defend the territory against the Rouran nomadic tribe, the central government not only granted them profitable earnings, but also waived their taxes and corvée. However, after Emperor Xiaowen relocated the capital to Luoyang, the six garrisons were no longer the darling protectors of the administrators. Those Xianbei nobles who moved with the Emperor to the new capital made an alliance with Han Chinese landowners. Together they controlled decision-making in the central government. Those Xianbei nobles who were left in the six northern garrisons were therefore neglected. Grievances grew as they could no longer ascend the hierarchy of power.

Also, the importance of northern defense was downgraded because the capital had been moved to the south. The new generals sent by the central government and newly drafted soldiers were not as good as before; these generals were greedy and cruel, exploiting local residents without restraint.

In AD 503, Emperor Xuanwu sent a minister named He Huai to examine the administration of the officials and to provide aid to the poorer people so as to ease the intensifying conflicts within the six northern garrisons. He was surprised that he could not find a single honest and law-abiding official among the six garrisons, as Yu Zuo, the general of Wayo garrison, and Yuan Nixu, the general of Huaishuo garrison, were all corrupt officials and they were much hated by the people. Many people complained to He Huai about them every day. This showed that there were many problems looming in these six garrisons.

In AD 523, after the Rouran tribe had robbed local residents, they asked the garrison general, Yu Jing, for food to survive. Yu Jing refused. The soldiers as well as residents became so furious that they rebelled and killed Yu Jing. This triggered great upheaval in the northern six garrisons.

In March of the next year, Poliuhan Bailing, a Xiongnu people from Woye garrison, conducted a rebellion. They first killed the king of Gaoque and the general of the garrison, then occupied the garrison. Seeing this, people of all ethnic groups in other garrisons responded and started uprisings in other garrisons.

The army led by Poliuhan Baling defeated the Northern Wei army, and even once captured the garrisons of Wuchuan and Huaishuo. However, it was finally suppressed. The uprisings in the six garrisons failed one after another, and the garrisons and lands were gradually deserted. The "Zhen-Shu" system of the Northern Wei Dynasty finally came to an end.

CHAPTER FIVE

TERRITORIES OF THE "KING OF HEAVEN"

—Territories and Administrative Divisions in the Sui, Tang, and the Five Dynasties and Ten Kingdoms Era

1. **ADMINISTRATION REFORMS AND TERRITORIAL EXPANSION IN THE SUI DYNASTY**

In AD 577, Northern Zhou defeated Northern Qi, unifying northern China. Soon afterward, Yang Jian took control of the central government. In AD 581, Yang forced Emperor Jing of Zhou to abdicate his throne. Yang Jian then established the Sui Dynasty and became Emperor Wen. In AD 589, the Sui defeated the Chen in southeast China; China was again unified, ending 300 years of turmoil.

(1) Removal of All Commanderies

In AD 583, on the eve of Sui's unification of the country, Emperor Wen completed a major reform of the local administrative system. As we have already mentioned, in the late Northern and Southern dynasties, the proliferation of states and commanderies had reached an unprecedented level, especially the increase of states, which made the prefecture-level division exist in name only. Faced with this situation, Emperor Wen Xuan of Northern Qi had a major reorganization during his reign, merging 33 states, 153 commanderies, 189 counties, three garrisons and 26 Shu, which was almost half of all the commanderies and counties at that time. However, this could not stop the worsening chaos in these political regions. An overhaul of the administrative system was imperative. After destroying the Northern Zhou Dynasty, minister Yang Shangxi of the Sui Dynasty submitted a proposal to Emperor Wen, saying that the number of commanderies and counties was many more times than in the past. Some places that were less than a hundred miles in circumference had several counties, and some places with less than a thousand households were even managed by two commanderies. In response to this abnormal phenomenon, he suggested that the administrative divisions should be reformed, "saving the important ones and merging the small ones."[1] Emperor Wen of Sui paid great attention to Yang Shang's opinions, but after careful consideration, he did not adopt the simple method of merging states and commanderies. Instead, he removed the middle level of the three-tier system of states, commanderies, and counties, that is, "removal of all commanderies,"[2] allowing states to directly administer counties. This simplified the hierarchy of administrative divisions and brought the administrative divisions back to a two-tier system. After the Sui Dynasty annihilated the Chen Dynasty, this measure was implemented nationwide. The greatest advantage of implementing a two-tier Commandery-County system is that it enables the central government's edicts to easily reach the local level, thereby strengthening centralization and avoiding the emergence of local separatism.

While Emperor Wen of Sui's reform was successful, it still did not completely solve the problem of too many states and counties. After the Wei, Jin, and Southern and Northern Dynasties, the number of states and counties had become very large, and the divisions of states and counties could not be made smaller. In the early Sui Dynasty, there were more than 300 states in total. Such a large scale made it difficult for the central government to govern directly. Therefore, adjusting the number and scope of states and counties became another important task for the central government of the Sui Dynasty.

This task was ultimately completed by Emperor Wen's son, Emperor Yang. In the third year of the Daye era (AD 607), Emperor Yang ordered the consolidation of states and counties, and then changed the states back to commanderies, returning to a situation similar to that of the Qin and Han dynasties. After this adjustment, by the fifth year of the Daye era, the whole country was divided into 190 commanderies and 1,255 counties. Compared with the Southern and

---

1. Book of Sui · Biographies of Yang Shangxi.
2. Book of Sui · Annals of Gaozu.

Northern Dynasties, the organizations above the county level were greatly streamlined.

During the Sui Dynasty, commanderies were governed by Taishou, who were assisted by officials called "Zanwu" (later changed to "Cheng"). In addition, a position called "Commandant" (Tongshou) was created beneath the prefect and above the "Cheng" to check the Taishou's power. At the end of each year, each prefecture had to send the Taishou or a senior officer to the capital to report on their work, a practice known as the "Imperial Envoy." Moreover, the positions of "Commandant" and "Deputy Commandant," who were military officers not under the jurisdiction of the prefecture, were created, resulting in a system of separate governance of military and civilians at the local level.

Additionally, Emperor Yang of Sui greatly admired the systems of the Han Dynasty. Therefore, he also followed the practice of Emperor Wu of Han and set up the positions of "Sili" and "Regional Inspector" above the commanderies to inspect the conditions in various places.

(2) Territorial Expansion
Since the Eastern Jin Dynasty, the south and the north had been separated for a long time. Most of the wars took place around the Yangtze and Huai Rivers. Although the Southern Dynasty was determined to recover the Central Plains as soon as possible, it failed to achieve this goal, let alone expand its territory. After the fall of the Northern Wei Dynasty the East and the West were in a confrontational attitude, therefore there was also no time to expand the territory. This situation finally changed during the reign of Emperor Yang of the Sui Dynasty.

Emperor Yang was an emperor who wanted to do great things and was greedy for achievements. At that time, the country had been unified, but he was not satisfied with the status quo. He was determined to expand the territory of the empire.

In AD 605, Emperor Yang sent General Liu to conquer the Kingdom of Linyi in the south, forcing its king to flee. Linyi was located in modern Vietnam. Previously it was a part of Xianglin County in the Rinan Commandery of Han Dynasty.

In AD 192, the local people declared independence and established Linyi. After that, it expanded north and eventually conquered all of Rinan Commandery. After Liu Fang conquered Linyi, three commanderies were set up. After a few months,

General Liu and his army went back home. The King of Linyi sent delegates to apologize to the Emperor of Sui and paid annal tributes from then on.

In addition, the Sui Empire also retrieved Hainan Island. As mentioned earlier, during the reign of Emperor Wu of the Western Han Dynasty, Hainan Island was included in the territory for the first time. At that time, Emperor Wu set up the Zhuya and Daner commanderies on Hainan Island. During the reign of Emperor Zhao and Emperor Yuan, the two commanderies were abandoned due to the resistance of the local people. The Wu Kingdom in the Three Kingdoms Period and the Liang Kingdom in the Southern dynasties also set Zhuya Prefecture and Liangzhou Prefecture respectively, but neither was established on Hainan Island. The reason why Hainan Island became one part of the Central Plains during the reign of Emperor Yang of the Sui Dynasty was closely related to the Xian clan, the leader of the Li ethnic group in the local island.

The Xian family had been the leaders of Southern Yue for generations, "ruling over more than 100,000 households in mountain and cave tribes," and "over a thousand caves in Hainan's Daner pledged their allegiance to them."[3] They were highly regarded in the region. During the Datong era of the Southern Dynasty Liang, Feng Bao, the Taishou of Gaoliang (modern western Yangjiang, Guangdong), married a woman from the Xian family. This woman is the famous Lady Xian in history. At the beginning of the Sui Dynasty, Lady Xian welcomed the Sui general into Guangzhou. Emperor Wen of Sui named her the Lady of Colony Prefecture and gave her command over the troops of six states, including Hainan Island. After the death of the Lady of Colony Prefecture, Emperor Yang of Sui annexed the territories controlled by the Xian family to the central government. In the sixth year of Daye (AD 610), the Sui Dynasty established the commanderies of Zhuya, Daner, and Linzhen on Hainan Island. Thus, after Emperor Yuan of the Western Han Dynasty gave up Zhuya Prefecture, Hainan Island once again became part of the territory of the Central Plains Dynasty after 750 years.

In the north, one major rival of the Sui in the north was Tujue, a branch of the Xiongnu people. The Tujue were originally a branch of the Xiongnu. In AD 552, the Tujue destroyed the Rouran and established the Turkic Khanates. At the end of the Northern Zhou Dynasty, Sha Bolue became the leader of the Tujue and married Princess Qianjin, the daughter of a Northern Zhou aristocrat named

---

3. *Book of Sui · Lady of Qiao State.*

Yuwen Zhao. After Emperor Wen of the Sui destroyed the Northern Zhou, Princess Qianjin was very angry. She persuaded Sha Bolue to send troops to fight with the Sui so as to avenge the Northern Zhou. Forty thousand Turkic troops invaded the northwest border of Sui in AD 583 and plundered a large number of people and livestock. When Emperor Yang of the Sui Dynasty learned the news, he sent Yang Hong, Gao Jiong and Yu Qingze to defend the country. They achieved a decisive victory in Baidao (now Hohhot, Inner Mongolia). After that, the Tujue fell into internal disorder and finally split into two countries, the Eastern Tujue and the Western Tujue. The Eastern Tujue was located in the Mongolian plateau east of the Altai Mountains, and the Western Tujue was located in the Leizhu Sea (now the Caspian Sea, or the Aral Sea) west of the Altai Mountains. The territory of the Western Tujue includes today's Junggar Basin, Ili River Basin, and Chu River Basin.

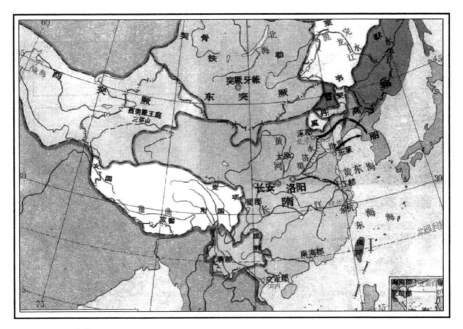

Territories of the Sui Dynasty[4]

The Sui central government adopted a strategy of divide and conquer to turn the two khans of Eastern Tujue against one another. Dulan Khan proposed to

---

4. Sketchmap based on Tan Qixiang, *Atlas in Chinese History* (Beijing: SinoMaps Press, 1982).

marry Princess Anyi of Sui. But the Emperor married her off to Dulan's brother Tuli Khan—the two brothers then fought. In AD 599, Tuli Khan was defeated by his brother and surrendered to the Sui. He was then crowned Qimin Khan. Later, Dulan Khan was killed by his subordinates. Qimin Khan occupied the entire land of Eastern Tujue. In this way, the Sui managed to control Eastern Tujue.

Datou Khan of Western Tujue wanted to annex Eastern Tujue, but he was defeated by the Sui armies. In AD 611, Chuluo of Western Tujue surrendered to Sui, after being defeated by his uncle Xiekui Khan. After settling the Eastern and Western Tujue issue, the Sui Empire then conquered the Hetao District and set up Wuyuan and Yulin commanderies.

In the early years of Emperor Wen of the Sui Dynasty, Tuyuhun often attacked Sui's borders. Later, they controlled the Shanshan District of the Western Regions, obstructing Sui routes. In AD 609, Emperor Yang of Sui sent armies west and defeated Tuyuhun. In the fifth year of the Daye era (AD 609), Emperor Yang of the Sui Dynasty sent Yang Xiong and Yuwen Shu to defeat the Tuyuhun. They then claimed a territory "from the city of Xiping, Linqiang (present-day Huangyuan, Qinghai) to the west, and from Qiemo to the east, south of the Qilian Mountains, and north of the Xue Mountains (present-day Minshan, Gansu), a territory of 4,000 *li* from east to west, and 2,000 *li* from north to south, all belonged to the Sui."[5] The Sui Dynasty then set up the four commanderies of Xihai (administered from present-day Fusi City, west of Qinghai Lake), Heyuan (administered from present-day Xinghai, southeast of Qinghai), Shanshan (administered from present-day Ruoqiang, Xinjiang), and Qiemai (present-day Qiemo, south of Xinjiang) on the former lands of the Tuyuhun. In the sixth year of the Daye period (AD 610), a new prefecture, Yiwu (with its administrative center located in modern Hami, Xinjiang), was established on the land of the Yiwu Tutun, which had separated from the control of the Turkic Khaganate and had submitted to the central government.

The above five commanderies included the eastern part of Xinjiang and most of Qinghai today. It was the first time in Chinese history that a central empire had set up commanderies and counties so far away from its capital.

The Sui Empire reformed and perfected its administrative divisions, and the

---

5. Du You et al. proof, "Border Defense Six," in *Tongdian*, vol. 190 (Beijing: Zhonghua Book Company, 1988), 5165.

country became prosperous again after the reigns of Emperor Wen and Yang. However, the dynasty did not last long. History repeated itself, and the Sui ended in a way similar to that of the Qin.

There were many factors that brought about this downfall. One important one was that Emperor Yang was too ambitious. He was also cruel, exploiting people to the extreme. In AD 611, Wang Bo and his men were the first to rebel against the Sui government in present-day Zhouping, Shandong. In a few years, hundreds of rebellions broke out across the country bringing down the empire. In AD 618, Emperor Yang was killed by Imperial Army leader Yuwen Huaji. The Sui Dynasty only lasted for 38 years.

In the year of the Emperor's death, his regent in Taiyuan, Li Yuan, declared himself Emperor in Chang'an (Xi'an), and established the Tang Dynasty.

2. Circuits in the Tang Dynasty

Li Yuan's second son Li Shimin became his successor, naming himself Emperor Taizong of Tang. From AD 626 to AD 649, the Tang expanded their territories westwards after defeating various nomadic tribes. Its territories then expanded north of the Yin Mountains and present-day Xinjiang. The Tang set up administrative divisions to govern these regions. Local tribe leaders regarded Emperor Taizong as "Khan of Heaven,"[6] because of his lenient policies. Later, Emperor Taizong's son, Emperor Gaozong, defeated Western Tujue, Baiji, Tianshan, and Goryeo, expanding Tang's territory significantly.

After the Tang Dynasty was established, it renamed commanderies as prefectures, thus its administrative divisions went back to the "Prefecture-County" system. In AD 742, prefectures were renamed as commanderies, and in AD 758, the name was again changed back to prefectures. One challenge for administrators was handling the number of prefectures, which rose quickly after its territories had expanded. Emperor Taizong tried to tackle the problem by combining some prefectures, however it was not very effective. In AD 639, the number of prefectures under direct control of the central government reached 358—almost three times that of the Han Dynasty.

---

6. *Old Book of Tang · Annals of Emperor Taizong.*

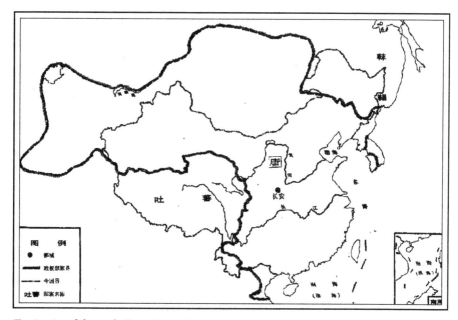

Territories of the early Tang Dynasty[7]

At that time, the territory of the Tang Dynasty was larger than that of the Han Dynasty, and the management of the country in the Tang Dynasty was more comprehensive. Although the Han Dynasty and the Tang Dynasty both implemented a two-tier system, the number of states in the Tang Dynasty could not be reduced to around 100, as the Han Dynasty did. However, it was indeed a significant challenge for the central government to manage these more than 300 states. There was an anecdote about Emperor Taizong. In order to have a clear grasp of every prefecture regional inspector, and to decide whether to reward or punish them based on their performance, Emperor Taizong of Tang came up with a method. He had his subordinates write the names of more than 300 prefecture regional inspectors on the screens in his daily office so that he could familiarize himself with these regional inspectors during his free time reviewing memorials. Although this reflects that Emperor Taizong was a diligent emperor, it ultimately revealed the difficulty in managing the prefecture regional inspectors. At that time, some ministers reminded the authorities from the perspective of official appointments that selecting one hundred good Taishou in the Han Dynasty

---

7. Sketchmap based on Tan Qixiang, *Atlas in Chinese History* (Beijing: SinoMaps Press, 1982).

was already a very difficult task, let alone the problem we now face in choosing more than 300 prefecture regional inspectors. This situation has made the central government have to consider setting up a supervisory district above the two-level system of states and counties, to monitor the actions of local regional inspectors and report local officials' situation to the central government at any time. Although the method of setting up supervisory districts can be an effective measure, the emperors of the early Tang Dynasty clearly understood from the experience of previous generations that once the supervisory districts are set up, there is a risk that they will become a formal administrative district. At that time, it will be difficult to revoke them, so it is necessary to find an alternative method. The Patrol Envoy established during the Zhenguan era of Emperor Taizong was an attempt in this regard.

In AD 627, Emperor Taizong divided the country into ten administrative units or "Dao" (circuits). They were:

a. Guannei Circuit: present-day central and northern Shaanxi Province, Longdong in Gansu, and Hetao District in Mongolia;
b. Henan Circuit: present-day south of the Yellow River in Henan and Shandong, north of the Huai River in Jiangsu and Anhui;
c. Hedong Circuit: present-day Shanxi and the northwestern part of Hebei;
d. Hebei Circuit: present-day south of the Great Wall in Hebei, the northern part of the Yellow River reaches in Henan and Shandong;
e. Shannan Circuit: present-day east of Sichuan, south of Shaanxi and Gansu, southwest of Henan, and west of Hubei;
f. Longyou Circuit: present-day Long Mountain in Gansu, west of Liupang Mountain, east of Qinghai Lake, and east of Xinjiang;
g. Huainan Circuit: present-day the part between Huai River and the Yangtze River in Anhui and Jiangsu;
h. Jiangnan Circuit: present-day Zhejiang, Fujian, Jiangxi, and Hunan Provinces, the southern part of the Yangtze River region in Anhui, a part of Hunan and Sichuan, and the northeastern part of Guizhou Province;
i. Jiannan Circuit: present-day central Sichuan and northern Yunnan;
j. Lingnan Circuit: present-day Guangdong and Guangxi provinces and northeastern Vietnam.

Emperor Taizong sent touring surveillance commissioners to inspect these ten circuits. However, the commissioners were only sent occasionally. In AD 711, the Surveillance Commissioner became a permanent position. The commissioners were sent by the central government to each of the circuits as coordinators.

In AD 733, Emperor Xuanzong wished to improve the system of existing circuits. He parted the prosperous Jiangnan Circuit into three: Eastern Jiangnan, Western Jiangnan, and Central Qian. The circuits' governing areas are:

a. Eastern Jiangnan Circuit: present-day Zhejiang and Fujian, as well as the southern part of the Yangtze River in Jiangsu;
b. Western Jiangnan Circuit: present-day Jiangxi and Hunan, south of Anhui, east of Hubei to the south of the Yangtze River;
c. Central Qian Circuit: present-day Guizhou and areas on the borders with Sichuan, Hunan, and Guangxi provinces, as well as the southwest tip of Hubei.

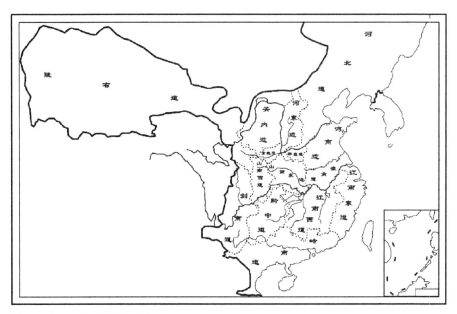

The 15 circuits in the Tang Dynasty[8]

---

8. Sketchmap based on Tan Qixiang, *Atlas in Chinese History* (Beijing: SinoMaps Press, 1982).

Emperor Xuanzong further divided Shannan Circuit into Eastern Shannan and Western Shannan. The two circuits were divided by present-day Chongqing and the eastern part of Shaanxi. In addition, he established a new circuit called the Metropolitan Circuit in which the dynastic capital Chang'an was located. Duji Circuit was added to govern Luoyang and neighboring prefectures. Hence, there were 15 circuits in total (see *The 15 circuits in the Tang Dynasty*).

The establishment of the supervisory districts showed that Emperor Xuanzong of the Tang Dynasty was highly optimistic and confident during the Kaiyuan heyday period. He did not need to think carefully about the impact of the supervisory districts on the centralization of power as Taizong did. On the other hand, the establishment of the supervisory districts was also necessary during that time. Without supervisory districts, it will not only bring a lot of inconvenience to the work of supervision, but also made the supervising officials tired of running between the capital and the area supervised, thus affecting the effect of the supervision. However, after the establishment of the supervisory districts, touring surveillance commissioners became permanent posts. Therefore, the Touring Surveillance Commission could become an administrative division and the its officials administrative officials. Based on the decree issued by Emperor Xuanzong of Tang in AD 750, the ninth year of the Tianbao period, emphasizing that the Censorate Envoys only needed to be responsible for investigating good and evil, and that the affairs within the prefectures should be handled by the prefecture regional inspectors and not be interfered with, it can be seen that the trend of the supervisory officials meddling in governance and becoming local administrative officials had already become significant at that time.

3. Three Types of "Fu"

Apart from circuits, the Tang also set up a new system called "Fu," which exerted great influence on the dynasties to come and had an important influence on the development of the Fu system in later times. The Fu can be divided into three types based on their conditions and statuses. Let's take a look at each of them separately.

(1) Metropolitan Prefecture (京、都所在的府)

The first type is the Metropolitan Prefecture (Fu in the capitals and the emperor's whereabouts). Starting from the first year of the Kaiyuan era of Emperor Xuanzong of Tang (AD 713), in order to elevate the status of the places where the capitals were located and to distinguish them from ordinary prefectures, they were called "Fu." At first, only Yongzhou, where the capital Chang'an was located, was called Jingzhao Fu, and Luozhou, where the Eastern Capital Luoyang was located, was called Henan Fu. Later, Bingzhou, where the Northern Capital Taiyuan was located, was called Taiyuan Fu, Qizhou, where the Western Capital Fengxiang was located, was called Fengxiang Fu; and Jingzhou, where the Southern Capital Jiangling was located, was called Jiangling Fu. Even the places where the emperor had been were also promoted to Fu, such as Puzhou being promoted to Hezhong Fu, Huazhou to Xingde Fu, Shanzhou to Xingtang Fu, Yizhou to Chengdu Fu, and Liangzhou to Xingyuan Fu. In this way, by the end of the Tang Dynasty, a total of ten Fus ad appeared.

The chief official of the prefecture was called the "Mu," and it was nominally led by a prince of the Tang Dynasty, but in actuality, the prefecture was administered by the "Yin." Under the Fu Yin, there were officials such as the Vice Yin, the Registrar and Military Affairs Consultant, and the Six Cao Military Affairs Consultants. The affairs these officials were in charge of were the same as those in other states, only their grades were slightly higher.

(2) Government-General (都督府)

Government-generals were located in the regions with strategic importance. As early as the Han Dynasty, the position of Commander-in-Chief already existed. It became a permanent position during the Wei Dynasty and then government-general came into being.

In AD 624, a commander-in-chief would govern military and administration in several prefectures. The prefecture, where the commander-in-chief was seated, was called government-general while the others were called branch prefectures.

In AD 711, Wu Zetian merged all the government-generals. And states and counties in the country were governed by 24 government-generals. In addition to serving as the prefecture regional inspector, the commander-in-chief was also the chief military officer. The commander-in-chief was also responsible for supervising the work of officials below the surveillance regional inspector. At that time, many people opposed this practice, believing that it would give too much power to the local government and would do harm to centralized rule. Therefore, it was not long before the system of 24 government-general was abolished.

In AD 729, Emperor Xuanzong set up three layers of hierarchy for the position of commander-in-chief—namely the first rank, second rank, and third rank. There were 40 government-generals in the country. Later the functions of commander-in-chief were replaced by prefectural ministers, and the title of commander-in-chief disappeared.

(3) Protectorate-General (都护府)

Protectorate-generals were located on the borders of the Tang Dynasty to defend against nomadic tribes. In the first 100 years or so, the empire defeated many nomadic tribes, such as, the Eastern Tujue, Xueyantuo, and Goryeo. Many other tribes also surrendered to the Tang.

The Tang adopted the protectorate system of the Han Dynasty in the Western Regions. In AD 640, Emperor Taizong established Anxi Protectorate-General in Gaochang. By the end of AD 756, there were altogether six protectorate-generals: Anxi, Andong, Annan, Anbei, Chanyu, and Beiting.

The following is a detailed description of the six protectorate-generals:

a. Andong Protectorate-General:

This protectorate-general was located on the northeastern border of the Tang Dynasty. As early as the 4th Century, there were three kingdoms on the Korean Peninsula—Goryeo, Baiji, and Xinluo. Goryeo and Baiji formed an alliance and often attacked Xinluo, which turned to the Tang for help.

In AD 644, Emperor Taizong sent troops to fight against Goryeo. The following year, Tang armies conquered several cities but met with strong resistance in Anshi (Haicheng, Liaoning). Eventually, the Tang had to retreat because of the extreme cold and food deficiencies.

Emperor Gaozong adopted a different strategy. His troops travelled by sea from Chengshan (eastern tip of Shandong) to the Korean Peninsula, and defeated the Kingdom of Baiji first. The Tang set up five protectorate-generals in the area. Top officials such as commanders-in-chief, regional inspectors, and district magistrates were appointed from suitable Baiji locals. After the Tang armies had settled down in Baiji, together with Xinluo armies, they could sandwich the Kingdom of Goryeo from both sides.

In AD 666, there were upheavals in Goryeo, so Emperor Gaozong took the opportunity and sent troops led by Li Ji to invade Goryeo. In AD 668, Goryeo was defeated and surrendered to the Tang. Nine government-generals, with 42 states and 100 counties, were set up. The Koryo people served as the commander-in-chiefs, regional inspectors, and district magistrates and jointly managed with the Han officials. Later, the Andong Protectorate-General was established in Pyongyang. The territory of Andong covered a vast area. At that time, the Andong Protectorate-General covered a large area, ranging from the east of Liaohe River in Liaoning Province, Songhua River in Jilin Province, and south of Toudao River to the northern and western regions of North Korea today. But in less than ten years, that is, in AD 676, the Andong Protectorate-General was moved to Jiucheng, Liaodong (present-day Liaoyang City, Liaoning Province) due to the resistance of the local people. The next year, it was moved to Xincheng (present-day north of Fushun, Liaoning Province). Later, it was again moved to Pingzhou (present-day Lulong, Hebei Province).

During the Kaiyuan period, the Tang Dynasty set up the Bohai Government-General and the Heishui Government-General in places where the Mohe ethnic group lived and set up the Shiwei Government-General in places where the Shiwei ethnic group lived. The three government-generals were all under the management of the Andong Protectorate-General. Because the southern part of the Koryo's land was occupied by the Xinluo Kingdom, the jurisdiction of Andong Protectorate-General contained the present-day Heilongjiang River Basin and the Okhotsk Sea in the north, the Bohai Sea and the West Korean Bay in the south, the Da Sea and the north of Korea in the east, and it bordered with Khitan in the west. In AD 742, the first year of the Tianbao era, the government-generals of Bohai, Heishui, and Shiwei were transferred to the jurisdiction of the Pinglu prefectural minister, and the jurisdiction of the Andong Protectorate-General was restricted to the former territory of Goguryeo (ancient Korea). Furthermore, at this time, the position of Duhu was also concurrently held by the Pinglu prefectural minister. In AD 761, Yingzhou (Chaoyang, Liaoning) was conquered by the Qidan people, and the Andong Protectorate-General was abolished.

b. Anbei and Chanyu Protectorate-Generals:
Anbei and Chanyu Protectorate-Generals were set up on the northern border of the Tang. When Tang was newly established, Eastern Tujue often attacked and once even reached the vicinity of Chang'an. Emperor Gaozu almost re-located the capital. After Emperor Taizong had ascended the throne, he fought back. By that time, the Tujue had been weakened by in-fighting and consecutive snowstorms. In AD 629, the Emperor sent some 100,000 soldiers, led by General Li Jing, to attack the Tujue. Tuli Khan surrendered. The following year, Jieli Kahn was captured and the entire Tujue tribe surrendered. The Tang expanded its territories to the Yin Mountains and the Gobi Desert.

After the fall of the Eastern Tujue, some of them came to Xue Yantuo, some emigrated to the Western Regions, and more than 100,000 people surrendered to the Tang Dynasty. Therefore, the Tang Dynasty set up four government-generals in the area previously controlled by Tuli Khan, and two government-generals in the area previously controlled by Jieli Khan.

During the Zhenguan period, Chebi, one of the Turkic tribes, rose in revolt. In AD 650, Gao Kan led the Tang army to capture Chebi Khan alive. The Tang government placed those who surrendered in Yudujun Mountain (now Hangai Mountain in Mongolia) and set up the Langshan Government-General to manage them. In addition, the Hanhai Protectorate-General was set up to manage three government-generals, including the Langshan Government-General, and fourteen states so as to manage the Turkic people. In AD 647, the Tang Dynasty established the Yanran Protectorate-General, which governed six protectorate-generals and seven states that accommodated the surrendered eleven northern minorities in Huihe. The administrative center was located 40 li northeast of Xishouxiang City (now in Northeast Jinhang Banner, Inner Mongolia, on the north bank of the Wujia River) at the old Chanyu platform. By the first year of the Yonghui era, the Yanran Protectorate-General had become the governing body for seven government-generals and eight states.

In AD 663, the third year of Emperor Gaozong's Longshuo era, the Tang government relocated the Yanran Protectorate-General to the Huihe yurt in the north of the desert (now northwest of Harhorin, Mongolia, on the west bank of the Orkhon River), renaming it the Hanhai Protectorate-General. The original Hanhai Protectorate-General was moved to Yunzhong Ancient City (now Tuchengzi, northwest of Helingeer, Inner Mongolia) and renamed the Yunzhong Protectorate-General. These two protectorate-generals were divided by the desert, with the Yunzhong Protectorate-General south of the desert and the Hanhai Protectorate-General to the north. Thus, the region around today's Hetao and Yinshan in Inner Mongolia was under the jurisdiction of the Yunzhong Protectorate-General. Meanwhile, the vast areas of southern Siberia in Russia and Mongolia, stretching from the northern part of Lake Baikal and the upper reaches of the Yenisei River to the Gobi Desert, fell under the jurisdiction of the Hanhai Protectorate-General. In AD 664, the first year of the Linde era, the Yunzhong Protectorate-General was renamed the Chanyu Protectorate-General. In AD 669, the second year of Emperor Gaozong's Zongzhang era, the Hanhai Protectorate-General was renamed the Anbei Protectorate-General.

In AD 784, Anbei Protectorate-General was abolished. In AD 845, Chanyu Protectorate-General was renamed as Anbei Protectorate-General, and it remained so until the 10th century.

c. Anxi and Beiting Protectorate-Generals:
The two protectorate-generals were located in the Western Regions. After the Gobi Desert was under his control, Emperor Taizong set out to unify the Western Regions. His major rivals were the Western Tujue and the Kingdom of Gaochang.

In AD 639, Emperor Taizong sent troops led by the Minister of Personnel, Hou Junji, to fight the Gaochang. In AD 640, Hou defeated Gaochang and Emperor Taizong established Anxi Protectorate-General. In the same year, Yehu Khan of Western Tujue surrendered. Emperor Taizong then set up Ting Prefecture in the area (north Jimusa'er in Xinjiang).

In AD 657, the commander-in-chief of Yaochi and Ashna Helu from the Western Tujue occupied the western region and rebelled against the Tang. They were defeated by Su Dingfang, the general of Tang. The Tang government then split the eastern part of the Western Tujue and set up the Kunling Protectorate-General (the area from the east of the Lake Balkhash to the Zungarian Basin and Ili River Basin in Xinjiang Uygur Autonomous Region today). The Mengchi Protectorate-General (the area from the west of the Chu River in Russia to the Aral Sea) was set up in the western part of the Western Tujue. The Tang government also set up government-generals and states in the area and tribes controlled by the Western Tujue, and the Anxi Protectorate-General was made responsible for their management. In the third year of the Xianqing period the Anxi Protectorate-General was moved to Qiuci. Four garrisons were relocated, and the Suiye garrison was replaced by Yanqi garrison. In the first year of the Longshuo period of Emperor Gaozong (AD 661), the Tang Dynasty also appeased the sixteen countries west of Yutian and east of Persia, setting up commander-in-chiefs, prefectures, and counties, all of which were under the jurisdiction of the Anxi Protectorate-General. They were all governed by the Anxi Protectorate-General, which then covered an area from the Altai Mountains to the present-day Caspian Sea, including Congling Mountain and Amu River, including the eastern and western parts of the Pamirs and the countries on both sides of the Amu Darya.

In AD 670, the Tibetans captured the four garrisons of Anxi, and the Anxi Protectorate-General was forced to move to Xizhou city. Nine years later, it moved to Suiye. In AD 692, the Tibetans were defeated by the Tang army led by Wang Xiaojie. The four garrisons of Qiuci, Shule, Khotan, and Suiye were recovered. The Anxi Protectorate-General was again moved to Qiuci. From then, to the end of the Tianbao period, Qiuci, Khotan, and Shule, which were located in the south of Tianshan Mountain, were under the control of the Tang Dynasty. Suiye, on the other hand, changed hands several times due to changes in the situation in the area north of the Tianshan Mountains, the strength of the Türgesh, and the westward expedition of the later Tujue. By AD 719, the seventh year of Emperor Xuanzong's Kaiyuan era, Suiye had finally become the headquarters of the Türgesh, and the Four Garrisons of Anxi were changed to Kucha, Shule, Yutian, and Yanqi.

In AD 702, during the second year of Wu Zhou's Chang'an era, the Beiting Protectorate-General was established, splitting from the Anxi Protectorate-General. The Beiting Protectorate-General was based in Tingzhou, commanding over the ten tribes of the Turkic, Türgesh, and Karluk tribes. Its jurisdiction stretched east to today's Altai Mountains, west to the Caspian Sea, north to Lake Balkhash and the upper reaches of the Irtysh River, and south to the Tianshan Mountains. Thus, the jurisdiction of the Anxi Protectorate-General was only the city-states to the south of the Tianshan Mountains and east of Persia.

During the Tianbao period, the west of the Pamirs was occupied by Dashi Kingdom, and the area under the administration of Anxi Protectorate-General was limited to four garrisons east of the Pamirs and south of Tianshan Mountain. In AD 756, Anxi Protectorate-General was renamed Zhenxi Protectorate-General.

In AD 767, the name was changed back to Anxi Protectorate-General again. Later, the Tubo occupied Hexi and Longyou, and then attacked Anxi and Beiting Protectorate-Generals. In AD 790, the Ting state, where the Beiting Protectorate-General was located, was first conquered by the Tubo. Soon, the Anxi Protectorate-General was also captured by the Tibetan. The two protectorate-generals were destroyed one after another.

d. Annan Protectorate-General:
This protectorate-general was located on the southern border of the Tang. At the end of the Sui Dynasty, Xiao Xian declared himself king, ruling an area from Jiujiang in the east and the Three Gorges in the west. Its northern border reached Hanchuan, and its southern border reached Jiaozhi (present-day Vietnam).

In AD 621, Emperor Gaozu sent General Li Jing to fight Xiao Xian and forced him to surrender. The following year, prefectures such as Ningyue, Yulin, and Rinan also surrendered. By then, the Tang Empire had the entire Jiaozhi region under its control, and Emperor Gaozu established Jiaozhou Protectorate-General. In AD 679, Emperor Gaozong renamed it Annan Protectorate-General, with its seat located in present-day Songping of Hanoi, Vietnam. The position of head of the protectorate was assumed by Jiaozhou prefectural inspector. The protectorate's territory included where would be present-day Honghe and Wenshan Autonomous Districts in Yunnan Province. Its southwestern border reached Laos.

In AD 757, the Annan Protectorate-General was renamed Zhennan Protectorate-General. In AD 766, it was changed back to the Annan Protectorate-General. During the Dazhong period, the northern border of Annan Protectorate-General was gradually occupied by the Nanzhao Kingdom. By the end of the Tang Dynasty, the border between the Central Plains and Nanzhao Kingdom was similar to the border between Yunnan and Vietnam today. In December, AD 861, the place where the governmental institution of the Annan Protectorate-General located was captured by the Nanzhao Kingdom. Although the place was recovered two years later, it was again captured by Nanzhao Kingdom in the fourth year of Xiantong period. The seat of the government of the Annan Protectorate-General had to be set up in the nearby Haimen garrison, Jiaozhou (now northwest of Haiphong, Vietnam). Three years later, the Tang Dynasty recovered the original area of the Annan Protectorate-General and set up the

Jinghai prefectural minister who also served as the governor of the protectorate-general. This arrangement lasted until the end of the Tang Dynasty.

The above six protectorate-generals had distinct differences, even though they shared the same title. For example, Anbei, Chanyu, Beiting, and Annan governed prefectures and districts. They were not much different from prefectures in central China. However, Andong and Anxi were more or less military administrations, ruled according to the habits of local tribes.

4. The Prefectural Divisions

Ever since the Han Dynasty, there had been explicit records of administrative division hierarchies in China. The classification was based on the number of families within the area. The prefectures governing the capital city and its vicinities were given special names to differentiate them. For example, where Western Han's capital Chang'an was located, its prefecture was called "Jingzhaoyin" (京兆尹). Its two neighboring prefectures were called "Zuopingyi" (左冯翊) and "Youfufeng" (右扶风). Together they were called "San Fu" (三辅, literally meaning three supporting prefectures).

In Eastern Han, where capital Luoyang was located, the prefecture was called "Hennan Yin" (河南尹). The Wei, Jin, Southern, and Northern dynasties all followed suit. However, it was difficult to find a definite answer to the criteria of their hierarchy structure. For example, the Sui classified their prefectures into three ranks, its criteria unknown.

Hierarchies of administrative divisions in the Tang Dynasty were based on population size and geo-politics. For example, where its capital Chang'an was located, the prefecture was called "Jingzhaofu" (京兆府). Some other important prefectures were grouped into four categories according to their distances to the capital, namely Fu (辅), Xiong (雄), Wang (望), and Jin (紧). The four Fu referred to the four prefectures of Tong, Hua, Qi, and Pu near Jingzhaofu; Six Xiong referred to the six prefectures of Zheng, Shan, Bian, Jiang, Huai, and Wei near Henan Fu; Ten Wang referred to the ten prefectures of Song, Hao, Hua, Xu, Ru, Jin, Ming, Guo, Wei and Xiang in the periphery of Six Xiong; Ten Jin referred to the ten prefectures of Bin, Long, Jing, Qin, Tang, Deng, Xi, Ci, Fen and Yan, which located in the vital communication line. Since the division of

Fu, Xiong, Wang, and Jin was based on the geographical locations of the states, the population and economy of these states were usually not on the same level. According to population size, all prefectures in the country were classified into three ranks. However, regardless of their population size, the "Fu," "Xiong," and "Wang" prefectures, as well as metropolitan prefectures belonged to the first rank. In addition, "Fu" was a special division above the Fu, Xiong, Wang, Jin, upper, middle, and lower levels. Since Fu has been discussed earlier, we won't go into much detail here.

The Tang government also stipulated the method for grading different counties, that is, by the status of the county, the number of residents, and the geographical location. The counties where the capital and the second capital located were called Chi County. The counties near Jingzhaoyin, Henan, and Taiyuan Fus, except for counties belonged to the capital, were called Ji County. Other counties were further divided into five levels—Wang, Jin, Upper, Middle, and Lower. The four-tier grading system of Chi, Ji, Wang, and Jin was different from the three-tier grading system of Upper, Middle, and Lower. The former system emphasized political status, while the latter focused on the number of residents, namely economic strength. This grading system was similar to the classification of states in the Tang Dynasty mentioned above. Therefore, the Tang government also stipulated that the counties graded as Chi, Ji, Wang, and Jin were also Upper counties no matter their population.

In the late Tang Dynasty, the number of Chi counties increased, and two levels of Minor Chi and Minor Ji therefore emerged. After Emperor Xuanzong of the Tang Dynasty fled to Chengdu to dodge the An-Shi Rebellion, his son Suzong succeeded to the throne. Chengdu therefore became the South Jing, and the status of Chengdu County was greatly improved. Chengdu's level was elevated to Minor Chi, and the counties belonged to Chengdu had also become Minor Ji.

5. The Jimi System

Jimi (羈縻) prefectures, located on the borders of Tang, were subordinate prefectures under loose rein. "Ji" (羈) literally means to rule with military force and political pressure; "Mi" (縻) literally means to reward with economic benefits. In other words, to rule with carrots and sticks.

The jurisdiction of these Jimi protectorate-generals and prefectures covered the original territories of the minority tribes. The positions like commander-in-chief and regional inspector in these Jimi protectorate-generals and prefectures were also held by the leaders of the original tribes. Those chiefs included kings, Khans, Yabghus, Irkinands, and other leaders. They maintained their original titles, and their powers remained too. However, they were also given such titles as commander-in-chief and regional inspectors by the Tang government. Most Jimi Fu and the state did not need to pay tributes to the Tang. In other words, they only belonged to the Tang Empire in theory.

In fact, as early as the Sui Dynasty, the government set up the chief manager in the southwest border areas to manage the minority nationalities in the southwest. In the early years of the Tang Dynasty, Emperor Gaozu adopted the Jimi Policy to settle the surrounding minorities. The focus of this Policy was to let the minorities retain their original way of life without imposing the ideology of the Tang by force or administrative means. During the reign of Emperor Gaozu Wude, the government set up government-generals and states within the tribes of Xi, Qidan, and Mohe in Youzhou (present-day Beijing) and Yingzhou (present-day Chaoyang, Liaoning). In addition, nearly 40 prefectures and counties were set up in Sichuan, Yunnan, and Guizhou provinces today, and these states and counties were all under the control of the local government-general. However, at that time, the government did not distinguish these states and counties from ordinary ones. And these states and counties were not decided as separate administrative divisions yet.

The first record of an official Jimi prefecture was in AD 630. In that year, Eastern Tujue was defeated by Tang armies. More than 50,000 Tujue people, including Jieli Khan, were captured. This was the end of Eastern Tujue.

It was a great challenge for the Tang government to relocate this gigantic number of prisoners of war. The solution was to put them in the vicinities. Four government-generals were established for this purpose, covering an area stretching from Youzhou in the east to Lingzhou in the west. Meanwhile, six prefectures were set up in what used to be the land of Jieli Khan.

Emperor Taizong adopted the advice of Wen Yanbo, who suggested that Tujue people should keep their customs. The Emperor rewarded chiefs at all levels in the Tujue tribe with affluent benefits, yet at the same time ruled with an iron hand. Consequently, the chiefs no longer wanted to, or couldn't, rebel against the Tang Empire. Later, tribal chiefs were given positions of high rank and they dwelled in Tang's capital Chang'an.

After that, Jimi prefectures became common practice. Until the end of AD 741, there were over 850 Jimi prefectures, including the Black Water Government-General. In comparison, those inland prefectures were often referred to as "Zhengzhou" (正州, normal prefectures).

Jimi prefectures in the Tang Dynasty could be grouped into five categories:

a. Some Jimi prefectures were directly set up by the Tang government. Those Jimi prefectures were large in size, e.g., those set up after Eastern Tujue was conquered.
b. Some Jimi prefectures were set up by delegates sent by the Tang government. In AD 658, Emperor Gaozong sent delegates to the Western Regions, who established such prefectures as the Kangju Government-General. However, these prefectures must be authorized by the central government.
c. Some prefectures were set up by military leaders during their expeditions. The Jimi prefecture and state established after the Tang Dynasty's eastern expeditions to Baiji and Goguryeo are typical examples of this setup method. In the fifth year of Xianqing (AD 660), Su Dingfang, a general of the Tang Dynasty, pacified Baiji on the Korean Peninsula and established five Jimi government-generals in the area. He then returned to the Tang Dynasty with more than 10,000 Baiji nobles and common people. Consequently, except for the Xiongjin Government-General guarded by Liu Rengui, the areas governed by the other four government-generals were all occupied by Silla. In the first year of Zongzhang (AD 668), Li Ji also pacified Goguryeo with his troops, dividing it into nine protectorate-generals and forty-two states. All these belong to the Jimi prefectures and states. However, it should be noted that although the Xiongjin Protectorate-General mentioned above is nominally a Jimi prefecture and state, it was guarded by the Tang general Liu Rengui. Therefore, in reality, the Xiongjin Protectorate-General was merely a military fortress established by the Tang Dynasty in Baiji, and such a form of Jimi rule could not last long. Therefore, after the Tang troops withdrew from the Korean Peninsula, the Jimi prefectures and states established in Baiji and

Goguryeo were also abandoned.
d. Some prefectures were set up by government-generals on the borders. In AD 622, General Li Jing was sent to Guizhou in South China. Li Jing set up some "Zhengzhou" as well as Jimi prefectures. This was to recruit local landowners and reward them with titles, thus their land would become part of the Tang Empire.
e. Some Jimi prefectures were set up by the chieftains of minority tribes. Those established in this way were relatively few and appeared in remote and inaccessible areas. During the reign of Tang Emperor Gaozong, such an incident happened. At that time, Wang Renqiu, a chieftain of the Bai minority in Yunnan, sought to consolidate his own position and requested the Tang court to establish more than twenty Jimi states (i.e., semi-autonomous regions) in the area he controlled around the Erhai Lake. History has shown that establishing Jimi states in this way was not only extremely beneficial to the local chieftain but also allowed the Tang Dynasty to gain a large swath of territory without any military expenditure. Therefore, the Tang government would readily agree to the chieftains' requests when faced with such situations.

These were the several ways to set up Jimi prefecture and state in the Tang Dynasty. Now let's look at the different divisions of Jimi prefecture and state. The highest level of Jimi prefecture and state was called Jimi Protectorate-General. After the pacification of the West Tujue during the reign of Emperor Gaozong, Mengchi and Kunling Jimi Protectorate-Generals were set up one the land of the West Tujue. These two Jimi Protectorate-Generals were responsible for the management of the Turkic tribes and their subordinate Jimi prefectures, which were located in the west and east of Shayechuan. At first, the two Jimi Protectorate-Generals were under the control of the Anxi Protectorate-General, while later, it belonged to the Beiting Protectorate-General. It was not until Wu Zetian's reign that this area was occupied by the Turgesh people, and the two Jimi Protectorate-Generals of Mengchi and Kunling were abolished. The level of division under Jimi Protectorate-General was Jimi Government-General, followed by Jimi state, and the last level was Jimi county. Although there were four levels of divisions, they were still customarily called Jimi prefectures or Fanzhou as a whole.

In summary, Jimi prefecture and state in the Tang belonged to government-generals or protectorate-generals on the borders. Among all circuits during Emperor Taizong's reign, Huainan Circuit was the only one that did not set up a Jimi prefecture and state. Relationships between the central government and Jimi prefecture, and state varied. Some Jimi states were treated like "Zhengzhou," while some stayed loose and largely existed in name only. For example, the Persian Government-General at that time was the most remote Jimi prefecture in the Tang Dynasty. During the reign of Emperor Gaozong, Persia was in turmoil and was attacked by the Dashi Kingdom (now Arabia). After the king of Persia was killed, Prince Belus traveled a long way to Chang'an, the capital of the Tang Dynasty, to ask for help. So the government of the Tang Dynasty appointed Belus as the commanders-in-chief of Persia and sent troops to escort him back home. However, due to the long journey, Belus finally failed to return to Persia, but stayed in the country of Tuhara on the way. In AD 661, the Persian Government-General was located in Jiling City (now Sistan in Iran). Although the Persian Government-General was destroyed after two or three years, the tribal people still sent envoys to pay tribute until the Kaiyuan and Tianbao period. Therefore, the name of the Persian Government-General had also been listed in the list of Jimi prefecture and state in the Tang Dynasty.

Since the mid-era of the Tang, most of the Jimi prefectures had either been abolished or moved inland.

6. Ten Prefectural Ministers of the Tianbao Period

In the mid-Tang era, prefectural ministers were set up to guard against nomadic tribes on the borders. The area governed by prefectural ministers were called "Fanzhen" (藩镇) or "Fangzhen" (方镇), literally meaning "buffer town." They were chosen for strategic military deployment. As early as in Emperor Gaozong's era, leaders governing bordering prefectures were given the title of Commander-in-Chief with extra power.

In AD 711, Emperor Rui appointed Heba Yansi, Commander-in-Chief of Liangzhou (Wuwei in Gansu) as the Hexi Prefectural Minister. In the years between AD 846 and AD 859, the number of prefectural ministers reached ten. Following is a brief introduction of the ten prefectural ministers:

a. Anxi Prefectural Minister:
The minister governed four towns in the Western Regions, with its seat in Qiuzi (present-day Kuche, Xinjiang). The post was successively held by Gao Xianzhi, Wang Zhengjian, and Feng Changqing.

b. Beiting Prefectural Minister:
The minister governed Beiting Protectorate-General, with its seat in Tingzhou (Jimusa'er North Pochengzi, Xinjiang). The post was successively held by Lai Zhuo, Wang Anjian, Cheng Qianli, and Feng Changqing.

c. Hexi Prefectural Minister:
The minister governed an area that defended against the Tubo and Tujue, with its seat in Liangzhou (Wuwei in Gansu). The post was successively held by Wang Chui, Huangfu Weiming, Wang Zhongsi, An Sishun, and Geshuhan.

d. Shuofang Prefectural Minister:
The minister governed an area that repelled the Tujue, with its seat in Linghzou (southwest of Lingwu, Ningxia). The post was successively held by Wang Zhongsi, Zhang Qiqiu, and An Sishun.

e. Hedong Prefectural Minister:
The minister governed an area that organized defense with Shuofang Prefecture against the Tujue, with its seat in Taiyuanfu (Jingyuan County in southwest Taiyuan, Shanxi). The post was successively held by Tian Renwan, Wang Zhongsi, Han Xiulin, and An Lushan.

f. Fanyang Prefectural Minister:
The minister governed an area that defended against Qidan, with its seat in Youzhou (present-day Beijing). The post was successively held by Pei Kuan and An Lushan.

g. Pinglu Prefectural Minister:
The minister governed an area that defended against Shiwei, with its seat in Yingzhou (present-day Chaoyang). The post was held by An Lushan.

h. Longyou Prefectural Minister:
The minister governed an area that defended against the Tubo, with its seat in Shanzhou (Ledu, Qinghai). The post was successively held by Huangfu Weiming, Wang Zhongsi and Geshuhan.

i. Jiannan Prefectural Minister:
The minister aimed to defend against the Tubo and pacify the barbarians; its seat was located in Yizhou (present-day Chengdu, Sichuan); it had jurisdiction over the troops of Tuanjie Battalion, Tianbao Army, Pingrong Army, Kunming Army, Ningyuan Army, Chengchuan garrison, Nanjiang Army and Yizhou, Maozhou, Weizhou, Zhezhou, Songzhou, Dangzhou, Yazhou, Lizhou, Yaozhou, Xizhou, and other counties. During the Tianbao period, the post was successively held by Zhangchou Jianqiong, Guo Xuji, Xianyu Zhongtong, Yang Guozhong, and others.

j. Lingnan Prefectural Minister:
The minister aimed to repel the southern minority tribes; the seat was located in Guangzhou (Nanhai County, now Guangzhou, Guangdong) and it was responsible for the management of the strategic army and the Qing navy, and directly managed the army in charge of the prefectures and counties, and also managed the army in charge of the prefectures and counties in Gui, Rong, Yong, and Annan. During the Tianbao period, Pei Dunfu served as the governor of the five Fu.

A Fanzhen was usually composed of several prefectures governed by one prefectural minister. At first, a prefectural minister was only responsible for defense on the borders. However, prefectural ministers gradually took on such responsibilities as court, farming, and budgeting. Regional inspectors also became their subordinates. Therefore, prefectural ministers were regarded as the most important official on the borders, mastering military forces, administration, finance, and surveillance. Often they would govern several garrisons for better defense against nomadic tribes. Prefectural Minister An Lushan was a good example. He earned the trust of Emperor Xuanzong, who appointed him as Supervisor of the Hebei Circuit. An Lushan was already the prefectural minister of three garrisons (Fanyang, Pinglu, and Hedong). This made it possible for An Lushan to dominate one part of China. In the late years of the Tianbao era, it was under this favorable background that An Lushan launched a violent rebellion that posed a great threat to the Tang Dynasty. Take Wang Zhongsi, for example, he, serving as the Prefectural minister (military commissioner) of Hexi and Longyou, concurrently managed affairs in Shuofang and Hedong, holding four commands in one, "controlling thousands of miles, the world's strong soldiers and important garrisons, all in his grasp."[9] These military commissioners' power was concentrated on the border, which eventually led to a situation where the tail was wagging the dog.

7. An-Shi Rebellion and the Shrinkage of Tang Territory

In AD 755, An Lushan led 150,000 soldiers to rebel against the Tang in Fanyang (present-day Beijing). After An Lushan died, his subordinate, Shi Siming, continued the rebellion. This was known in history as the An-Shi Rebellion.

While the Tang government was focused on suppressing the rebellion, the Tubo people took advantage of the chaos and occupied vast amounts of land in the empire. By AD 763, when the rebellion was finally appeased, the Tubo had captured the following regions: present-day Long Mountain, Liupan Mountain, west of Sichuan Basin, and west of the Yellow River. At first, the Hexi Corridor district was still governed by Tang officials, but soon it fell completely into the hands of the Tubo. Meanwhile, the Kingdom of Nanzhao expanded its territory to the entirety of Yunnan, south Sichuan, and west Guizhou. The Dadu River became the border between the Nanzhao and Tang empires. Some minority groups in southwest China also turned against the Tang government. Thus, by the end of the Tang Dynasty, modern Guizhou, southwestern Hubei, western Hunan, and western Guangxi were all beyond the jurisdiction of the Tang central government. In addition, with the rise and expansion of the Bohai State,[10] the northeastern territory of the Tang Dynasty had also retracted to the central part of present-day Liaoning.

---

9. *Zizhi Tongjian*, vol. 215 (Beijing: Zhonghua Book Company, 1956), 6871.
10. At that time, the Bohai State was a prosperous country in the east of the sea, ruling over 5 Jing, 15 Fu, and 62 states. Its territory extended east to the sea, neighbored the Blackwater Mohe to the north, bordered Silla to the south, and connected with the Khitan and Tang's Liaodong to the west.

During the reign of Xuanzong, the territory of the Tang Dynasty continued to change. In AD 848, Zhang Yichao, a native of Shazhou (present-day southwest of Dunhuang, Gansu Province), gathered the people of the Han, Huihe, Qiang, Tuyuhun, and other ethnic groups who had been oppressed by the Tubo, and launched an uprising during the upheaval of Tubo. They expelled the Tubo soldiers and recovered Shazhou. Then, Guazhou (present-day in the southeast of Anxi, Gansu Province), Suzhou (present-day in Jiuquan, Gansu Province), and Ganzhou (present-day in Zhangye, Gansu Province) were recovered. In the fifth year of Dazhong, Zhang Yichao returned to the Tang Dynasty under the leadership of eleven states, including Sha, Gua, Yi, Xi, Gan, Su, Lan, Shan, He, Min, and Kuo. He was appointed as the prefectural minister of the Guiyi Army by the Tang government. Before that, the Tang Dynasty had recovered Longyou, Qinyuan, and three other prefectures and seven passes in the three years of Dazhong. At this point, the western territory of the Tang Dynasty was restored to the Turpan region of Xinjiang and the Hexi Corridor and was connected with Longdong and Guanzhong.

In AD 875, a rebellion led by Huang Chao severely weakened the Tang regime. It also suffered continuous losses to the Tubo and Huihu, who occupied the Longdong and Hexi districts in the West. Only Guazhou and Shazhou were still ruled by the Tang. Later, Cao Yijin's Cao regime replaced the Zhang regime, and it was not until the Northern Song Dynasty that it was destroyed by the Western Xia.

8. The Rise of Fanzhen

The An-Shi Rebellion, in particular, was a catastrophe the Tang had never experienced the likes of before. The poet Bai Juyi wrote in his famous poem "Song of Eternal Regret" that "The drums of Yuyang come with earth-shaking power, startling and breaking the serenity of the 'Rainbow Skirt and Feathered Robe' melody." In order to quell the rebellion as fast as possible, the central government granted the tittle of Prefectural Minister to standout generals and rebel leaders who had surrendered. As a result, Fanzhen, which used to be on the border, flourished inland. Some bigger Fanzhen governed over ten prefectures, while smaller ones governed two or three.

The attitude of the central government toward these Fanzhen varied with the region. For those located in Shaanxi, Sichuan, and south of the Yangtze and Huai, the government ruled with an iron hand, because these prosperous regions were the Tang's major revenue sources. As soon as signs were detected that prefectural ministers had any intention to rebel, they would be wiped out immediately. During the reign of Emperor Daizong, the military governor of Shannan East Circuit (covering a region roughly equivalent to today's Fuling and Wanzhou in Chongqing, and Yang County in Shaanxi, and areas east of this line), Lai Tian, acted arbitrarily and disregarded the central government. As a result, Daizong used a eunuch to frame Lai Tian, demoting him and ordering his execution. During the reign of Emperor Daizong, the military governor of Shannan East Circuit (covering a region roughly equivalent to today's Fuling and Wanzhou in Chongqing, and Yang County in Shaanxi, and areas east of this line), Lai Tian, acted arbitrarily and disregarded the central government. As a result, Daizong used a eunuch to frame Lai Tian, demoting him and ordering his execution. There was another figure, Zhou Zhiguang, who was the military governor of Tonghua Circuit (covering an area roughly equivalent to today's Hua County and Dali region in Shaanxi). He believed he had enough power to confront the central government, so he was extremely arrogant. He boasted that if he stretched his leg while sleeping, he could flatten the capital city of Chang'an in an instant. In the face of such a dangerous individual, the Tang government decisively ordered General Guo Ziyi to lead an army to suppress him, and Zhou Zhiguang was quickly eliminated.

However, for those located in Heshuo, Emperor Daizong (reign: AD 762–779) adopted a policy of appeasement. After the An-Shi Rebellion was suppressed, the Tang government did not have enough strength to wipe out the remaining forces of An Lushan and his subordinates. As a conciliatory gesture, the central government gave the title of prefectural minister to rebel leaders in the Heshuo district.

The new prefectural ministers were:

a. Lulong Prefectural Minister Li Huaixian, governing northeastern Hebei;
b. Chengde Prefectural Minister Li Baocheng, governing central Hebei;
c. Weibo Prefectural Minister Tian Chengsi, governing southern Hebei and northern Shandong;

d. Xiangwei Prefectural Minister Xiao Hao, governing southwestern Hebei and some parts of Shandong and Henan.

Later, Tian Chengsi annexed Xiangwei Fanzhen. It became known in history as the "Three Fanzhen in Heshuo." In name, the three prefectural ministers were governed by the Tang central administration. In fact, they didn't pay any taxes and could select their own officers. A similar situation also existed in such regions as Shandong, Henan, Hubei, and Shanxi. However, the central government was not strong enough to make any changes. The only choice was to let the prefectural ministers do whatever they wanted so long as there were no rebellions.

After Emperor Dezong (reign: AD 779–805) ascended the throne, he adopted the Yan's proposal to reform the revenue system. In essence, the new system was to draft copper coins as tax rather than cloth or wheat. Since the tax was to be collected twice a year, the new revenue system was known as the Biannual Tax Law. In order to implement the new revenue system, the central government decided to slash the numbers of Fanzhen because they did not pay any taxes. What the central government didn't expect was this policy to trigger great grievances among prefectural ministers. Those in the Heshuo District turned against the government and declared themselves kings; Huaixi and Jinyuan prefectural ministers rebelled. Emperor Dezong finally killed the two rebel ministers and deprived Heshuo ministers of their titles as kings. However, he had to abandon the original plan of reducing the number of Fanzhen. This made Heshuo prefectural ministers even bolder than before.

By the era of Emperor Xianzong (reign: AD 805–820), revenue of the central government had significantly increased due to the implementation of the Biannual Tax Law. On the other hand, the central government trained elite troops. Well-prepared, Emperor Xianzong was able to defeat the prefectural ministers one by one. After the Huaixi Prefectural Minister was defeated, the rest submitted to the central government. Xianzong was therefore referred to as the "Emperor of Rejuvenation." Unfortunately, Emperor Xianzong was killed by one of his eunuchs while the remaining forces of the prefectural ministers were still strong.

Xianzong's successor Emperor Muzong (reign: AD 820–824) reduced military force in order to cut government expenditure. This again triggered great grievances among prefectural ministers in Heshuo district, who turned against the central government. Prefectural ministers in Chengde and Lulong were either killed or detained by the rebels. Without enough strength to fight back, the central government had to give in. Since then, rebellions took place frequently, and prefectural ministers became their own masters. The status quo continued until the end of the Tang Dynasty.

9. Chaos of the Five Dynasties and Ten Kingdoms Period

Most of the revenue collected by the Tang central government came from Jianghuai and Guandong. The heavy tax burdens eventually became unbearable. In AD 875, a group of farmers led by Wang Xianzhi rebelled against the government. Huang Chao followed suit with several thousands of people. After Wang Xianzhi was killed, Huang Chao became the rebel leader. Although the Tang government mustered soldiers from different prefectures to fight back, most of the prefectural ministers took advantage of the chaos to recruit soldiers and strengthen their own forces. In AD 880, Huang Chao and his men occupied Tang's capital of Chang'an, and Emperor Xizong fled to Chengdu. The Tang government called on the Shatuo people to fight against Huang Chao, who was eventually defeated. However, the Tang Dynasty also collapsed. By now, it was effectively the walking dead. In the meantime, several other forces appeared, breaking the original balance of prefectural ministers. These forces fought with each other constantly. Zhu Wen and Li Keyong were the most powerful in the north. Zhu Wen occupied Bianzhou (present-day Kaifeng, Henan) and Huazhou (present-day Huaxian East, Henan), and Li Keyong occupied Taiyuan and Shangdang (present-day Changzhi, Shanxi). In the struggle between these two forces, Zhu Wen finally took the lead.

In AD 907, Zhu Wen deposed Emperor Ai of Tang (reign: AD 904–907) and declared himself the Emperor of Liang. It was known in history as Later Liang. And this marked the beginning of the Five Dynasties and Ten Kingdoms Period. The Five Dynasties were Liang, Tang, Jin, Han, and Zhou. In order to distinguish them from previous dynasties with the same name, the five dynasties were referred to as "Later." Please see details below.

The Five Dynasties

Name	Reign
Later Liang	AD 907–923
Later Tang	AD 923–936
Later Jin	AD 936–947
Later Han	AD 947–950
Later Zhou	AD 951–960

It was recorded that within the 53 years of the five dynasties, there were 14 Emperors. Their capitals were all in the northern part of China. Later Tang had its capital in Luoyang and the other four settled in Bianjing (present-day Kaifeng, Henan).

Starting from the end of the Tang era, some circuits in southern China such as Jiangnan, Lingnan, Jiannan, and Hedong were occupied by prefectural ministers, who later declared themselves as kings. Altogether there were ten kingdoms. Please see details below.

The Ten Kingdoms

Name	Reign
Wu	AD 892–937
Wuyue	AD 893–978
Min	AD 897–945
Chu	AD 896–951
Southern Han	AD 905–971
Former Shu	AD 891–925
Later Shu	AD 925–965
Jingnan	AD 907–963
Southern Tang	AD 937–975
Northern Han	AD 951–979

All ten kingdoms were based in southern China, except the Kingdom of Northern Han. It was established in what would be present-day Shanxi. The five dynasties and ten kingdoms were a natural consequence of the growing Fanzhen. In terms of administrative divisions, they all copied the Tang system of "Circuit-Prefecture-County."

At that time, the territory of Houliang was only part of the six circuits in the Tang Dynasty, including Guannei, Henan, Hedong, Hebei, Shanxi, and Huainan. It is equivalent to most of today's Henan, Shandong, Shaanxi, Hubei, and part of Anhui, Jiangsu, Hebei, Shanxi, Gansu, and Ningxia.

Later Tang was the largest kingdom. In AD 923, Li Keyong's son, Li Cunxu, defeated Later Liang and declared himself Emperor Zhuangzong of Tang. Li Cunxu was a military genus. He conquered 123 prefectures and nine circuits of Tang. However, Li Cunxu was killed in a mutiny only three years after founding Later Tang.

Shi Jingtang, the Supervisor of Hedong in the Later Tang Dynasty, took advantage of the internal turmoil in the Later Tang Dynasty, destroyed the Later Tang Dynasty in AD 936, and established Later Jin. After Shi Jingtang ascended to the throne, in order to repay the Khitans for their help, he ceded sixteen prefectures to the Khitan leader Yelü Deguang. These prefectures were roughly centered around today's Beijing and Datong in Shanxi, extending east to Zunhua in Hebei, north to the Great Wall, west to Shenchi in Shanxi, and south to an area north of a line through Tianjin, Hejian, and Baoding in Hebei, and Fanshi and Ningwu in Shanxi. The sixteen prefectures included You, Ji, Zhuo, Tan, Shun, Ying, Mo, Wei, Shuo, Yun, Ying, Ru, Xin, Gui, Wu, and Huan. After the late Northern Song period, these sixteen prefectures were also referred to as the "Sixteen Prefectures of Yanyun."

After Shi Jingtang ceded the 16 prefectures, the Later Jin Dynasty lost its defense in the northern region, providing convenient conditions for the invasion of the Qidan, Nüzhen, and other ethnic minorities. Sang Weihan, a meritorious general, admitted afterward that the Qidan army was cavalry, which was advantageous in the flat land, and the Later Jin army were infantry, which was advantageous in complex terrain. After ceding the 16 prefectures, the area south of Yanji became a flat plain spanning thousands of miles. In such terrain, it is obvious without comparison who between the infantry and the cavalry has the advantage. As expected, the Later Jin inevitably fell to the Khitan. Aside from the sixteen prefectures of Youji, the territory of Later Jin was roughly the same as that of Later Tang, with 109 prefectures.

In AD 947, Liu Zhiyuan, Hedong Prefectural Minister of Later Jin, declared himself Emperor of Han in Taiyuan (Later Han). He occupied the land of Later Tang, except that Later Shu had taken Qin, Feng, Cheng, and Jie prefectures in the West.

The struggle for the throne heated up in the Later Han period. In AD 951, Guo Wei, then regent in Yedu, forced the Emperor to abdicate. Then Guo established the Zhou Dynasty, known as "Later Zhou." Its territory was almost the same as that of the Later Han, excluding northern Shanxi. In AD 954, Chai Rong, the adopted son of Guo Wei, succeeded to the throne. Chai, known as Emperor Shizong of Zhou, had great ambitions. He wanted to "expand Zhou's territory within the next ten years, make people rich in another ten years and unify China in another ten years."[11] Emperor Shizong implemented vigorous reforms and simultaneously tried to unify China. His efforts paid off. In the second year of Xiande (AD 955), Emperor Shizong, Chai Rong, dispatched troops to conquer the west and seized the four states of Qin, Feng, Cheng, and Jie from Later Shu, which deterred Later Shu from taking any reckless actions. Later on, Zhou forces also carried out a southern expedition, taking control of fourteen states and sixty-four counties north of the Yangtze River from Southern Tang. In the sixth year of Xiande, Shizong reclaimed two states—Ying (present-day Hejian in Hebei) and Mo (present-day Renqiu in Hebei)—out of the sixteen states of Youji that were occupied by the Khitans, as well as the region of Yi (present-day Yi County in Hebei), and the three locations of Yijin, Waqiao, and Yukou. By the end of Later Zhou, it had a total of one hundred and eighteen states.

At the end of Tang Dynasty, Yang Xingmi became the Huainan Prefectural Minister, governing Yangzhou. In AD 902, Emperor Zhaozong of Tang granted Yang the title Prince of Wu. His territory included 30 prefectures such as Yangzhou and Chu.

In AD 927, Yang Pu, the fourth son of Yang Xingmi, declared himself Emperor of Wu. However, he was killed ten years later by Xu Zhigao, who proclaimed himself Emperor of Tang (which became known as Southern Tang). Later,

---

11. *Old History of the Five Dynasties · Annual of Zhou Shizong* quotes *Five Dynasties History Supplement*.

Xu changed his name to Li Bian and claimed that he was the heir of the Tang Emperors. Its territory "extended east to Qu and Wu, south to the Five Ridges, west to Hunan, and north to the Huai River, encompassing over thirty states and spanning thousands of miles."[12] The territory of the Later Tang Dynasty is equivalent to that of today's Jiangsu, Anhui, south of the Huaihe River, and Fujian, Jiangxi, Hunan, and eastern Hubei. The territory of the Southern Tang was the largest among the southern Kingdoms. In AD 958, the Later Zhou took the northern part of the Yangtze that belonged to the Southern Tang. In AD 975, the Southern Tang was abolished by the Song. By then, it still had 19 prefectures and 108 commanderies.

Qian Liu was the prefectural minister of Zhenhai and Zhendong at the end of the Tang. In AD 902, Qian was appointed Prince of Yue by the Tang government. Two years later, the title was changed to Prince of Wu. After Later Liang was established, Qian Liu yielded and was granted the title King of Wuyue in AD 907. King Qian divided the land among his sons, but the territory of Wuyue was very small. In AD 978, Wuyue surrendered to the Song Empire.

At the end of Tang, Prefectural Minister Ma Yin, governed an area of Tanzhou (present-day Changsha in Hunan) and Heng (Hengyang, Hunan). In AD 907, Later Liang granted Ma Yin the title King of Chu. At its prime, Chu owned over 20 prefectures, covering present-day Hunan, a large part of Guangxi and some parts of Guizhou and Guangdong. In AD 951, Chu was ended by Later Tang.

At the end of the Tang Dynasty, brothers Wang Chao and Wang Shenzhi occupied the five prefectures of Minling (equivalent to Fujian Province today). In AD 892, the Tang government appointed Wang Chao as the supervisor of Fujian and his brother Wang Shenzhi as the deputy supervisor, governing an area of five prefectures in Minling (Fujian). Four years later, Wang Chao became the prefectural minister. After his death, his brother succeeded in his position. In AD 909, Wang Shenzhi accepted the title granted by Later Liang to become King of Min. In AD 933, Wang's son, Wang Ling, declared himself the Emperor of Min. In AD 945, the kingdom was ended by the Southern Tang.

Lingnan Prefectural Minister Liu Yin also yielded to Later Liang and was granted the title King of Nanhai (South Sea), governing the entire area of Lingnan (present-day Guangdong and Guangxi). After his death, his brother Liu Yan

---

12. *Li Jing* attached to the *Old History of the Five Dynasties · Jiewei Liezhuan · Li Sheng*.

succeeded his position. In AD 917, Liu Yan declared himself the Emperor of Han, known as "Southern Han." In AD 971, it was ended by the Song Empire. By then, Southern Han had amassed 60 prefectures and 214 counties.

In AD 907, Gao Jixing, the general of the Later Liang Dynasty, became the Supervisor of Jingnan with his seat in Jiangling. Later, he was granted the title of Prince of Bohai. In the Later Tang Dynasty, he was granted the title of King of Nanping, and his reign was known as Jingnan or Nanping. Nanping is flat on all sides and vulnerable to attack, so it is the smallest of the ten countries. At first, it had only Nanping Prefecture. Although it occupied the Xia Prefecture and Gui Prefecture later, there were only three prefectures and seventeen commanderies in total, with an area similar to that of today's Jiangling and Gong'an areas in Hubei. In AD 963, Nanping was easily captured by the army of the Song Dynasty.

In AD 891, Wang Jian conquered western Sichuan in Jiannan Prefecture, and then east Sichuan. In AD 907, at the end of the Tang period, Wang Jian declared himself the Emperor of Shu—known as "Former Shu." Its territory covered 64 prefectures and 249 counties, which would be present-day Sichuan, south of Shaanxi, southeast of Gansu, and west Hubei. Ten Supervisors were set up in the Former Shu. After the collapse of the Wu Dynasty, the territory of the Former Shu was second only to that of the Southern Tang Dynasty.

In AD 925, Later Tang's Emperor Zhuangzong dispatched Guo Chongtao and other generals to lead troops to conquer Former Shu. In AD 934, Meng Zhixiang, who was previously granted the title King of Shu by Later Tang, declared himself as the Emperor of Shu, known as the "Later Shu." Its territory was more or less the same as the Former Shu. After Meng Zhixiang died, his son Meng Chang ascended the throne. At that time, the Central Plains was in chaos. Shi Jingtang destroyed the Later Tang Dynasty and established the Later Jin Dynasty. He ceded 16 prefectures to the Qidan. Later, the Qidan army attacked the Central Plains and aroused the people's resistance, so the Later Shu took the opportunity to retrieve the four prefectures of Qin, Feng, Cheng, and Jie, marking his territorial size at its peak. In AD 965, the Later Shu was ended by the Song Empire. By then, it had 46 prefectures and 198 counties.

The only kingdom located in the north was the Northern Han. In AD 951, Hedong Prefectural Minister Liu Chong declared himself the Emperor of the Han in Taiyuan. He was the brother of Liu Zhiyuan, Emperor Gaozu of Later Han.

The territory of Northern Han was small, encompassing only about twelve prefectures such as Bing, Fen, and Xin. It wasn't even as large as the Hedong Circuit during the Tang Dynasty, roughly corresponding to today's northern Shanxi and parts of Shaanxi and Hebei. The weakness of the nation's power speaks for itself. Despite this, Northern Han still appointed a number of military commissioners. As a result, these commissioners could only enjoy a monthly salary of thirty *min*. This weak kingdom was ended by the Song Empire in AD 979.

In addition, during the Five Dynasties and Ten Kingdoms period, there was also the Bohai Kingdom in the northeast, the emerging Qidan Kingdom (Liao) in the north, the Nanzhao Kingdom (Dali) and Tubo Kingdom in the southwest border, and the Gaochang Kingdom in the northwest. Inter-state wars among these kingdoms were incessant.

CHAPTER SIX

"STRENGTHEN THE TRUNK AND WEAKEN THE BRANCHES"

—Territories and Administrative Divisions in the Northern and Southern Song Dynasties

1. Unification of the Song Dynasty and the Implementation of the Route System

Zhao Kuangyin, a distinguished military leader of Later Zhou, was sent in AD 960 by Emperor Gong to fight the Liao Kingdom. Liao was originally the Kingdom of Qidan, but was renamed in AD 947. When Zhao's army came to Chenqiaoyi, Zhao Kuangyi, Zhao's younger brother, solicited his fellow soldiers to stage a coup d'etat. They put a yellow robe on Zhao Kuangyin and urged him to be the new Emperor. In ancient China, the color yellow was a symbol of emperors.

Zhao Kuangyin drove his army back to Kaifeng (the capital) and forced Emperor Gong of Later Zhou to abdicate. The Emperor was only seven years old. Thus, Zhao was able to claim power without much effort. He then declared himself as the Emperor Taizu of Song, which became known as the Northern Song Dynasty. When Song was established, its rivals in the North included the Liao Kingdom and Northern Han, which was supported by Liao. In the South, there was the Southern Tang, Wu, Later Shu, Southern Han, and Nanping.

Zhao Kuangyin didn't follow Emperor Shizong steps in fighting his northern rivals. Instead, he mustered all his strength to fight with the southern kingdoms. It took him 13 years to wipe them all out. Later, Emperor Taizu's brother, Zhao

Guangyi, ascended the throne. In AD 979, he defeated the Northern Han Kingdom and finally re-unified China. One day in AD 960, Emperor Taizu of the the Song Dynasty asked the minister Zhao Pu, "Since the end of the Tang Dynasty, there have been 12 emperors from eight families in a short period of time. The war is endless, and the people are suffering from it. I want to eliminate the war and formulate a strategy to make the country long and stable. Do you have any good methods?" Zhao Pu was proficient in the methods of governing the country and had long considered these issues. After listening to the question of Taizu, he replied that the key to this question was that the power of Fangzhen was too great, and the power of the emperor was greatly learned. As long as the emperor weakened the power of local officials, limited his money and food, and incorporated his army, the world would naturally be stable. Before Zhao Pu could finish his words, Emperor Taizu of Song interrupted, saying, "You don't need to say more; I already understand."[1] That is how a plan to rebuild the centralized autocracy was formed and gradually implemented.

Zhao Kuangyin established his own dynasty through a coup; thus, he was well aware of the potential danger of generals with too much power. He was always thinking about how to constrain the power of local governments most effectively, and how to implement centralization and thereby avoid the chaos which arose from buffer towns in the Tang Dynasty.

One day in July AD 961, his second year as Emperor, he invited all his top military leaders, like Shi Shouxin and Gao Huaide, to a banquet. While they were dining, Emperor Taizu first praised all the generals and gave them credit for helping him establish the dynasty. Then he made them a most generous offer, which they could not refuse. The generals accepted and later retired on account of illness; otherwise, their lives and the lives of their families would be threatened. This incident was known in history as "Seizing Power through a Banquet."

Second, the government adopted the method of "Strengthen the Trunk and Weaken the Branches" to govern magistrates with military power. The Tang Dynasty was finally destroyed by the separatist forces, and its disaster lasted Five Dynasties and Ten Kingdoms, resulting in a long-term split. This period of history made Song Taizu strongly realize that the three-level administrative division

---

[1]. Chen Bangzhan, "Recalling Military Power," in *Chronicle of the Song Dynasty*, vol. 1 (Beijing: Zhonghua Book Company, 1977).

system of Cicuit-State-County was absolutely impossible for the centralized government. Song Taizu believed that a new and effective method must be adopted to change this situation.

In order to weaken the power of the original regional inspector, Song Taizu Zhao Kuangyin first took back the states managed by the envoy, other than his residence, to the central government. In the early years of the Western Han Dynasty, the prefectures of the vassal kingdoms were called Zhijun. For example, the regional inspectors of Shannan Dongdao managed the four prefectures of Xiang, Jun, Fang, and Fu. Regional inspectors live in Xiangzhou, and the other three states were called Zhijun. At the same time, civil officials dispatched from the central government took on the role of local governors, known as "Zhizhou," responsible for managing affairs of each province. However, the original prefecture regional inspector of each prefecture were retained. The full title of "Zhizhou" was "Quan Zhi Jun Zhou Shi" (权知军州事) which means "temporarily in charge of the military and civil affairs of the prefecture." In fact, this position was a permanent office, but at the time, to make it more acceptable to the existing military governors, a playful tweak was made in its naming. Later, when the regional inspectors were abolished, the word "Quan" (meaning "temporary") in the title was also omitted. The "Zhizhou" would be replaced every three years and reported directly to the central government, no longer taking orders from the local military governors. As for the officials at the county level, the situation was similar to that of the provinces. Officials dispatched from the central government took on the role of "Zhixian" to replace the original district magistrate. For some military governors who had been in power since the Five Dynasties period, Emperor Taizu of Song employed the same old trick, seizing power through a banquet, to dismiss them one by one. Later, to prevent the "Zhizhou" from having too much power locally, a "Tongpan" (deputy governor) was set up as a deputy to the "Zhizhou" to balance their power, thus achieving the purpose of dividing the power of the governor.

Emperor Taizu of the Song Dynasty intended to centralize control of various states governed by prefectural ministers under the central government, aiming to establish a two-tier administrative division system, directly controlling states and counties. However, he quickly realized that in a country with such a vast territory, the implementation of a pure two-tier system had almost become a dream. Especially when there are many states, which govern counties, it's impossible for the central government to operate effectively without setting up supervisory regions above the two-tier system. However, once supervisory regions are established, it is hard to avoid the development of a three-tier system, which could weaken the centralization of power and lead to the reoccurrence of divisive situations.

Emperor Taizu finally drew inspiration from the Transport Commissioner system of the Tang. Previously, transport commissioners were called water and land transport commissioners, responsible for the transportation of food supply between Luoyang and Chang'an. Later, the Jiang and Huai District transport commissioners managed the transportation of food and tax from the Jiang and Huai Circuits to the rest of the country. In the era of Emperor Daizong of Tang, the government created an ad hoc position of Transport Commissioner responsible for both salt and iron transportations. It was a temporary financial management position. During the reign of Qiande (AD 963–967), Emperor Taizu adjusted the system to his own needs. First, the Transport Commissioner became a permanent position. At the same time, the commissioners were to collect tax and transport goods on land and via water ways. For better management the rulers of the Song Dynasty re-divided the jurisdiction according to the geographical situation of the country. Different transport commissioners were responsible for the management of different routes, whereas Prefecture officers were in command. At that time, the routes co-existed with the circuits in the Tang. In AD 977, Emperor Taizong ordered the 18 Prefecture ministers to return their power to the central government. The system of branch commanderies was completely abolished. As time went by, transport commissioners took charge of local administrations and thus were of a higher rank than prefectures. Consequently, circuits became redundant. In AD 994, Emperor Taizong abolished the circuit system. Henceforth, Route became a new genre of administrative division.

As transport commissioners controlled vast areas of land—managing the military, civilians, finance, and legal systems—they became a potential threat to the central government. Emperors tried their best to disperse the power of transport commissioners. In AD 1007, Emperor Zhenzong officially established the Bureau for Judicial Commissioners. The officers were named as judicial commissioners of certain routes. They were responsible for legal affairs, imprisonment, and supervision. They could also recommend officials to the central government.

Besides transport commissioners and judicial commissioners, the route officials also included fund commissioners and military commissioners. Fund commissioners were responsible for food supply and price regulations, while the latter was responsible for militia on the route. The Military Commission was often called "Shuaisi." In addition to "Shuaisi," the transport commission (Caosi for short), the judicial commission (Xiansi for short), and the fund commission (Cangsi for short) were generally referred to as "Zhujian commissions." The Song Dynasty was the first in history to divide military, civilian, finance, and legal affairs of one area into four different commissions. In this way, routes couldn't be a single administrative hierarchy. In previous dynasties, a single local government was set up in one administrative area with one chief administrator.

Geographically, even though the jurisdictions of these supervisory offices were all referred to as "routes," the route under each office were not identical but rather intersected. What was considered one route under the Transport Commissioner might be viewed as two routes by the Judicial Commissioner. From the standpoint of the Pacification Commissioner, it could even be divided into four or as many as six routes. For clarity, let's examine a specific example. In the northwest region at the time, the Transport Commissioner established a single route called "Shaanxi Route." However, from the perspective of the Judicial Commissioner, it was divided into two routes: "Yongxing Army Route" and "Qinfeng Route." Yet, if viewed from the Pacification Commissioner's standpoint, it was further divided into six routes: "Yongxing Army Route," "Fuyan Route," "Huanqing Route," "Qinfeng Route," "Jingyuan Route," and "Hexi Route." Furthermore, even if two supervisory offices had circuits that perfectly aligned in terms of their jurisdictional territories, the administrative centers of those routes were intentionally set up in two different locations. This arrangement allowed them to maintain separate spheres of authority.

In general, while from a power distribution perspective, the Song Dynasty implemented a two-and-a-half-tier or a quasi-three-tier system, from an administrative division standpoint, the Song Dynasty practiced a three-tier system of Route-State-County.

The reform of the local administrative system in the Song Dynasty was different from that of the previous generation. On the one hand, the changes of administration were effective in preventing the routes from becoming a single administrative section. As a result, it would be hard for route officials to become warlords. On the other hand, the central government controlled the nomination of officials in routes, prefectures, and counties, preventing any possibility of decentralization.

Due to the reasons mentioned above, the Song had a high degree of centralization; the power of local governments significantly weakened. This was put in place to "strengthen the trunk and weaken the branches." The "trunk" referred to the central government, while the "branches" referred to the local governments. However, the downside of this practice was the great weakening of local government security defense systems. Therefore, the Song might be insulated from inner rebellions and prefectural chaos, but it couldn't guard itself against foreign invasion. This issue was manifested later, as the Northern Song was ended by the Kingdom of Jin, while the Southern Song was ended by the Mongolian tribes.

2. THE 24 ROUTES OF THE CHONGNING PERIOD

In the Northern Song Dynasty, routes were divided according to the functions of transport commissioners. In the early days, there were many changes in the route divisions. It was not until AD 997 that Emperor Taizong settled on 15 routes. In the era of Emperor Zhenzong, the number of routes increased to 18. Under Emperor Shenzong, it increased to 23. And finally, in AD 1105, the number reached 24 under Emperor Huizong. They were called the Chongning 24 routes.

Below is a chart of the 24 routes in detail.

Route	Seat	Present-day
Jingji Route	Chenliu	Chenliu, Southeast of Kaifeng, Henan
East Jingdong Route	Qingzhou	Yidu, Shandong
West Jingdong Route	Yingtianfu	South of Shangqiu, Henan
South Jingxi Route	Xiangzhou	Xiangfan, Hubei
North Jingxi Route	Henanfu	East of Luoyang, Henan
East Hebei Route	Damingfu	East of Daming, Hebei

(Continued)

Route	Seat	Present-day
West Hebei Route	Zhendingfu	Zhengding, Hebei
Hedong Route	Taiyuanfu	Taiyuan, Shanxi
Yongxingjun Route	Jingzhaofu	Xi'an, Shaanxi
Qinfeng Route	Qinzhou	Tianshui, Gansu
Liangzhe Route	Hangzhou	Hangzhou, Zhejiang
East Huainan Route	Yangzhou	Yangzhou, Jiangsu
West Huainan Route	Shouzhou	Fengtai, Anhui
East Jiangnan Route	Jiangningfu	Nanjing, Jiangsu
West Jiangnan Route	Hongzhou	Nanchang, Jiangxi
South Jinghu Route	Tanzhou	Changsha, Hunan
North Jinghu Route	Jianglingfu	Jiangling, Hubei
Fujian Route	Fuzhou	Fuzhou, Fujian
Chengdufu Route	Chengdufu	Chengdu, Sichuan
Zizhou Route	Zizhou	Santai, Sichuan
Lizhou Route	Xingyuanfu	Hanzhong, Shaanxi
Kuizhou Route	Kuizhou	Fengjie, Sichuan
East Guangnan Route	Guangzhou	Guangzhou, Guangdong
West Guangnan Route	Guizhou	Guilin, Guangxi

Hebei and Shaanxi were of extreme importance in defense because they bordered with Liao and Western Xia. Therefore, four military commissions were set up in Hebei, in addition to two transport commissions. In Shaanxi, six military commissions were set up, in addition to two transport commissions. Please see the ten military commissions below.

Throughout Chinese history, there have been two main principles of administrative divisions. The first was borne out of geographic convenience: literally, it was to divide administrative regions along the edges of mountains and rivers. The second was called the "Criss-crossing Principle." It was about meeting the needs of rulers, instead of following the natural divisions of mountains and rivers. On the contrary, they made the borders of administrative divisions as zigzag as dog's teeth. The Song followed the second principle. The purpose was to enhance centralization and prevent the potential threat of warlords, who might take advantage of the natural defense of mountains and rivers. By adopting the second principle, the centralization of the Song Dynasty was effectively strengthened, and the control ability of the central government was greatly improved.

Route		Seat	Present-day
East Hebei Route	Damingfu Route	Damingfu	Daming, Hebei
	Gaoyangguan Route	Hejianfu	Hejian, Hebei
West Hebei Route	Zhendingfu Route	Zhendingfu	
	Dingzhou Route	Dingzhou	Ding County, Hebei
Yongxingjun Route	Yongxingju Route	Jingzhaofu	
	Fuyan Route	Yan'an	Yan'an, Shaanxi
	Huangqing Route	Qingzhou	Qingyang, Gansu
Qinfeng Route	Qinfeng Route	Qinzhou	
	Xihe Route	Xizhou	Lintao, Gansu
	Jingyuan Route	Weizhou	Pingliang, Gansu

For example, the East Huainan Route was named after Huainan, meaning south of Huai River. However, half of its governing area was located north of the river. What was more, it shared a zigzagging border line with the East Jingdong Route. Another example was present-day Jiangxi Province. It had always been under the control of a single administrative division. However, the Song divided it in half. Its northeastern part was governed by the East Jiangnan Route, while the rest was governed by the West Jiangnan Route. In addition, most of the Yongxingjun Route in the northwest was located in today's Shaanxi Province, but it also included parts of the east of the Yellow River and the west of Henan Province, as well as Shangzhou in the south of the Qinling Mountains, making Yongxingjun Route the first administrative division in history that set across the north and south of the Qinling Mountains.

The area division of some routes is the result of military factors. For example, during the Xining reign of Emperor Shenzong of the Song Dynasty (AD 1068–1077), Zhang Dun led his troops from the Jinghu North Route to the south along the Yuan River in today's Hunan Province, calming the southern and northern Jiangman areas in western Hunan. The original three states of Yi, Qi, and Ding were renamed as Chen, Yuan, and Jing, which were managed by Jinghu North Route. As a result, the regions along the Yuan and Li Rivers in present-day Hunan did not belong to the nearby Jinghu South Route or Kuizhou Route, but instead were under the jurisdiction of Jinghu North Route to the north. This made the jurisdiction of Jinghu North Route appear very unique, as it extended southwest from present-day Hubei, wedging itself between Jinghu Route and Kuizhou Route, and bordering Guangnan West Route to the south.

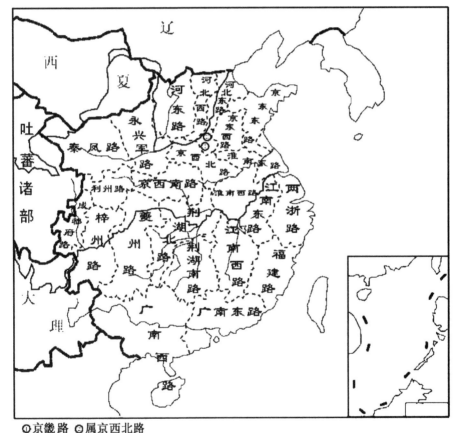

❶京畿路 ❷属京西北路

The 24 routes of Northern Song Dynasty[2]

---

2. Sketchmap based on Tan Qixiang, *Atlas in Chinese History* (Beijing: SinoMaps Press, 1982).

The second tier of administrative divisions in the Song was grouped into four categories: Fu (superior prefecture), Zhou (prefecture), Jun (military), and Jian (supervision). All of them governed counties. The names of Fu and Zhou stemmed from Tang Dynasty systems. The Fu was a superior Prefecture, and there were two different types of Fu: one was Jing-Fu, literally meaning where the capital or auxiliary capital was. In the Northern Song, there were four capitals, respectively: Eastern Jing-Fu (present-day Kaifeng in Henan), Western Jing-Fu (present-day Luoyang), Northern Jing-Fu (present-day Daming, Hebei), and Southern Jing-Fu (present-day Shangqiu, Henan). The other was Ci-Fu, meaning a superior Prefecture of the second class. It had the same status as superior Prefecture. The chief administrator was called Yin (governor of superior Prefecture). Since Emperor Taizong was once the Yin of Kaifengfu, the name was changed to Zhifu in order to show respect to the Emperor. One prominent Zhifu was Bao Zheng, who was then-governor of Kaifengfu. He was regarded as one of the most righteous governors in history and there were many stories and anecdotes about him. For example, as Bao smiled little, people joked that one would have to wait till all the seas ran dry to see him smile.

Prefectures in the Song were much smaller than those in previous dynasties. One-tenth of all the Prefectures had only one county. This was also a method to prevent local governments from accumulating too much power. One consequence of this approach was that it weakened the power of local governments. When rebellions occurred locally or when there were external invasions, these governments often appeared powerless. During the Song Dynasty, zhous (provinces) were categorized based on geographical importance, the size of their jurisdiction, and their level of economic development. Zhous near the jing shi (capital) were ranked as Fu, Xiong, Wang, or Jin, and regardless of their population, they were considered top-tier zhous. Zhous in other lu (regions) were categorized as upper, middle, or lower based on their population. The chief officials of these zhous followed a jun zhi (military system). The central government appointed Jing guan (officials from the capital) to manage the affairs of these zhous, with the title "Quan Zhi Jun Zhou Shi" commonly referred to as Zhizhou. These Zhizhou had full authority to manage both military and civil matters in their state and could report directly to the central government.

There were also two categories in the "Jun" and "Jian" units. One was directly under the hierarchy of the routes, registering the same rank as superior Fu and prefecture. The other category was below that of superior Fu, prefecture, registering the same rank as county. The Jun was originally a border garrison institution in the Tang Dynasty, and its governors were called "Shi." The place where the army was based were call "Jun." After the An-Shi Rebellion, due to the need of military operations, the mainland also began to set up "Jun." However, at this time, the Jun was only a military unit under the control of the Prefectural Minister, not an administrative division. In the Five Dynasties, military activities increased, and the government set up Jun in some counties, which often interfered with the power of the county officials. Because of the chaotic political situation and the great power of the local officers, the government abolished the district magistrates and let the officials of Jun manage the affairs of the county. Therefore, Jun became an administrative division that had the same status as prefectures. The Jun units in the Song stemmed from the old systems in previous dynasties. The Song administration set up Jun on borders and in inland areas for the purpose of national defense and inland security. Jun that had affiliated counties enjoyed the same status as prefecture. If the political status of some Jun units was upgraded, then they might officially be seen as prefectures. If the political status of some prefectures was downgraded, then they might be registered at the same rank as "Jun," a lesser rank than prefectures.

The Jian units stemmed from the period of Five Dynasties. They were set up to supervise on mineral ores, money casting, salt mines, etc. In the Song, the Jian units were also responsible for civic affairs, hence they were regarded as an official administrative division. Those Jian units governing counties were at a lower rank than Jun units. However, if the political status of some Jian units were upgraded, they could also be seen as Jun. The following is a specific example: the Guiyang Jian under the jurisdiction of South Jinghu Route in the Northern Song Dynasty was set up to manage the local mining industry. In the Southern Song Dynasty the Guiyang Jian was upgraded to Guiyang Jun due to the rise of its political status, not because of changes in the local mining industry.

3. Wars between the Song and Liao Dynasties

In AD 936, Shi Jingtang, Emperor of Later Jin in the Five Dynasties, ceded 16 prefectures to the Kingdom of Qidan (renamed as Liao in AD 947). Qidan had been using the prefectures as a base to invade central China. Among them, seven prefectures (You, Ji, Ying, Mo, Zhuo, Tan, and Shun) were dubbed "Shanqian" (山前, meaning in front of the mountains), while the remaining nine prefectures were dubbed as "Shanhou" (山后, meaning behind the mountains), according to their location in relation to the Taihang Mountain region.

For governments in central China, if they lost these "Shanhou" prefectures, they could still rely on Yanmenguan of the Great Wall along the Taihang Mountain range as a natural defense. However, if they lost the "Shanqian" areas, then all natural defenses in the Hebei area would be lost and northern invaders could conquer the central plains with ease. Dynasties in central China had realized the extreme geopolitical importance of the 16 prefectures. Therefore, ever since Later Zhou, much effort was made to secure this area.

In AD 960, Zhao Kuangyin replaced Later Zhou with the Song. Although he focused on unifying South China first, he never forgot his ambition to retrieve the 16 prefectures in the North. After he had appeased states in the South, Emperor Taizu personally led the fight against the Northern Han twice. However, he was defeated because the Liao Dynasty was behind the Northern Han military forces.

It wasn't until AD 979 that Northern Han was defeated by Emperor Taizong of Song. In the same year, he personally led 100,000 soldiers to fight the Liao armies, aiming to retrieve Youzhou. After winning the first battle, the Emperor was overwhelmed by his victory and lost the next battle by Gaoliang River (near Xizhimen Gate in Beijing). Emperor Taizong himself was hit by arrows and had to flee in a donkey-driven cart. In the years afterward until AD 982, the Liao armies tried many times in vain to invade Song borders.

In AD 986, Emperor Shengzong of Liao ascended the throne. As he was still a child, his grandmother, Empress Xiao, was the real acting power. Emperor Taizong of Song took advantage of the unstable transition period, sending armies from three different routes to attack Liao. The eastern route was to seize Zhuozhou (present-day Zhuo County in Hebei); the central route Weizou (Wei County in Hebei); and the western route to seize the nine prefectures dubbed "Shanhou."

The central and western route armies were largely successful in their objectives. However, the eastern route army was severely damaged by the Liao armies. Therefore, a complete retreat was necessary and the Song armies had to give up their conquest. Yang Ye, one of the most famous generals in the western route army, was seriously injured in an ambush by the Liao. He was captured but refused to surrender. After three days of fasting, the hero died.

After two defeats, Emperor Taizong decided to give up on his ambition of retrieving the 16 prefectures. However, Liao armies took advantage of the low morale of the Song armies and invaded several prefectures, including Shenzhou (present-day Shen County), Qizhou (present-day Anguo), and Yizhou (present-day Yi County) in contemporary Hebei. They were rewarded with vast amounts of gold and other valuables. Ever since, Liao armies kept invading the borders of the Song Empire.

In AD 997, Zhao Heng ascended the throne as Emperor Zhenzong of Song. In autumn AD 1004, Empress Xiao and Emperor Shengzong of Liao led armies to attack the Song once again. The Liao armies evaded direct confrontation with the Song armies, instead taking a detour and making for Tanzhou on the Yellow River border, posing a direct threat to the security of the Eastern capital of Kaifeng.

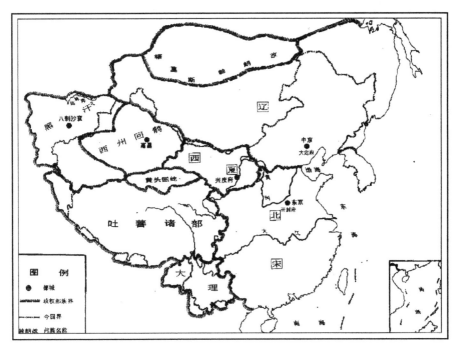

Territories of the Northern Song Dynasty and Liao Dynasty[3]

---

3. Sketchmap based on Tan Qixiang, *Atlas in Chinese History* (Beijing: SinoMaps Press, 1982).

The Song administration was divided. Fearing they would lose the battle, one group of officers proposed to relocate the capital to Yizhou (present-day Chengdu). The rest wanted to defend the capital at all costs. The new counsel-in-chief, Kou Zhun, convinced the Emperor, who eventually went to Tanzhou in person to raise the morale of soldiers. The Song soldiers killed Xiao Daling, general of Liao, with flying arrows. This was a great set-back for the Liao armies.

The purpose of Liao's invasion was to blackmail the Song administration and claim resources. Therefore, they quickly halted the fighting and proposed a ceasefire. Emperor Zhenzong, who went to Tanzhou unwillingly, wanted to strike a treaty at all costs. Consequently, Song and Liao settled on Baigou River as the border. Furthermore, Song had to pay Liao 100,000 *liang* silver (两, one *liang* =31.25 grams) and 200,000 *pi* silk (匹, one *pi* ≈ 33.3 meters) annually. This was known in history as the "Treaty of Tanyuan."

The treaty was a humiliation for the Song administration and they didn't get the 16 prefectures back. On the contrary, they had to pay a huge sum to the Liao Dynasty. However, on the brighter side, the Treaty of Tanyuan ended 25 years of constant war between the two dynasties. And from the perspective of China as a nation in the long run, the ceasefire significantly increased economic development between the borders of the two empires.

4. Territories and Administrative Divisions of the Liao, Jin, and Western Xia Dynasties

(1) Five Capitals of the Liao Dynasty

The Qidan People came to power in northeast Inner Mongolia at the end of the Tang. In AD 907, Yelü Abaoji became the Kahn of Qidan. He united eight sub-tribes of Qidan and proclaimed himself Emperor in AD 916. He then defeated several other neighboring ethnic groups and ended the Bohai Kingdom in AD 926.

Yelü Deguang, the son of Abaoji, seized the 16 prefectures from Shi Jingtang of Later Jin in AD 936. In AD 983, Liao Shengzong changed the title of the country to Qidan, while Xingzong changed it back to Liao in AD 1066. The dynasty ended in AD 1125 when the Emperor Tianzuo was captured by the Jin army. The Liao administration altogether set up five capitals. Below is a detailed description.

- **Shang-Jing (上京) Linhuangfu**

In AD 918, Yelü Abaoji set up Linhuang (Boluo City of Inner Mongolia) as his capital. In AD 926, the city was expanded to accommodate his palaces. In AD 938, the capital was renamed Shang-Jing Linhuangfu. This was the early political center of the Liao Dynasty. This place was described in the history book as follows: "the mountain is behind, and the sea is ahead. The harsh natural environment secures this place. At the same time, the water and grass are abundant, making it convenient for grazing; the land is fertile, making it easy for cultivation."[4]

- **East-Jing (东京) Liaoyangfu**

In AD 919, the Emperor renovated Liaoyang and set up Dongping Commandery. In AD 928, Qidan transferred residents of the Bohai Kingdom to Dongping and made it a southern capital. After Qidan had acquired Youzhou in the South, the area was then renamed the Eastern Capital Liaoyangfu.

- **South-Jing (南京) Xijinfu**

In the eleventh year of the Tianxian era (AD 936), the Emperor of Later Jin, Shi Jingting, ceded the northern sixteen states of Youji to the Khitans. The Khitan rulers highly valued this region because the Youji sixteen states were a developed agricultural area. Its agriculture, handicrafts, and other cultural activities were more advanced than those in the Khitan's native regions. For this reason, they decided to elevate Youzhou (now southwest of Beijing) from the Youji sixteen states to the status of South-Jing (also known as Yanjing), calling it Youzhou Prefecture. They renamed their imperial capital to Shangjing and the original South-Jing (Liaoyang) to Dongjing. Numerous official positions were established in South-Jing Youzhou, treating it as their hinterland, thereby presenting themselves with the stature of a major power just beyond the northern borders of the Song Dynasty. In the first year of the Kaitai era (AD 1012), it was renamed Xijin Prefecture.

- **Zhong-Jing (中京) Dadingfu**

In AD 1007, Emperor Shengzong set up Dadingfu (present-day Damingcheng in Inner Mongolia). He relocated a good number of Han Chinese to its vicinity and

---

4. *History of Liao · Geography.*

then moved his capital from Linhuang to the area, making it the political center of Liao.

- WEST-JING (西京) DATONGFU

In AD 1044, Emperor Xingzong made Yunzhou (Datong, Shanxi) the Western Capital. He also ordered that only princes could govern this area, because of its geographic importance.[5]

The administrative divisions and political systems of the Liao Dynasty stemmed from the Tang. Emperor Taizong drafted all systems and divisions, and they were perfected in the era of Emperor Shengzong. The Liao administration set the five capitals as their political centers and divided the country into five circuits, dubbed the "Five Jing Circuits":

a. The Shang-Jing Circuit covered what would today be Mongolia, Liaoning and Jilin provinces, and the west of Heilongjiang Province, as well as the northern part of Inner Mongolia, and the southern part of Siberia in Russia.
b. The East-Jing Circuit covered eastern Heilongjiang, Jilin, and Liaoning, to the south of the Outer Khingan Range, Heilongjiang River, and from the east of Ussuri River to Sakhalin, as well as the northeastern part of North Korea.
c. The Zhong-Jing Circuit covered what would be present-day southern Inner Mongolia, western Liaoning, and northern Hebei.
d. The South-Jing Circuit covered what would be the present-day northern part of Hebei, Beijing, and northern Tianjin.
e. The West-Jing Circuit covered what would be present-day northern Shanxi, southern Inner Mongolia, and the northwestern tip of Hebei.

Most of the time the Liao regime overlapped with the Northern Song, hence the latter also influenced the former in setting up its political systems, e.g., the separation of powers. The power of circuits was divided into three branches.

The Supervisor-in-Chief was in charge of military affairs, with his counterpart being the Military Commission in the Northern Song administration; the Supervisory Commissioner was in charge of legal affairs, inspection and supervision,

---

5. *History of Liao · Geography.*

with his counterpart being the Judicial Commissioner in the Song administration; and there was also the Transport Commissioner in both dynasties. The name varied in different circuits.

The administrative division below the Circuit was divided into four categories: Fu, Zhou, Jun, and Cheng. Xian (County) was the lowest level. The Fu and prefecture under the jurisdiction of Circuit in the Liao Dynasty roughly had the same status, but there were some slight differences. The Fu had its own directly-controlled county and it also governed prefectures. In the Liao Dynasty, there were five levels of prefectures: Jiedu, Guancha, Tuanlian, Fangyu, and Ci Shi. In addition, there were prefectures without title that had the lowest status. Jiedu prefecture and the Fu had the same status, and they were both inferior to the "Circuit"; the status below the Guancha Prefecture varied. Some directly belonged to "Circuit," and some were subordinate to "Fu" or "Jiedu Prefecture." All prefectures could govern counties, but "Jiedu Prefecture" could govern other prefectures in addition to managing counties.

Furthermore, during the Liao Dynasty, for the nomadic tribes in the north, they did not adopt the traditional county system of the central plains dynasties. Instead, they were categorized into tribes and vassal states. For the tribes, prefectural ministers were appointed. They fell under various frontier military offices such as the Dongbei Route Zhaotao Office, Dongbei Route Tongjun Office, Dongbei Route Bingma Office, Dongjing Du Buzheng Office, Xibei Route Zhaotao Office, Xinan Route Zhaotao Office, Huanglong Prefecture Du Buzheng Office, Wugudi Lie Tongjun Office, and so on. The vassal states "did not have a regular tribute schedule. When there was a need, envoys were dispatched to summon troops, or a decree was issued for a specific conscription. Those who did not comply were attacked. The number of troops provided, whether many or few, varied according to their convenience, without a set quota."[6] According to the *History of Liao · Geography*, there were five capitals, six Fu, 156 Provinces, Jun and Cheng, 209 Counties, 52 tribes, and 60 dependencies in the Liao Dynasty.

(2) The Touxia Garrison and Woluduo Systems
In terms of military affairs, the Liao administration had two distinct systems. They were called the Touxia Garrison and Woluduo.

---

6. *History of Liao · Binwei.*

- THE TOUXIA GARRISON SYSTEM

Researchers have not been able to determine what "Touxia" meant exactly. It can only be deduced it was a term in the Qidan language. At the end of the Tang, the Qidan grew in strength. They constantly invaded the borders of Tang and captured Han Chinese who were relocated to fortresses set up according to the Tang "Prefecture-County" system. The early fortresses, known as "Touxia," belonged to different military nobles.

After Qidan established its kingdom, those Touxia fortresses, owned by various nobles, became Touxia Garrisons so long as they were given the title of "Zhou" and "Jun" from the central government. This system was implemented from the beginning of Nüzhen Abaoji's reign. The residents of the Touxia Garrisons were mostly people captured from wars. However, after the Treaty of Tanyuan was signed between the Song and Liao dynasties, far fewer Han were captured, as there were fewer wars. The central government of Liao also tightened its control on the number of divisions and regiments in the Touxia Garrisons. Consequently, the number of garrisons dropped significantly. Fengzhou, granted by Emperor Shengzong of Liao in AD 995, was the last of its kind recorded in history books. There were more than 40 known Touxia Garrisons in the Liao Dynasty. The names of the Touxia Garrisons were usually the same with the surnames of the captured Han people; for example, the Touxia Garrison where people once resided in Weizhou was called Weizhou.

Prefectural sizes in Liao were small, and those of the Toxia Garrisons were even smaller. Some bigger ones boasted a population of over 1,000 or even 10,000 families. However, most Toxia Garrisons only had less than 100 families. Shen Kuo vividly described the bleak scene of Chengzhou, which was then under the jurisdiction of the Touxia Garrison: "The state has an earthen wall, about six or seven feet high, spanning a distance of a mile. Half of it is empty, with only about one or two hundred households inside. Most houses are mud-clad, with only a few covered with tiles."[7] According to the size of the population, the Touxia Garrisons could be categorized into five types: Zhou, Jun, Xian, Cheng, and Bao. The scale of the latter three was smaller than the former ones, while there were more Xian, Cheng, and Bao, than Zhou and Jun.

---

7. Shen Kuo, "Xi Ning Envoy to the Liao Illustrative Excerpts," in *Yongle Encyclopedia*, vol. 10877, under the phonetic category for the character "虏."

Geographically speaking, Toxia Garrisons were usually located in the Shang-Jing, Zhong-Jing, and East-Jing circuits. Most of them clustered around the Huang River area. According to archaeologists, most of the garrisons were located along the borders of prairies. This was mainly because the Han could not survive outside the farming regions while Qidan lords could not build houses far away from the prairies. Therefore, the Qidan nobles made a compromise by building fortresses near the farming land and the prairie.

- WOLUDUO SYSTEM

Woluduo was a term in Qidan for an officer with a certain position. It referred to the palaces of Emperors and Empresses. The Liao Dynasty had 12 palaces and one Fu in total. The nine Emperors had nine palaces; two regent Empresses, Yingtian and Chengtian, had two; the Emperor's brother had one palace; and Consul-in-Chief Yelü Longyun had one Fu.

Those prefectures set up to govern the servants were in fact Touxia Garrisons of the Emperors. And the governors were called Woluduo. Such prefectures were usually located in the Shang-Jing, Zhong-Jing, and East-Jing circuits—in other words, the central part of Qidan. The purpose was to protect the core of the Liao administration.

(3) The Five Capitals of Jin Dynasty and Its 17 Routes

The Jin Dynasty was established by the Nüzhen people. They were one of the oldest nomadic tribes in North China. It had different names in different historical periods. During the Spring and Autumn Period, it was called "Su Shen"; In the Han Dynasty, it was called "Yi Lou"; in the Northern and Southern dynasties, it was called "Wu Ji"; in the Sui and Tang dynasties, it was called "Mo He." It was not until the confrontation between Liao and Song dynasties that it was called "Nüzhen." They were active in the present-day Heilongjiang River Basin and Songhua River Basin.

It had different names in different historical periods. During the Spring and Autumn Period, it was called "Su Shen"; In the Han Dynasty, it was called "Yi Lou"; in the Northern and Southern dynasties, it was called "Wu Ji"; in the Sui and Tang dynasties, it was called "Mo He." It was not until the confrontation between Liao and Song dynasties that it was called "Nüzhen." They were active in the present-day Heilongjiang River Basin and Songhua River Basin.

In the mid-11th century, a chief called Wanyan from Sheng Nüzhen formed a coalition with other tribes. In AD 1114, Wanyan Aguda, head of the coalition of tribes, led soldiers to rebel against the Liao. In AD 1115, Aguda, drawing from the Han Chinese system, proclaimed himself Emperor, established a reign title, and founded the Jin Dynasty. He constructed Huining Prefecture (present-day Acheng County, south of Heilongjiang) as the capital, formally establishing a regime in opposition to the Liao. Aguda is also known as Emperor Taizu of Jin.

In September, AD 1116, Aguda attacked and captured Huanglongfu (present-day Nongan, Jilin Province), an important garrison in northern Liaoning. In response, Emperor Tianzuo led more than 100,000 troops to fight back, and he was defeated by the Jin army in Hubudagang (now west of Wuchang city in Heilongjiang Province). Since then, the Jin had taken the lead. In the second year of Shouguo period, the Jin conquered Liaodong and occupied East-Jing Liaoyangfu of the Liao Dynasty.

As Jin continuously defeated Liao in battles, the Northern Song administration wished to form an alliance with Jin, aiming to retrieve the key 16 prefectures. In AD 1120, the Jin and Song administrations made a deal—the "Covenant on the Sea"—to fight the Liao, shifting the balance of power. In May, the Jin captured Shang-Jing Linhengfu, and in the sixth year of the Tianfu period, Zhong-Jing Dadingfu was conquered. Emperor Tianzuo hurriedly fled to Jiashan Mountain (present-day northwest of Tumd Left Banner, Inner Mongolia). The Jin army captured South-Jing Xijinfu with ease at the end of the year.

After succeeding to the throne, Emperor Taizong collaborated with the Western Xia to fight against Emperor Tianzuo of Liao. In AD 1125, the last Emperor of Liao was captured by Jin when he fled to Dangxiang, and his dynasty collapsed. The Jin army took only ten years to conquer all of the land.

In AD 1127, after the Northern Song Dynasty was abolished, its capital was still called Bianjing (present-day Kaifeng, Henan). Therefore, during the reign of Emperor Xizong, there were seven capitals: Shang-Jing Huiningfu, North-Jing Linhengfu, Zhong-Jing Dadingfu, East-Jing Liaoyangfu, West-Jing Datongfu, Yan-Jing Xijinfu, and Bian-Jing Kaifengfu.

In AD 1153, the Jin administration relocated its main capital to Yan-Jing and renamed it Zhongdu Daxingfu (present-day southwest Beijing). The purpose was to strengthen its rule by moving closer to central China. Then Zhong-Jing was renamed North-Jing, and Bian-Jing was renamed South-Jing. Thus, the five capitals of Jin were: Zhongdu Daxingfu, North-Jing Dadingfu, West-Jing Datongfu, East-Jing Liaoyangfu, and South-Jing Kaifengfu.

In terms of local administration, Jin maintained the tribe system in its base where the empire started. In the rest of the country, they copied the Northern Song system. Like the Song, the Jin administration also set up routes to manage different areas. In the second year of Jin Xizong's reign (AD 1142), there were seventeen routes established: Upper Jing Route (capital at Upper Jing Huiningfu), Northern Jing Route (originally Liao's Upper Jing region, renamed in AD 113, capital at Beijing Linhuangfu), Eastern Jing Route (originally Liao's Eastern Jing region, capital at Eastern Jing Liaoyangfu), Central Jing Route (originally Liao's Central Jing region, capital at Central Jing Dadingfu), Western Jing Route (originally Liao's Western Jing region, capital at Western Jing Datongfu), Yanjing Route (originally Liao's Southern Jing region, capital at Yanjing Xijinfu), Bianjing Route (originally Song's Henan region, capital at Bianjing Kaifengfu), Eastern Hebei Route, Western Hebei Route (Song's four Hebei Routes were split into East and West, Eastern Route's capital at Hejianfu, Western Route's capital at Zhendingfu), Southern Hedong Route, Northern Hedong Route (Song's Hedong Route divided into South and North, Southern Route's capital at Yangfu, Northern Route's capital at Taiyuanfu), Eastern Shandong Route, Western Shandong Route (following Song's Eastern and Western Routes in Jingdong, Eastern Route's capital at Yidufu, Western Route's capital at Dongpingfu), Shaanxi's Four Routes (Jingzhaofu Route with its capital at Jingzhaofu, Qingyuan Route with its capital at Qingyangfu, Xi-Qin Route with its capital at Lintaofu, Fuyan Route with its capital at Yan'anfu).

Like the Song, the Jin administration also separated power among the route offices. The difference was that the latter had four branches. They were: the Supreme Supervisor-in-Chief, which stemmed from the Liao. At first, it was responsible for military affairs. Later it turned to civil affairs after the Military Commission was set up; the Transport Commissioner, responsible for financial management, as in the Song Dynasty; the Judicial Commissioner responsible for legal affairs; and the Military Commissioner responsible for military affairs. In terms of the division of routes, the Supreme Supervisor-in-Chief, Transport Commissioner, and Judicial Commissioner had different ways of dividing routes.

There were four categories of administrative divisions that were governed by Route: Sanfu, Jiezhen Prefecture, Fangyu Prefecture, Regional Inspector Prefecture, and Jun. Shang-Jing Route was responsible for Puyu Route, Helan Route,

Supin Route, and Huligai Route. The East-Jing Route was responsible for the Hesuguan Route and the Posu Route. Since there were no residents in the East-Jing Route, it could not be upgraded to a prefecture. In addition, Shang-Jing, the North-Jing, and West-Jing Routes were responsible for the management of the tribes on the border.

The 17 routes of Jin were expanded to 19 routes in AD 1157 and to 20 routes in AD 1187. The number of routes was changed back to 19 in AD 1208. According to historical materials, under the administration of the 19 routes, there were nine Sanfu, 36 Jiezhen prefectures, 22 Fangyu prefectures, 23 Regional Inspector prefectures, 16 juns, and 632 counties.

(4) Meng'an Mouke
Meng'an Mouke was a local administrative agency. The residents of Meng'an Mouke were mainly composed of the Nüzhen people and the rest of them were the Qidan people and the Xiongnu people. "Meng'an" was a transliteration of Nüzhen language, meaning "thousand," whereas "Mouke" meant "hundred."

One year before Wanyan Aguda founded his empire (AD 1114), he stipulated that the 300-household was a "Mouke" unit; ten "Mouke" was a "Meng'an" unit. The primary organization was Cunzhai (village), and the head of Cunzhai was called "Zhaishi," who was responsible for more than 50 households. In the early years of the Jin Dynasty, the Nüzhen rulers once settled the Qidan, Bohai, and Xiongnu people who had surrendered to Jin in "Meng'an" and "Mouke." After occupying the Central Plains, Jin applied this system to the areas where the Han people lived. During the reign of Emperor Xizong, this system evolved into a full-fledged feudal primary organization, which functioned as a military establishment, production unit, and local administrative organization. During the reign of Emperor Hailing, a large number of residents of Meng'an and Mouke living in Shang-Jing moved south. They mainly resided near Zhongdu, Hebei, and Shandong. In AD 1189, there were 202 Meng'an units and 1,878 Mouke units. Later, because these residents were unwilling to engage in agricultural production and military training, their fighting capacity gradually declined.

(5) The Territory and Administrative Divisions of the Western Xia Dynasty
A nomadic tribe called the Dangxiang established the Dingnan Kingdom in Xiazhou. They were on friendly terms with the Northern Song as it became estab-

lished. In AD 982, a Dangxiang tribe chief called Li Jipeng submitted himself to the Song. In return, he was granted the position of regional governor in Xiazhou.

However, Li's brother, Li Jiqian, turned against the Song and often defeated them in battle. His grandson, Li Yuanhao, proclaimed himself Emperor of Daxia in AD 1038—known as Western Xia in history. He set the capital in Xingqingfu (present-day Yinchuan in Ningxia). Its territory covered an area that stretched from the Yellow River in the East to Yumenguan (Dunhuang in Gansu) in the West. Its southern border reached Xiaoguan (north Huan County in Gansu) and its northern border reached the Gobi Dessert.

In AD 1044, the Western Xia made peace with the Northern Song. Soon afterward the Xia defeated Liao and the two called a ceasefire after negotiations. It was a period in which China was divided among the three dynasties. The Western Xia administration adopted the "Prefecture-County" system. Records show that in AD 1111, during the reign of Yuan Hao's great-grandson, Qianshun, the Western Xia had a total of twenty-two prefectures: nine in Henan (Ling, Hong, You, Yin, Xia, Shi, Yan, Nanwei, and Hui), nine in Hexi (Xing, Ding, Huai, Yong, Liang, Gan, Su, Gua, and Sha), and four outside the river (Xining, Le, Kuo, and Jishi). However, in reality, the number of prefectures in Western Xia was greater than 22. Currently, there are 36 known Western Xia prefectures. In addition, the Western Xia set up 12 Jianjun Commissions in places where prefectural government and other military strongholds were located.

The Western Xia also set up prefectures in border areas, such as the Wuyuan Prefecture, the Lingwu Prefecture, the Fanhe Prefecture, and the Zhenyi Prefecture, managing civil and military affairs.

5. General Yue Fei and His Northern Expeditionary Armies

"The Humiliation of the defeat was still waiting to be wiped out," wrote General Yue Fei's in his poem. Yue was the most famous military leader of the Southern Song. The defeat he referred to happened in AD 1127, when both Emperor Huizong and Emperor Qinzong, as well as their wives and relatives, were captured by Jin forces.

To understand this story one must go back to AD 1125. After Jin had defeated the Liao, it turned its focus to the Song. In November, Wanyan Sheng, Emperor

Taizong of Jin, led an army attack on the Song, aiming to take their Eastern capital, Kaifengfu. The western route of Jin's army was stopped in Taiyuan, however, its eastern route conquered Yanshanfu. They successfully crossed the Yellow River, close to the capital.

Emperor Qinzong of Song had only just ascended the throne. He wanted to flee but was stopped by his Minister of Defense, Li Gang. The Emperor stayed and ordered Li to defend the Eastern capital. However, Emperor Qinzong was afraid of the Jin armies and wanted to strike an appeasement. The first step he took was removing Li Gang. And then he sent delegates to negotiate with the Jin. The Song administration agreed to cede three towns (Taiyuan, Zhongshan, and Hejian) to the Jin Empire. Satisfied, the Jin armies retreated.

In AD 1126, the Jin armies attacked Song again on the excuse that they did not honor their treaties. They were soon threatening to take the Eastern capital. Song's central government was then dominated by officers who opted for appeasement rather than combat. Emperor Qinzong of Song accepted every request made by the Jin armies, which essentially amounted to drawing the borders along the Yellow River. The Emperor had thought the Jin armies would retreat after the agreement. On the contrary, the Jin armies continued to attack and eventually conquered Kaifengfu. The Emperor and his father were taken as captives and that was the end of the Northern Song Dynasty. It was known in history as the Humiliation of Jingkang.

Zhao Gou, Prince Kang of Song, was the only royal family member not captured by the Jin. Therefore, in AD 1127, the officers of the previous Song regime made him Emperor in the southern capital of Yingtianfu (present-day Shangqiu, Henan). In AD 1138, the capital was moved to Lin'anfu (Hangzhou). It was known as the Southern Song and Zhao Gou was called Emperor Gaozong. He had hoped to keep his empire in South China. However, the Jin appetite was too large and his hopes were soon broken; there were continuous wars between the two dynasties.

General Yue Fei of Song constantly defeated Jin armies and was regarded as a hero. At the end of the Northern Song, Yue Fei had been enlisted to fight against Liao armies. In the early years of the Southern Song, Yue fought in the defense of Kaifengfu and was held in high regard by Zong Ze, regent of the Eastern capital. In AD 1132, Yue became a general at the age of 30 and was responsible for defending the middle part of the Yangtze.

In AD 1134, General Yue was ordered to retrieve land in the North, specifically Henan and Shaanxi, which had been taken by the Jin four years ago. General Yue set out from Yuezhou (Wuchang, Hubei), and quickly retrieved Xiangyang (Xiangfan, Hubei), Yinzhou (Zhongxiang, Hubei), Suizhou, Dengzhou, Tangzhou (Tanghe, Henan), and Xinyangjun (Xinyang, Henan). This was the first time the Southern Song retrieved such a large territory. Later the general retrieved west Henan and a large part of southern Shaanxi.

When he was about to take Caizhou (present-day Runan, Henan), the Jin and Song administrations struck a peace agreement—Jin would return Henan and Shaanxi to the Southern Song. General Yue was against this and submitted several proposals to the central government in the hope of retrieving all land taken by the Jin. However, his efforts were in vain. Emperor Gaozong and his counsel-in-chief, Qin Kuai, had their own plans.

In AD 1140, the Jin administration tore up the peace agreement with the Southern Song. Jin armies quickly took over Shaanxi and Henan and headed toward Huainan. Emperor Gaozong was scared and sent General Yue to fight back from Xiangyang. General Yue and his armies marched in two routes. One force took a detour to Jin's Eastern capital. He himself led the majority of his soldiers to retaliate in central China and quickly retrieved Yingchangfu, Huainingfu, Zhengzhou, and Jin's Western capital of Henanfu (present-day Luoyang). The two branches cooperated to threaten the security of Jin's Eastern capital. Later, General Yue won victories in the battles of Yancheng and Yingchang. The Jin armies could only agree that "it was easier to shake a mountain than to shake General Yue's army."[8]

As General Yue was about to cross the Yellow River and continue north, Emperor Gaozong ordered him to retreat because he wanted to make another peace agreement with the Jin administration. General Yue had to give up on his ambition. In November AD 1141, an agreement was made in which the Southern Song administration was to yield to the Jin by paying ransom and ceding land. The two empires were divided by the Qinling Mountains and the Huai River. The two prefectures in between (Tangzhou and Dengzhou) belonged to Jin. This agreement was known in history as the "Shaoxing Agreement." After this, the two administrations divided China in half.

---

8. *Book of Song · Annals of Yue Fei.*

164 | Chapter Six

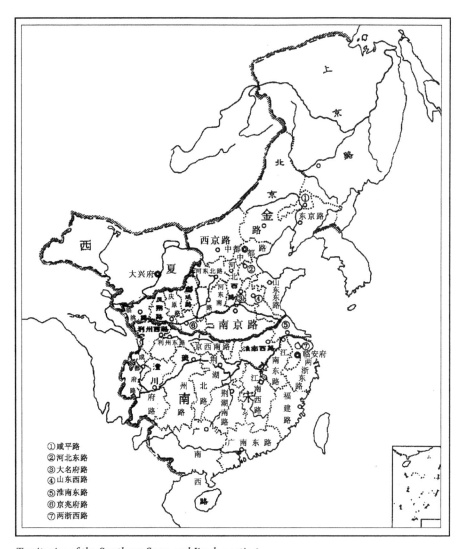

Territories of the Southern Song and Jin dynasties[9]

9. Sketchmap based on Tan Qixiang, *Atlas in Chinese History* (Beijing: SinoMaps Press, 1982).

6. THE 16 ROUTES OF THE SOUTHERN SONG DYNASTY

The Southern Song inherited the route system from the Northern Song. In AD 1142, there were 16 routes. Every route was equipped with a military commission responsible for military and civic affairs in that region. This was different from the Northern Song, which had transport commissioners at the core in routes. Please see the table below for details.

Route	Seat	Present-day Location
West Liangzhe Route	Lin'anfu	Hangzhou, Zhejiang
East Liangzhe Route	Shaoxing	Shaoxing, Zhejiang
East Jiangnan Route	Jiankangfu	Nanjing, Jiangsu
West Jiangnan Route	Hongzhou	Nanchang, Jiangxi
East Huainan Route	Yangzhou	Yangzhou, Jiangsu
West Huainan Route	Luzhou	Hefei, Anhui
South Jinghu Route	Tanzhou	Changsha, Hunan
North Jinghu Route	Jianglingfu	Jiangling, Hubei
South Jingxi Route	Xiangyangfu	Xiangfan, Hubei
Fujian Route	Fuzhou	Fuzhou, Fujian
Chengdufu Route	Chengdufu	Chengdu, Sichuan
Tongchuanfu Route	Tongchuanfu	Santai, Sichuan
Kuizhou Route	Kuizhou	Fengjie, Sichuan
Lizhou Route	Xingyuanfu	Hanzhong, Shaanxi
East Guangnan Route	Guangzhou	Guangzhou, Guangdong
West Guangnan Route	Jingjiangfu	Guilin, Guangxi

Apart from military commissions, the Southern Song administration also set up transport and judicial commissions. Even though the three branches shared the same route, their seats might be located in different areas.

It could be seen from the names of the 16 routes that the Southern Song copied the names of routes in the Northern Song. The only two changes were that the

Liangzhe Route was divided into East and West, and Zizhou Route was renamed Tongchuanfu Route. In addition, in the history of more than one hundred years in the Southern Song Dynasty, the number of routes had not changed much. The Lizhou Route was sometimes divided into one East Route and one West Route; the North and South Jinghu Routes were once renamed the East and West Jinghu Routes. Therefore, the total number of routes in the Southern Song Dynasty fluctuated between 16 and 17.

The Southern Song also set up Fu, Zhou, Jun, and Jian underneath Route. The county was at the bottom of the hierarchy. Only the number of Fu was larger than those in the Northern Song Dynasty.

CHAPTER SEVEN

THE CRISSCROSSING BORDERS
—Territories and Administrative Divisions in the Yuan Dynasty

1. The Largest Territory in History

In AD 1206, Tiemuzhen, a Mongol tribe chief, united all tribes on the Mongolia Plateau and established the Kingdom of Mongolia. He was known as Genghis Khan. Ancestors of Mongolian tribes used to live on the northern part of Greater Xing'anling, and east of Eergu'na River. The name Mongolia was first recorded in history books of the Tang. Later, the tribes moved to the Mongolia Plateau.

After the Kingdom of Mongolia was established it continued to expand. By the time of Mongke Qayan Khan, it had already defeated other kingdoms such as Western Liao, Western Xia, Jin, and Dali. Mongolians also attacked the Southern Song Empire several times. After Mongke Qayan died, his brother, Kublai Khan, ascended the throne in AD 1260 in Kaiping (east of Zhenglan Banner of Inner Mongolia). In AD 1271, Kublai Khan renamed the kingdom "Da Yuan," which was the name of the roots of world creatures described in *The Book of Changes*. Kublai Khan became Emperor Shizu and the following year he moved the capital to Dadu (present-day Beijing).

In AD 1276, Yuan armies conquered Lin'an (present-day Hangzhou), forcing the Southern Song Emperor to surrender. Three years later, Yuan armies wiped out the remaining forces of the Southern Song Dynasty in Yashan (south Xinhui, Guangdong), which marked the end of the Southern Song. The Yuan conquered all other kingdoms including the Jin, Xia, and Liao. Territories of the Yuan Empire had expanded to become the largest in Chinese history, stretching from the seas in the East to Xinjiang in the West. Its southwestern part included Tibet and Yunnan, while its southernmost tip reached Vietnam and northern Thailand. Its northern part included most of Siberia in Russia and to the northwest it reached the Sea of Okhotsk.

2. Branch Secretariat System and the 11 Provinces in the Mid-Yuan

The top rank of Yuan administrative divisions was different from previous dynasties. It contained the Secretariat and branch secretariats. This system stemmed from the Jin Dynasty. Previously, Yuan's ancient royal palaces were called "Sheng" (province), and they were forbidden to the common people.

In the era of the Wei and Jin dynasties, the central government usually set up three provinces called "Sheng." They were to help Emperors with daily political affairs. Hence, Sheng became a name for officers. When local areas needed special attention, the central government would send officers to local governments. The local areas were referred to as provinces. As we mentioned before, Sima Zhao built up Xingtai (make-shift provinces) when he began fighting against the Zhuge Dan during the Three Kingdoms Period. However, these organizations were temporary. When the officers finished their business, provinces would be canceled. Therefore, Xingtai Sheng did not have any actual jurisdiction.

During the Northern Wei and Northern Qi dynasties, the governments set up too many prefectures and counties, making them difficult to manage. In order to strengthen central control, the government adopted the Xingtai system to manage the prefectures. Xingtai, therefore, became a first-level administrative division above the Zhou, prefecture and county. The Xingtai system was implemented from the Sui Dynasty to the early Tang Dynasty. In the Zhenguan period of Emperor Taizong of the Tang Dynasty, the Xingtai system was gradually abolished.

In the Jin Dynasty, the Xingtai system was extensively utilized. After the Jin Dynasty occupied the territory of the Northern Song, it inherited the Song Dynasty's route system but divided the regions of the routes into slightly smaller areas. However, since the capital of the early Jin Dynasty was located in Huining, which was far from the Central Plains, it was very inconvenient to control this region. So, in the fifteenth year of Tianhui (AD 1137), after Jin Xizong Wanyan Dan abolished the Liu Yu Qi Kingdom, he set up the Xingtai Shangshu Sheng (Office of the Chancery) in the former Qi Kingdom's territory, Kaifeng. Later, to cope with the military operations of the Southern Song and Western Xia, a number of temporary Xingtai Shangshu Sheng were also established. By the late Jin Dynasty, especially after the outbreak of the Mongol-Jin war, the Jin army suffered consecutive defeats, and the route governors could no longer handle regional affairs. To manage local military and political matters, the Jin central government dispatched ministers to various routes to "act in the capacity of the Shangshu Sheng," establishing offices and overseeing one or several regions. These institutions were called "Xing Shangshu Sheng," commonly referred to as Xingsheng (Province, Branch Secretariat). These provinces were still dispatch agencies of the Shangshu Sheng, representing its authority with a temporary nature. Once their tasks were completed, they were abolished.

During the conquest of the Central Plains, the Mongol Yuan Dynasty adopted this system of the Jin as a temporary wartime measure. Yuan Shizu, Kublai Khan, oversaw national affairs with the Zhongshu Sheng and used the Xing Zhongshu Sheng (sometimes Xing Shangshu Sheng) as the administrative body governing newly conquered areas. Over time, the territorial scope managed by this institution became associated with the name of the Xing Zhongshu Sheng, commonly referred to as Province or Sheng. At the same time, the Zhongshu Sheng, as a central government institution, also directly governed a large area, including the capital.

The Secretariat in Yuan was also called the Capital Secretariat (Dusheng, 都省). The top administrative division in local areas were called branch secretariats, abbreviated as "Xingsheng" or "Sheng." In order to prevent any potential warlords, the Yuan administration also set up an organization called the Censorate. There were 22 branch censorates in total, providing censorial surveillance over provincial-level branch secretariats.

The branch secretariat system set up by the Yuan was a great development in terms of centralization—it was a phenomenal reform in the history of Chinese administration. With its establishment, the power of the central government was strengthened. It not only solidified unification, but also exerted great influence on future dynasties—the name "province" has been kept until today. Most significantly, the geographic divisions in the Yuan Dynasty also set a blueprint for the provinces of China today.

In AD 1280, when the Southern Song was completely wiped out by the Yuan Empire, there were seven provinces across the territory, including one Secretariat and six branch secretariats. The Capital Secretariat governed an area including Hebei, Henan, Shandong, Shanxi, Monan (漠南), Mobei (漠北), Liaodong, and the regions which used to be Western Xia. Details of the six Branch Secretariats are below:

a. Shaanxi and Sichuan: It was set up in AD 1260 and was also known as Qinshu Province. With its seat on the Anxi Route (Xi'an), it covered an area which used to be the Shaanxi Route of Jin and the Sichuan Route of Southern Song.

b. Yunnan: It was set up in AD 1274. With its seat on the Zhongqing Route (present-day Kunming), it covered what used to be the Kingdom of Dali.

c. Huguang: It was set up in AD 1274. With its seat on the Tanzhou Route (Changsha, Hunan), it covered Hunan, Hubei, southwest of Jing, and four routes in Guangxi.

d. Jianghuai Province: It was set up in AD 1276. With its seat on the Yangzhou Route, it covered an area which used to be the Lianghuai and Liangzhe Routes in the Southern Song era.

e. Jiangxi Province: It was set up in AD 1277. With its seat on the Longxing Route (Nanchang, Jiangxi), it covered an area which used to be Jiangxi, and the Guangdong routes in the Southern Song era.

f. Fujian Province: It was set up in AD 1278. With its seat on the Quanzhou Route (Quanzhou, Fujian), it covered an area of which used to be Fujian Route in the Southern Song era.

From the information listed above, it can be seen that the sizes of these seven provinces (the Zhongshu Sheng and six provinces) vary greatly, with significant differences. The main reason for this is that the regions of these seven provinces were primarily formed based on the process and routes of military operations. The territories occupied by a single campaign or along a particular route were designated as one province. For example, the Yunnan Province was established by the Yuan Dynasty after the conquest of the Dali Kingdom, ruled by the Duan clan. Kublai Khan set it up based on the original jurisdiction of the Dali Kingdom and appointed the senior official Saidianchi as the Chief Minister to handle the affairs of the Yunnan Province. These wartime-formed regions proved inconvenient for administration during peacetime. Therefore, by the middle of the Yuan Dynasty, adjustments were made to the jurisdictions of the aforementioned seven provinces, gradually forming a new layout of eleven provinces on the Yuan Dynasty's map, which consisted of one Zhongshu Sheng and ten Xing Zhongshu Shengs:

a. Secretariat
The size of the Secretariat had been reduced to the area of Hebei, Monan (漠南), Shandong, and Shanxi.

b. Lingbei Province
In AD 1307, Helin Province was set up. It was renamed Lingbei in AD 1312. With its seat on the Hening Route (Ha'erhelin in Inner Mongolia), it covered an area stretching from Greater Xing'anling in the East to the Stone River of the Ye'er region in the West. Today, it would cover Mongolia and Inner Mongolia, part of Xinjiang, and Siberia. Some parts of this province were used for farming and pastoral activities. The rest was mostly granted to royal family members and grasslands for nomadic tribes.

c. Liaoyang Province
Liaoyang Province had been set up and abolished several times. Finally, officers in the central government made Liaoyang official in AD 1287. With its seat on the Liaoyang Route, it covered an area of the previous Jin's Eastern capital, Xianping and Shang-Jing routes, and a large part of the Northern-Jing Route. Today, it would cover Heilongjiang, Jilin, and Liaoning. Some parts of this province were used for farming, while the rest was mostly granted to royals and nomadic tribes.

d. Henan-Jiangbei Province
It was set up in AD 1291. With its seat on the Bianliang Route (Kaifeng), it covered the area south of the Yellow River in modern Henan, and north of the Yangtze in modern Hubei, Anhui, and Jiangsu.

e & f. Shaanxi and Sichuan Provinces

In the 18th year of Zhiyuan (AD 1281), the combined Shaanxi-Sichuan Province was divided into two separate provinces: Shaanxi and Sichuan. They were briefly merged back into a single Secretariat, but in the 23rd year (AD 1286), they were again separated. The Shaanxi Province was initially administered from the Anxi Route, which was later changed to Fengyuan Route (present-day Xi'an, Shaanxi). Its jurisdiction was roughly equivalent to the five routes (administrative regions) of Jin's Shaanxi and parts of the South Song's Lizhou Route, starting from the Yellow River between today's Shanxi and Shaanxi in the east, encompassing the Heyao and Daba Mountains in the west and south, and including the Ordos grasslands of Inner Mongolia in the north. The Sichuan Province was administered from the Chengdu Route. Its jurisdiction corresponded to the Song Dynasty's Chengdu, Tongchuan, and Kuizhou routes, as well as one section of the Lizhou Route. Its area is roughly equivalent to today's Ganzi, Aba, and areas east of Yaan in Sichuan, as well as the Enshi region in Hubei.

g. Gansu Province

In AD 1261, the central government set up its capital in Zhongxing Province in the previous Kingdom of Western Xia, with its seat in Zhongxingfu. In AD 1286, the province was renamed Gansu and its seat was moved to the Ganzhou Route (present-day Zhangye, Gansu). It covered an area of what is today Ningxia, the Hexi District in Gansu and western Inner Mongolia.

h. Huguang Province

In AD 1281, the provincial seat was first moved to Ezhou, and then the Wuchang Route. Its size remained more or less the same, covering an area of what is today Hunan, Guangxi and Hainan, a large part of Guizhou, and parts of Hubei and Guangdong.

i. Jiangzhe Province

In AD 1284, Jianghuai Province was renamed Jiangzhe Province, with its seat moved to the Hangzhou Route. In AD 1299, Fujian Province was abolished and annexed to Jiangzhe Province. It covered an area of what is today Shanghai, southern Jiangsu, southeastern Anhui, Zhejiang, and Fujian provinces.

j. Jiangxi Province
This province remained the same. It covered most of Jiangxi and Guangdong provinces.

k. Yunnan Province
This province also remained the same. It covered an area of Yunnan, Mount Liang in Sichuan, western Guizhou, as well as some of Southeast Asia, including parts of Thailand, Laos, Vietnam, and Myanmar.

It needs to be stressed that the Yuan central government applied the crisscrossing principle in dividing up the Provinces. Major rivers and mountains, such as the Qinling Mountains, Taihang Mountains, and Huai River were shared by several Provinces. For example, Shaanxi Provinces vince owned the Hanzhong Valley, but was divided by the Qinling Mountains in the middle. Huguang Provinces covered Nanling Mountains, but owned only a tip of what is today Guangxi Province; Provinces Province crossed Nanling Mountains, but owned today Guangdong Province; Henan Jiangbei Provinces crossed Huai River; Jiangzhe Province covered Jiangnan and south of Fujian Mountain areas; the Province crossed the east and west side of Taihang Mountain, covering Shanxi Plateau, North China Plain and Shandong Hilly Region. In contrast, only Sichuan Provinces had natural barriers in all directions. However, its northern barrier, the Qinling Mountains, already belonged to Shaanxi Provinces. Therefore, the geographical advantage of Sichuan Provinces was lost. Chu Dawen of the Qing Dynasty said pointedly that the "Combine Henan and Hebei, and the natural barrier of the Yellow River is lost; combine Jiangnan and Jiangbei, and the natural barrier of the Yangtze River is lost; combine Hunan and Hubei, and the natural barrier of the Dongting Lake is lost; combine Zhejiang East and Zhejiang West, and the natural barrier of the Qiantang River is lost; Huaidong, Huaixi, Hannan, Hanbei, with their mixed county jurisdictions, and the natural barriers of the Huai and Han Rivers are lost; Hanzhong is subordinated to Qin, returning the administrative region to Chu, also combining the Inner and Outer Rivers, and the natural defenses of Sichuan are lost."[1] From this, if one looks at the map of the provinces during the Yuan Dynasty (see *Administrative Divisions of 11 Provinces*

---

1. Cited from Wei Yuan, *Shengwu Ji*, appendix vol. 12 (Beijing: Zhonghua Book Company, 1984).

in the mid-Yuan Dynasty), it will be evident that due to the application of the interlocking principle, the division of the provinces in the Yuan Dynasty was mainly longitudinal. This presents a sharp contrast to the Tang Dynasty, where the division of the administrative regions was primarily horizontal.

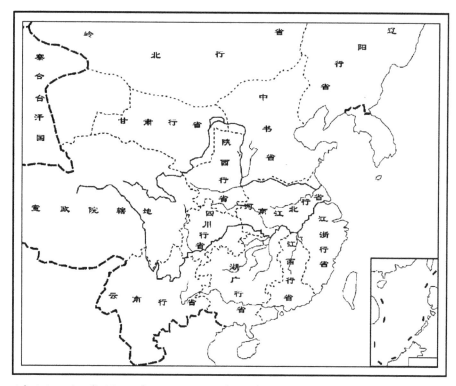

Administrative divisions of 11 provinces in the mid-Yuan Dynasty[2]

There were pros and cons in how the Yuan divided its administrative regions. On the one hand, it helped strengthen the centralization of power. On the other hand, its downsides were also obvious, and are described below:

a. The provinces were deprived of their natural defenses because most mountains and rivers were shared by different provinces. Once there was a rebellion from within or a foreign invasion, it would be hard for local

---

2. Sketchmap based on Tan Qixiang, *Atlas in Chinese History* (Beijing: SinoMaps Press, 1982).

governments to defend themselves.
b. One province usually had various territorial features, making it difficult to develop agriculture.
c. Many provinces were of gigantic size, making it difficult to govern.

It wasn't until the Ming Dynasty that administrators began to deal with these shortcomings.

Apart from the 11 provinces mentioned above, the Yuan administration also set up Zhengdong Province. In the third year of Dade (AD 1299), it was initially established in Goryeo but was soon abolished. By the first year of Zhizhi (AD 1321), the Zhengdong Province was re-established. However, since the prime minister of this Province was also held by the king of Goryeo, who could choose and appoint his officials, the original political institutions and systems were not changed, and governance continued according to the existing customs. These characteristics were different from the general nature of the Provinces established during the Yuan Dynasty. It was a Province in name only. Therefore, this Province should be regarded as a tributary state of the Yuan central government.

At the end of the Yuan Dynasty, there were uprisings in various provinces. The central government set up some extra provinces to quell those riots, such as the Province located in Jining (present-day Juye, Shandong), Zhangde (present-day Anyang, Henan), Jining (present-day Taiyuan, Shanxi), Baoding, Zhending (present-day Zhengding, Hebei), and Datong. The Shandong Province was also established separately. The Henan Jiangbei Province was divided to form the Huainan Jiangbei Province, and the Jiangzhe Province was divided to form the Fujian Province. Later, the Fujian Province further separated to establish provinces such as Jianning, Tingzhou, and Quanzhou. In general, Yuan's Province system was in chaos by this point.

3. The Multi-Level Administrative Divisions in Local Areas

Provinces in the Yuan Dynasty boasted much greater territory than previous dynasties. And they were set above the hierarchies of previous administrative structures such as routes and circuits. As a result, local areas had multi-level administrative divisions.

During the Yuan Dynasty, below the provincial level, there were several layers of local administrative divisions: route, Fu, state (prefecture), and county. In the most intricate regions, such as the Central Secretariat, the administrative tiers could extend to as many as five levels, which are province–route–Fu–state–county. In the simplest areas, the administrative levels consisted of only two tiers, such as province–route, province–Fu, or province–state. An example of this is the Lingbei Province, which only had the Hening route under its jurisdiction, with no further Fu, state, or county beneath the route. However, in most parts of the Yuan Dynasty, the administrative division was characterized by either a three-tier or four-tier system.

Moreover, during the Song Dynasty, both Fus and states were regarded as being on the same level, with the establishment of a Fu simply indicating a higher status. By the time of the Liao Dynasty, the Fu had become a tier above the state. The Yuan Dynasty borrowed from the Liao system, placing the Fu above the state. Typically, a Fu was on par with a route, but in certain situations, it might be ranked below a route. Concerning the states during the Yuan Dynasty, their scope was smaller than those of the Song Dynasty. Many states governed just one county or did not have any counties under them at all. In parts of Jiangnan, some counties, due to a surge in population, were even upgraded to the status of a state. Thus, in the Yuan Dynasty, counties, and states were almost equivalent in status. Essentially, the administrative structure of the Yuan Dynasty generally comprised three levels: province–route (Fu)–state (county).

The prefectures in Yuan were smaller than Song. Often there was only one county within one prefecture. And sometimes, the prefectures were just by themselves. In Jiangzhe Province, some counties were upgraded to prefectures because their population had increased. Therefore, counties were more or less the same level as prefectures in Yuan. In conclusion, the administrative divisions had basically three levels: province; routes/superior prefectures; prefectures/counties.

In addition, there were multi-levels of governance in the Yuan administration. The multi-level of governance stemmed from the Liao Dynasty. Before the Northern Song Dynasty, the hierarchical structure of administrative divisions was straightforward. A two-tier system was strictly two tiers, and a three-tier system was strictly three tiers. However, the Liao Dynasty developed multi-levels of government, that is, the two-level system and the three-level system coexisting in a higher-level administrative division. For example, the South-Jing Xijinfu (present-day Beijing) in the Liao Dynasty directly managed eleven counties, while it also governed six prefectures. These six prefectures also managed several counties. Details are shown in the following chart:

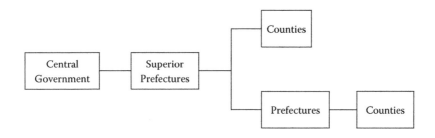

In this way, the county could be both the second level and the third level administrative division. It was the same case with the Route and Fu in the Yuan Dynasty. A county could be directly governed by the Route and Fu, and it could also be indirectly governed by prefectures.

Since the Yuan Dynasty had multiple administrative levels and adopted a composite jurisdictional relationship, it formed a complex and cumbersome administrative division system. The relationships between its various levels can be roughly illustrated in the following diagram:

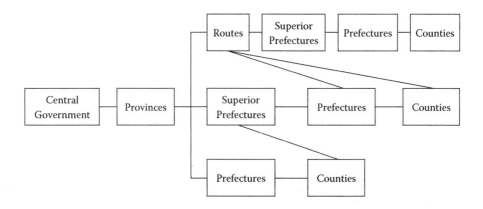

a. province–routes–superior prefectures–prefectures–counties
b. province–routes–prefectures
c. province–routes–prefectures–counties
d. province–routes–ounties
e. province–superior prefectures–prefectures–counties
f. province–superior prefectures–counties
g. province–prefectures–counties

The political structures were the most complex in Chinese history.

For routes, the Yuan adopted a Supervisor-in-Chief, like that of the Jin Dynasty. However, unlike previous dynasties, the supervisor-in-chief of Yuan brought many responsibilities under one umbrella, including legal affairs, administration, and finance etc. In other words, the system of routes had different functions.

Positions in this system included: one Darughachi/supervisorate (达鲁花赤) and one route commander. Darughachi is from Mongolian and literally means the one with the seals. Other members included one vice prefect, one Zhizhong (知中), one notary of the administrative assistant, and one or two military judges.

It was also worth noticing that Dadu Route was located in the Capital, therefore its Supervisorate-in-chief was called the Capital Supervisorate-in-chief.

In AD 1284, another general management office was established to handle civil affairs, while the Residence Office was responsible for guarding the imperial palace and the capital, controlling the gates, managing keys, and coordinating supplies for the region. The General Management Office of the capital had the same officials as the general management office of the regular routes, but it had two officials plus two deputy Darughachis. The Residence Office had five resident officials, under whom were positions such as deputy resident, assistant resident, and adjudicators.

There were not so many provinces in the Yuan Dynasty, and they did not play an important role in local administrative structures. Most were located in the previous territories of the Jin and Song dynasties, as well as the Kingdom of Dali. There were two kinds of superior prefectures. One was directly under provincial control, while the other was under route control. During the Yuan Dynasty, larger Fu were often promoted to the route. Although the remaining Fu still maintained their original establishment, their importance had greatly diminished. In the Yuan

Dynasty's Fu, positions included Darughachi, Prefecture Head or Household Head, Associate Prefect, Adjudicator, Examiner, Administrator, and Document Controller, with one official for each position.

In the Yuan Dynasty, states that were subordinate to the Central Secretariat and the Provinces were generally referred to as "directly administered states." Those subordinate to routes and independent prefectures were typically called "dispersed states." Some of these provinces governed counties, while others did not. Officials in these provinces included positions such as Darughachi, Chief Magistrate, Associate Officer, and Adjudicator.

The distribution of counties during the Yuan Dynasty was uneven. In the Lingbei area, where Mongolian tribes resided, there were no established provinces or counties, and the residents there maintained their original structures based on units of thousands or hundreds of households. A county in the Yuan Dynasty could be under the jurisdiction of a circuit, a Fu, or a province. Typically, each county had officials like Darughachi, Chief Magistrate, Assistant, Registrar, Lieutenant, and Record Keeper. If the county was of a middle or lower rank, it would not have an Assistant position.

Additionally, it should be noted that, in order to ensure control over conquered regions, the Mongol rulers of the Yuan stipulated that the position of Darughachi in the circuits, prefectures, provinces, and counties could not be held by Han Chinese. Instead, it was mainly occupied by Mongols and often also by Semu people (a specific non-Mongol, non-Han social class in the Yuan Dynasty). The implementation of this system was a unique creation of the Yuan rulers and a result of a minority group ruling over the Central Plains.

According to the *History of Yuan · Geography Records*, the Yuan Dynasty comprised 185 circuits, 33 prefectures, 359 provinces, and 1,127 counties.

4. Pacification and Military Commissions

The top administrative division was the Provinces. However, as they were gigantic, it was difficult for central government to manage them. Therefore, Pacification Commissions were set up in far flung areas to coordinate civic and military affairs of neighboring routes and superior prefectures. There were 11 Pacification Commissions in total:

Pacification Commissions	Seat
Shandong East-West Circuit	Yidu Route
North Jinghu Circuit	Zhongxing Route
Hunan Circuit	Tianlin Route
North Sea & South Sea Circuit	Leizhou Route
Hedong & Shanxi Circuit	Datong Route
South Sichuan Circuit	Chongqing Route
Guangdong Circuit	Guangzhou Route
Fujian Circuit	Fuzhou Route
East Huai Circuit	Yangzhou Route
East Zhe Circuit	Qingyuan Route
Guangxi & Liangjiang Circuit	Jingjiang Route

The top administrative division was the Provinces. However, as they were gigantic, it was difficult for central government to manage them. Therefore, Pacification Commissions were set up in far flung areas to coordinate civic and military affairs of neighboring routes and superior prefectures. There were 11 Pacification Commissions in total: Shandong East-West Circuit with its seat in Yidu Route; North Jinhu Circuit with its seat in Zhongxing Route; Hunan Circuit with its seat in Tianlin Route; North Sea and South Sea Circuit with its seat in Leizhou Route; Hedong and Shanxi Circuit with its seat in Datong Route; South Sichuan Circuit with its seat in Chongqing Route; Guangdong Circuit with its seat in Guangzhou Route; Fujian Circuit with its seat in Fuzhou Route; East Huai Circuit with its seat in Yangzhou Route; East Zhe Circuit with its seat in Qingyuan Route; and Guangxi and Liangjiang Circuit with its seat in Jingjiang Route. Pacification Commissions received orders directly from provincial officers and then passed them to different counties. Meanwhile, they also collected requests from counties and reported them to provincial officers. Pacification Commissions could be regarded as an administrative division below provinces because they functioned as coordinators between provinces and counties.

The Pacification Commission was also set up in the border areas where the minority people lived. For example, in Yunnan Province, there were seven Pacification Commissions: Luoluosi Pacification Commission with its seat in

Jianchang Route; Wusa Wumeng Pacification Commission with its seat in Wusa Route; Qujing Pacification Commission with its seat in Qujing Route; Yuanjiang Pacification Commission with its seat in Shuizhou; Yinsha Luodian Pacification Commission with its seat in Yinshaluodian; Jinchi Pacification Commission with its seat in Yongchang Superior Prefecture; and Babai Pacification Commission with its seat in Babai. Bafan Shunyuan Pacification Commission (its seat in Guizhou) was set up in Huguang Province. From the perspective of the number and scope of the Pacification Commission's jurisdiction, none of them can compare with the 11 Pacification Commissions mentioned above. Moreover, because these Pacification Commissions were mainly responsible for military affairs, they were often called Marshal's Pacification Commissions. Although the name had changed, its chief was still Pacification Commissioner.

In addition, in areas where the minority lived, the government also set up a Propaganda Commission and Military Commission governed by Pacification Commission. For example, in Huguang Province, Propaganda Commissions were set up in Shunyuan, Bozhou, Sizhou, and Military Commissions were set up in Nandan and Qianning; in Yunnan Province, Propaganda Commissions were set up in Lijiang Route, Weichu Kainan, and West Guangnan Route; in Sichuan Province, a Propaganda Commission was set up in Xunan and a Military Commission was set up in Yongshun.

In areas where minority tribes lived, the Yuan administration also set up ad hoc pacification and military commissions. Top rank positions in those organizations were called Daruqais. Deputy positions were assumed by locals dubbed "Aboriginal Offices." The Aboriginal Office system was a special policy only implemented in the regions of minority groups. This system was different from the Jimi System adopted since the Qin and Han dynasties which let the aboriginal offices manage the local affairs, instead of letting the central government set up administrative divisions there. Positions in aboriginal offices could only be inherited; however, they required approval from the central government. Otherwise, it would be considered a criminal offence. For example, in AD 1280, an aboriginal officer called Yixi Buxue became ill and passed his title to his nephew. When the Emperor Shizu of Yuan learned about the news, he was so angry that he even sent armies to the area. Yixi Buxue apologized, and the Yuan armies returned to the capital. This anecdote underscored the Yuan central government's bottom line when controlling aboriginal offices. In conclusion, the Aboriginal Office system of the Yuan was far more advanced than the Jimi system in previous dynasties, at least in terms of administration. The former was a form of direct control of the central government, while the latter was indirect. However, there was still a big gap between aboriginal offices and official administrative divisions.

5. Commission for Buddhist and Tibetan Affairs

After the Yuan Dynasty was established, Tibet yielded itself to Mongolia and became a part of Yuan territory. Even though China went through different dynasties and powers afterward, Tibet has always been under the rule of central administrations. In the Yuan, Tibet was called "Tubo."

In AD 1260, Kublai Khan ascended to the throne. In that year, Basiba, the nephew of Gongga Jianzan, a senior monk of the Sakya School, was titled Master of State. In AD 1269, he was granted the title of Imperial Master and responsible for the management of the Buddhist affairs of the country, in charge of Buddhist education and management of the Tubo region. Four years later, he set up the Supreme Control Commission in charge of Buddhist affairs in China, headed by the Mentor of State. In AD 1288, it was renamed the Commission for Buddhism and Tibetan Affairs, ranking at the same level in the central government as the Secretariat (for administration), Censorate (for supervision), and Bureau of Military Affairs. "Oversee and manage the Buddhist monks and the territory of Tubo and bring them under control."

The functions of the Commission for Buddhism and Tibetan Affairs were as follows:

a. It was responsible for the military management of Tibet. General military actions in Tibet must go through the Commission.
b. It could recommend officers to the central government, including pacification commissioners and military commissioners.
c. It was in charge of managing postal stations. Envoys were sent three times to check on the population in Tibet. Altogether over 30 postal stations were set up, responsible for receiving and dispatching documents, and providing accommodation and food for officers in transit.
d. It was responsible for Buddhist affairs in this region.

Tubo/Tibet was directly governed by the Commission for Buddhist and Tibetan Affairs, with the commission was at the same level as the other 11 provinces. Underneath the commission, the highest local administrative structures were composed of three Chief Military Command of the Pacification Commissions. They were set up in three Tubo regions.

Names of the three chief military commands were the following:

a. Chief Military Command of the Pacification Commission in Tubo and Neighbouring Areas;
b. Chief Military Command of the Pacification Commission in Tubo and Neighbouring Routes;
c. Chief Military Command of the Pacification Commission in Wusi, Zang, and Nalisugulusun.

In Tibetan, the area in Qinghai Province where Tibetan tribes lived were called "Duo." The eastern part of Qinghai was called "Duosima." The chief military command of the Pacification Commission in Tubo and Neighbouring Areas was set up in AD 1253. The jurisdiction excludes Xining State (since Xining State was designated as the fief of Fuma Changji, it does not belong to the Pacification Commission) and includes Duosima, which roughly corresponds to today's eastern and southern Qinghai, southwestern Gansu, and Aba Autonomous Prefecture in Sichuan. It was also called the "Duosima" Pacification Commission. With its seat in Hezhou (present-day Linxia in Gansu), it covered "Duosima," excluding Xining Prefecture.

The "Duosima" Pacification Commission governed several routes, including the Duosima Route, Hezhou Route, Jishizhou Military Command (Xunhua in Qinghai), and Guidezhou (present-day Guide in Qinghai). If anyone wanted to go to Wusizang Postal Station, they had to go via Duosima. Many delegates, monks, and merchants had left their footprints there.

The chief military command of the Pacification Commission was set up around AD 1280, mainly governing the Duogansi area and covering an area of today's Ganzi, Aba, and east of Changdu in the Tibetan Autonomous Region. Therefore, it was also dubbed Duogansi Pacification Commission. It governed Duogansi Chief Military Commission; Military and Civilian Pacification Commissions in Diaomen (present-day Tianquan, Sichuan), Yutong (present-day Kangding,

Sichuan), Li, Ya, Changhexi, Ningyuan; and Land Tax Commissions in Duogansi, Hada (present-day Taining, Sichuan), Litang (present-day Litang, Tibet), and Yutong. In addition, the government also set up Military Commissions in other places.

The chief military command of the Pacification Commission in Wusi, Zang, and Nalisugulusun was set up around AD 1280. In AD 1292, the central government merged Ali (Nalisu) with the area. This region would be present-day Tibet excluding the Changdu District. Wusi, Zang, and Nalisugulusun were all transliterations of Tibetan. They indicated the Former Tibetan, Later Tibetan, and Ali regions respectively. Wusizang Regional Military Commission governed 13 "Ten Thousand Households" units consisting of Buddhist monks and laymen.

According to the Tibetan historical books, the Yuan government divided the Tibetan region into three "Khas": one was from Ali region to Solajiawo (present-day Suo County, Nagqu region, Tibet); one was from Solajiawo to the Hequ Section of the Yellow River; and one was from the Hequ Section of the Yellow River to the Great Buddha Relic Tower in the Central Plains. These three "Chol-Kha" regions covered roughly the same areas as the three Chief Commander Pacification Commissions established in the Tibetan region in the Yuan Dynasty, which provided another way for us to understand the administrative divisions of Tibetan areas in the Yuan Dynasty.

Generally speaking, officers in the region were assumed by local Tibetans. However, they must be recommended by the commission and then appointed by the Emperor. The Yuan central government picked officers from military forces, civilians, lamas, and non-religious local natives. This was the beginning of the integration of religion and politics in Tibet.

6. BECHBALIQ, QARA-HOJA, HAMILI, AND PENGHU MILITARY INSPECTORATE

(1) Bechbaliq, Qara-hoja, and Hamili

In the area to the west of modern Gansu and the east of modern Xinjiang, there were three districts that didn't belong to any provinces but were under direct rule of the central government. They were Bechbaliq (Pochengzi, to the north of Jimusa'er County), Qara-hoja (present-day Turpan), and Hamili (present-day Hami).

At the end of Genghis Khan's rule in AD 1225, he granted a vast area of land in Xinjiang to his four sons. The land stretched from the Tianshan Mountains to the Altai Mountains west of Irtysh River. When Genghis Khan was still alive, all the tribes were united in awe of him. However, during the reigns of Mongke Qayan Khan and Kublai Khan, Mongolia was divided into four parts. They were Ögedei Khan, Chagatai, Ilkhanate, and the Golden Horde.

The area to the north of the Tianshan mountains in modern Xinjiang was the territory of Ögedei Khan. Mongke Qayan Khan once set up Amu River Province. However, it was too far from the capital and therefore was merged into Ilkhanate at the end of Mongke's reign. In AD 1251, after Möngke ascended to the Khanate, in order to strengthen control over Central Asia, he established the Bieshibali Provincial Government. People like Ne Huai, Tarahai, and Masuhu were appointed to manage the affairs of the Bieshibali and other provincial governments. The administrative center was set up in Bieshibali, which governed the area east of the Amu River and west of the Antai Mountains, including the former territories of the Western Liao and Khwarazm (present-day lower Amu River region and the northern part of Afghanistan).

In the battle for the throne between Ariq Böke and Kublai Khan, Bechbaliq was occupied by Ariq Böke. In AD 1264, Ariq Boke surrendered, and Bechbaliq became the territory of Kublai Khan, who set up a protectorate in the area. After the Yuan Dynasty defeated the Southern Song, in order to strengthen defenses against rebel kings such as Haidao in the northwest, the Yuan sent the pacification envoy Qi Gongzhi to lead a large number of Han troops and newly surrendered forces to be stationed and engage in agricultural colonization for military provisions. They also established foundries to produce agricultural tools. Simultaneously, a postal station was set up to ease the communications from Bechbaliq to inland areas. In AD 1283, the Yuan government set up Bechbaliq Pacification Commission to manage military and political institutions of the northern borders. In AD 1286, the Yuan army stationed in Bechbaliq was defeated by Duwa, the great-grandson of Tsagadai. After the withdrawal of Duwa army, the Yuan government recovered Bechbaliq.

In AD 1295, Emperor Chengzong set up Beiting Chief Military Command in Bechbaliq and Talin Chief Military Command in Quxian (Kuche). The two governed the northern and southern parts of the Tianshan mountains, respectively. In the early 14th century, Bechbaliq was occupied by Duwa, and then later Chagatai. However, Bechbaliq's importance was significantly reduced by then. The Ili River area in modern Xinjiang was not granted to anyone at the time of Genghis Khan. Kublai Khan set up Ali Mali Province in AD 1275, with its seat in Ali Mali. However, the province was abolished after two years and was merged into Chagatai Khanate.

(2) *Penghu Military Inspectorate*

Yuan administrators also set up Penghu Military Inspectorate to manage the Taiwan and Penghu islands. As early as the Three Kingdoms Period, Sun Quan, Emperor of Wu, sent over 10,000 soldiers to Taiwan—then called "Yizhou" (夷州). The expedition lasted for one year but ended fruitless. However, this was the first time in recorded history that the Han Chinese went to the island on a large scale.

In the Sui Dynasty, Taiwan was called "Liuqiu" (流求). Emperor Yang sent delegations to Taiwan three times. In the five hundred years or so between the Tang and Northern Song dynasties, Taiwan and mainland China had always communicated in cultural and economic exchange. In Southern Song, the ties between the two Straights became closer. Southern Song administrations had set up military camps in the Penghu Islands. The islands were then governed by Jinjiang County of Quanzhou in Fujian.

In the Yuan Dynasty, Taiwan was called "Liuqiu" (琉球—with the same pronunciation but different Chinese characters as the Sui). The Yuan government was keen on expanding overseas in the early years and sent armies to Taiwan twice. The first military expedition was in AD 1291 and ended in vain. At the turn of spring and summer in the next year, they set out from Penghu Islands. They arrived at a place where there were low hills stretching out. Several people went ashore to check. However, because of the language barrier, three people were killed by the local people, and they had to return. Regarding this action, there were differing opinions within their ranks at the time. Yang Xiang believed they had reached Liuqiu, but Ruan Jian and Wu Zhidou did not see it that way. Now, if we infer based on the circumstances, since Yang Xiang and the others set out from Penghu and then arrived at a maritime location described as a "long yet low mountain," and they didn't understand the local language, it should naturally be a place inhabited by indigenous people. Therefore, it might be a location on the western coast of Taiwan, not an island in the Penghu archipelago. This is because, at that time, only Han people lived in the Penghu archipelago, and there were no indigenous people.

The second was in AD 1297. At the time, the seat of Fujian had moved to Quanzhou, which was close to Liuqiu. Gao Xing, manager of Governmental Affairs in Fujian, expressed his wish to conquer the islands. After his proposal was approved, he sent his men to capture some 130 locals in Liuqiu. In the next year, the captives were allowed back home. To return the favor, they were asked to submit themselves to the Yuan administration. However, the story ended there.

Although the efforts of Yuan administrations to conquer Taiwan Islands ended in vain, Penghu Military Inspectorate was set up to manage all kinds of affairs in Taiwan and the Penghu Islands. The Tong'an County of Quanzhou Prefecture in Fujian Province (present-day Xiamen) was responsible for the management of the Penghu Military Inspectorate. Since then, Taiwan and Penghu had officially become part of China's territory. However, at present, there is no final conclusion as to when the Penghu Military Inspectorate was set up. During the reign of Emperor Shun at the end of the Yuan Dynasty, Wang Dayuan traveled to the Nanyang area twice for several years. In AD 1349, he wrote the *Annals of Taiwan Islands* based on his own experience. In the book, he mentioned that the Penghu Military Inspectorate was set up during the "Zhiyuan" period.[3] But there were two "Zhiyan" periods during the Yuan Dynasty: one was during the reign of Emperor Shizu (AD 1264–1294), and one was during the reign of Emperor Yuanshun (AD 1335–1340). It became a question as to which "Zhiyuan" Wang Dayuan was referring to. According to the Taiwanese chronicles recorded in the Qing Dynasty, the inspectorate was set up at the end of the Yuan era. According to the *Annals of Taiwan Islands*, the term "Zhiyuan" might have referred to Emperor Shun. The annals also recorded the fact that many residents moved from Quanzhou to the Penghu Islands.

In the early years of the Ming Dynasty, the government still set up the Penghu Military Inspectorate. However, bothered by the increasing prevalence of pirates, the Ming government thought that it was inconvenient to defend the

---

3. Wang Dayuan, Penghu section in *Annals of Taiwan Islands*, annotated and edited by Su Jiqing (Beijing: Zhonghua Book Company, 1981).

Penghu Islands since it was left alone overseas. Therefore, in AD 1387, the Ming government abolished the Penghu Military Inspectorate, which had a history of more than 100 years. Residents there were moved to Zhangzhou Prefecture and Quanzhou Prefecture, thinking that this would make it impossible for pirates to live in Penghu Islands.

CHAPTER EIGHT

THE RETREATING TERRITORIES
—Territories and Administrative Divisions in the Ming Dynasty

1. Changes in Territory

At the end of the Yuan Dynasty, there were several uprisings against the government. Some of the rebel troops established their own administrations. One of the most famous rebel leaders was Zhu Yuanzhang, who had previously been a monk.

In AD 1352, he participated in the Red Turban Rebellions. In AD 1356, he led his troops to conquer Jiqing (present-day Nanjing). Zhu made Jiqing his base and renamed it Yingtianfu. In AD 1368, he established the Ming Dynasty and proclaimed himself Emperor Taizu. In the same year, Ming troops conquered Yuan's capital and Emperor Shun of Yuan fled. In AD 1382, Yunnan Province yielded to Ming, and In AD 1387, Liaodong District was conquered—Zhu Yuanzhang had finally unified China.

Territories of the Ming were more or less the same as the Yuan. Between AD 1387 and AD 1399, the size of Ming territory reached its peak. It stretched from the Regional Military Commission of Liaodong District in the northeast to Jiayuguan in the West. It covered the Regional Military Commission of Shanxi and the Beiping branch in the North, the regional branch of Sichuan in the southwest, and the sea in the South.

In AD 1406, the Ming Empire sent troops to Annan, and set up Jiaozhi Provincial Administration Commission in northern Vietnam. Jiaozhi remained a part of Ming territory until AD 1427. Ming administrations also set up Duogan and Wusizang regional military commissions in Qinghai and the Tibetan Plateau. They were governed by the Jimi system.

According to the *Book of Ming*, its territory covered an area from Liaodong in the East to Jiayuguan in the West; and from Qiongya in the South to Yunshuo in the North. The records describe territory under direct Ming rule around the year AD 1403. Ming territories changed significantly over the course of time. Since AD 1573, the Later Jin Dynasty occupied a large part of the commission in Liaodong District as well as the Nurgan Regional Military Commission in northeastern China. In northwestern China, Turpan tribes continued to encroach the Ming frontiers.

During Emperor Xianzong's reign (AD 1465–1487), eight prefectures between Jiayuguan and Lop Nor either moved further inland or were absolved. By AD 1522 or so, those subordinated prefectures under loose control of the central government no longer existed. In southwestern China, many aboriginal offices in Yunnan were annexed into territories of Myanmar. By the year AD 1620, the land governed by the Provincial Administration Commission in Yunnan had significantly shrunk.

2. Regional Military Commissions, Provincial Administration Commissions, and Provincial Surveillance Commissions

The Ming administration adopted the provincial system of the Yuan Dynasty. However, Emperor Taizu thought branch secretariats had too much power so he made significant reforms for the purpose of centralization. He admired the highly centralized Song Dynasty and decided to copy its route system. He tried to balance the power of provincial governments by dividing the political structure into three branches: Regional Military Commissions, Provincial Administration Commissions, and Provincial Surveillance Commissions.

In AD 1375, Regional Military Commissions were set up as the top military agency in provinces. Positions in the commission included commissioner-in-chief, vice commissioner-in-chief, and assistant commissioner-in-chief. The Ministry of War topped this hierarchy and reported to the Emperor himself.

The following year, Emperor Taizu transformed branch secretariats into

Provincial Administration Commissions, undertaking the promulgation of imperial orders and disseminating government policies. Such positions as manager of Governmental Affairs were abolished, while the position of assistant administrator was changed into provincial administrator and dubbed "Fantai" (藩台). Unlike their counterparts in the Yuan, who handled both military and civil affairs, the provincial administrators in Ming were only in charge of civil affairs.

In AD 1380, Emperor Taizu abolished the Secretariat. Since then, the names of secretariats and branch secretariats no longer appeared in historical records. Provincial administration commissions in Ming had different levels of competence from their Yuan counterparts, yet in essence they were the same. Therefore, they were still called provinces. Provincial administration commissions topped the hierarchy of local administrative divisions. In order to balance power within commissions there were usually two top commissioners with additional assistants.

In the early years of the Ming, the central government also set up Provincial Surveillance Commissions to take charge of local judicial affairs. They were the top judicial organizations in the provinces. Provincial Surveillance Commissioner was often dubbed "Nietai" (臬台) or "Antai" (按台). There were also deputy provincial surveillance commissioners and assistants, responsible for surveillance in districts. In AD 1382, the government set up the Imperial Supervision Branch Office.

The Regional Military Commissions, Provincial Administration Commissions, and Provincial Surveillance Commissions mentioned above were collectively called the three commissions of "Du, Bu, and An," independent from each other. Regional Military Commissions reported to both the Ministry of War and the Five Chief Military Government-General. Provincial Administration Commissions reported to the Chief Surveillance Bureau and Six Ministries: the Ministry of Personnel, the Ministry of Revenue, the Ministry of Rites, the Ministry of War, the Ministry of Justice, and the Ministry of Works. Provincial Surveillance Commissions reported to the Ministry of Justice and Chief Surveillance Bureau. In this way, Emperor Taizu managed to divide the power of military, administration, and justice into the hands of three different officers. Furthermore, Emperor Taizu also made the administrative divisions of those commissions different from each other. This was well demonstrated in the divisions between the Regional Military Commissions and Provincial Administration Commissions. For example, the

Ming government set up the Liaodong Regional Military Commission while it was not included in the 13 Provincial Administration Commissions of the Ming Dynasty. The governing area of the Liaodong Regional Military Commission was taken over by Shandong Province. In addition, Yingzhou (present-day Fuyang, Anhui) was governed by the South-Jing Fengyangfu, whereas the Yingzhou Guard Station was governed by the Henan Regional Military Commission; the Kuizhou (present-day Fengjie, Sichuan) was governed by Sichuan Province whereas Qutang Guard Station (seat in present-day Fengjie) was governed by Huguang Regional Military Commission; the Cizhou (present-day Ci County, Hebei) was governed by the capital, while the "Thousand Household Office" of Cizhou Prefecture was governed by Shanxi Regional Military Commission. Emperor Taizu tried his best to balance the powers in local provinces and to prevent them from accumulating enough strength to stand against the central government.

3. Two Capitals and 13 Provincial Administration Commissions

Ming Taizu first established his capital in Nanjing. He transformed branch secretariats into Provincial Administration Commissions. And later in AD 1380 he abolished the Secretariat with its prefectures, making a previously subordinate group of six ministries the core of his central government.

Capital Nanjing had its seat in Yingtianfu. For the rest of the country, the land was divided into 12 Provincial Administration Commissions. They were: Beiping, Shandong (with its seat in Ji'nanfu), Zhejiang, Jiangxi, Fujian, Guangdong, Guangxi, Huguang, Sichuan, Shaanxi, Henan, and Shanxi (with its seat in Taiyuanfu). In AD 1382, Yunnan Provincial Administration Commission was set up, bringing the total to 13.

In AD 1403, Emperor Yongle created a Northern capital in Shuntianfu (present-day Beijing), dubbed "Xingzai." In February of the same year, the Beiping Provincial Administration Commission was abolished. In the nineteenth year of Yongle (AD 1421), Beijing's status as the secondary capital was abolished, and Beijing was renamed the "Capital City." The capital was officially moved to Beijing. After Emperor Chengzu of the Ming Dynasty relocated the capital to Beijing, Nanjing served as the secondary capital. Hence, during the Ming Dynasty, there were two capitals: Nanjing and Beijing. The prefectures, states, and counties under their jurisdiction were directly governed by the six ministries of the two capitals, and this system was referred to as "the two direct governorships of the South and North." Jiaozhi provincial administration commission was set up in AD 1407 by Emperor Chengzu and was abolished in AD 1428 by Emperor Xuande. Guizhou provincial administration commission was established in AD 1413 by Emperor Chengzu. Throughout Ming, there were 13 provincial administration commissions and two capitals directly attached to the central government. They were collectively called 15 Provinces under the Ming administration's direct rule.

During the Ming Dynasty, when transforming the Yuan Dynasty's Provinces into Provincial Administration Commissions, most of the areas under the Yuan Dynasty's northern Provinces were outside the jurisdiction of the Ming Dynasty. Additionally, the Liaoyang Province was divided between the jurisdiction of the Nurgan Regional Military Commission and the Shandong Provincial Administration Commission's Liaodong Command. The territorial jurisdictions of the Yuan Dynasty's Provinces essentially became the foundation for the delineation of the fifteen provinces during the Ming era. For instance, the territories under the governance of the Capital City, along with the Shandong and Shanxi Provincial Administration Commissions, originated from the Yuan Dynasty's Central Secretariat. Nanjing covered areas from the Yuan Dynasty's Henan Province, which includes today's northern Anhui and northern Jiangsu, as well as the Jiangzhe Province, encompassing present-day southern Anhui, southern Jiangsu, and Shanghai. The Guangdong Provincial Administration Commission was formed from territories previously under the Yuan Dynasty's Jiangxi and Huguang Provinces, which now consist of most of Guangdong, Qinzhou in Guangxi, the Hepu region, the Leizhou Peninsula in Guangdong, and Hainan Island. The areas held by the Shaanxi Provincial Administration Commission were previously under the Yuan Dynasty's Shaanxi and eastern Gansu Provinces. When establishing the Sichuan Provincial Administration Commission, parts of the Yuan Dynasty's Yunnan Province were incorporated. The Huguang Provincial Administration Commission was derived from areas under the Yuan Dynasty's Henan Province, although parts of Guangdong and Guangxi were subsequently separated. However, it retained its traditional name of Huguang. The Zhejiang Provincial Administration Commission largely took over the region controlled by the Yuan Dynasty's Jiangzhe Province. Last, the

Guizhou Provincial Administration Commission was created by merging parts of the neighboring regions of the Yunnan, Sichuan, and Huguang Provincial Administration Commissions (see *The two capitals and 13 Provincial Administration Commissions in the Ming Dynasty*).

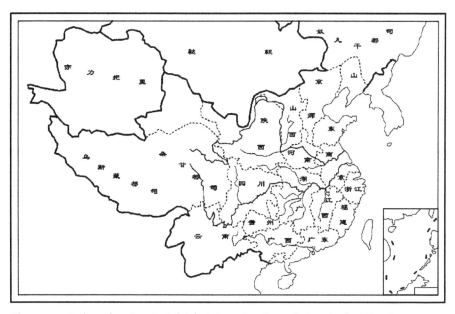

The two capitals and 13 Provincial Administration Commissions in the Ming Dynasty[4]

The Ming abolished provincial divisions made on the crisscrossing principle in Yuan. However, it created its own crisscrossing provincial divisions.

One example would be Ming's Southern capital. When the dynasty was established, Emperor Taizu made Jinling (present-day Nanjing, Jiangsu) his capital. Since his hometown was in Fengyang (present-day Fengyang, Anhui), he created a Greater Southern Jing Area, including Huaibei, Hunan, and Jiangnan, with Jingling and Fengyang at the center. The Yangtze and Huai Rivers were important administrative division lines in Chinese history. Never had any governments before the Yuan set their administrative divisions across these rivers. In the Yuan, however, Jianghuai Province had both the northern and southern parts of Huai in its territory. This was already extreme in terms of administrative division. However,

---

4. Sketchmap based on Tan Qixiang, *Atlas in Chinese History* (Beijing: SinoMaps Press, 1982).

it was nothing compared to what Emperor Taizu of Ming did. He crisscrossed over both the Yangtze and Huai. The size of the Southern capital area became too large, shrinking the land of neighboring Zhejiang. Consequently, Ming's provincial capital Hangzhou was almost next to its border. Emperor Taizu finally realized the problems he had created, so he merged two superior prefectures (Huzhou and Jiaxing) on the southern bank of Taihu Lake with Zhejiang. However, this created a new problem—the Taihu Lake area was then shared by two provinces. This disobeyed the principle of aligning administrative divisions with the natural borders of mountains and lakes. As a result, even though the problem of Zhejiang was resolved, what Zhu Yuanzhang did not anticipate was that this approach violated the principle of demarcating administrative regions based on geographical convenience, which took into account the natural layout of landscapes such as mountains and rivers. This decision split the Taihu Basin, a geographic unit that historically always fell under a single administrative region, into two separate jurisdictions, creating a divided situation for the Taihu watershed. When reflecting on this phenomenon, the Qing Dynasty scholar Gu Yanwu aptly compared it to cutting a person in half at the waist. By the Qing Dynasty, while it was recognized that the jurisdiction of Nanjing was too extensive, due to considerations of fiscal balance and other factors, there was no move to redistrict from south to north based on river basins. Instead, Nanjing's jurisdiction was divided from north to south into eastern and western parts, which led to the present-day boundary between Jiangsu and Anhui provinces.

One example would be Ming's Southern capital. When the dynasty was established, Emperor Taizu made Jinling (present-day Nanjing, Jiangsu) his capital. Since his hometown was in Fengyang (present-day Fengyang, Anhui), he created a Greater Southern Jing Area, including Huaibei, Hunan, and Jiangnan, with Jingling and Fengyang at the center. The Yangtze and Huai Rivers were important administrative division lines in Chinese history. Never had any governments before the Yuan set their administrative divisions across these rivers. In the Yuan, however, Jianghuai Province had both the northern and southern parts of Huai in its territory. This was already extreme in terms of administrative division. However, it was nothing compared to what Emperor Taizu of Ming did. He crisscrossed over both the Yangtze and Huai. The size of the Southern capital area became too large, shrinking the land of neighboring Zhejiang. Consequently, Ming's provincial capital Hangzhou was almost next to its border. Emperor Taizu finally realized the problems he had created, so he merged two superior prefectures (Huzhou and Jiaxing) on the southern bank of Taihu Lake with Zhejiang. However, this created a new problem—the Taihu Lake area was then shared by two provinces. This disobeyed the principle of aligning administrative divisions with the natural borders of mountains and lakes. As a result, even though the problem of Zhejiang was resolved, what Zhu Yuanzhang did not anticipate was that this approach violated the principle of demarcating administrative regions based on geographical convenience, which took into account the natural layout of landscapes such as mountains and rivers. This decision split the Taihu Basin, a geographic unit that historically always fell under a single administrative region, into two separate jurisdictions, creating a divided situation for the Taihu watershed. When reflecting on this phenomenon, the Qing Dynasty scholar Gu Yanwu aptly compared it to cutting a person in half at the waist. By the Qing Dynasty, while it was recognized that the jurisdiction of Nanjing was too extensive, due to considerations of fiscal balance and other factors, there was no move to redistrict from south to north based on river basins. Instead, Nanjing's jurisdiction was divided from north to south into eastern and western parts, which led to the present-day boundary between Jiangsu and Anhui provinces.

Another example would be Henan Province. The northern boundary of Henan Province in the Ming Dynasty was not the south bank of the Yellow River, but the north side of the Yellow River, forming a typical crisscrossing shape with the southern boundary of the Jing (see *The borders dividing two capitals and Henan Province in the Ming Dynasty*). This division method made Henan Province manage the Hebei area, which was the result of the Ming's military action from south to north in its establishment years. After the founding of the People's Republic of China, this crisscrossing boundary line was adjusted into a straight line, but Henan Province still governed the area north of the Yellow River.

Another is Guizhou Province. During the Ming Dynasty, the boundaries of Guizhou Province were quite peculiar. To its north, Sichuan Province was like a sharp dagger, piercing deeply south into the heart of Guizhou, annexing areas such as Zunyi, Weng'an, and Yuqing, which resulted in a significant inward concave in the northern boundary of Guizhou. The reason for this unusual delineation was mainly because Guizhou was a newly established provincial region at the time. The central government adopted this boundary design to strengthen its control over the area.

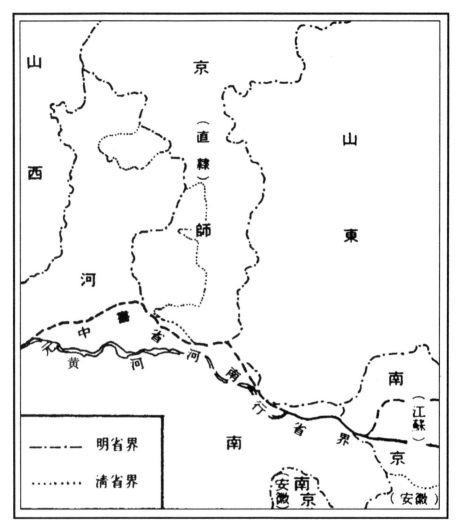

The borders dividing two capitals and Henan Province in the Ming Dynasty[5]

The last is Guangdong Province. During the Song Dynasty, the coastline of Guangdong could not be compared with that of Guangxi, as the areas of Gaozhou, Huazhou, Leizhou Peninsula, and today's Hainan Province were all under the jurisdiction of Guangxi at that time. When the Yuan Dynasty

---

5. Zhou Zhenhe, *General History of Chinese Culture · Local Administration Systems in China* (Shanghai: Shanghai People's Publishing House, 1998), 246.

established the Provinces of Huguang and Jiangxi, they inherited this boundary. However, the Yuan Dynasty once separated the coastal areas of Guangxi from the Song era, specifically the regions of Gao, Hua, Lei, Qin, Lian, and Hainan Island, and established the Northern and Southern Seas Comfort Administration, which was subordinate to the Huguang Province. After the establishment of the Ming Dynasty, even though Guangdong and Guangxi provinces were set up, the original boundary from the Song era was not restored. Instead, the territory under the jurisdiction of the Yuan Dynasty's Northern and Southern Seas Comfort Administration was incorporated into Guangdong Province. This led to an odd division where Guangxi had no coastline at all, and the Qin-Lian region was almost completely isolated from Guangdong. This zigzag boundary persisted until the Republican era. After the establishment of the People's Republic of China, this anomaly was rectified, returning the Qin-Lian region to the embrace of Guangxi Province.

Superior prefectures were in the second rank of the hierarchy, governed by capitals or provinces. Underneath superior prefectures, there were either prefectures or counties, or both. The Heads of superior prefectures were called Prefects (Zhifu), assisted by a Supervisor of Treasury, dubbed "Taishou." In the early years of Ming, there were altogether 159 superior prefectures. In AD 1373, the rules of the Ming government stated that the ranks of superior prefectures were to be categorized according to their revenue. For example, those that turned in 200,000 *dan* annually were of the first rank; those between 100,000 and 200,000 *dan* annually were of the second rank; and those under 100,000 *dan* were of the third. Superior prefectures were also categorized according to their geographic locations. Some were of strategic importance, while some were in remote and less important areas. In addition, the superior prefectures in charge of military affairs were called "Military and Civil prefectures" and had a higher rank than the others. Some of these prefectures were native offices.

The prefectures in Ming fell into two categories. The first kind was directly governed by capitals and provinces, called "Direct Prefectures." Their status was more or less the same as superior prefectures. They either governed counties or none. The second kind was governed by superior prefectures, called "Sub-Prefectures." Their status was more or less the same as counties. In fact, most of the sub-prefectures governed counties. Therefore, their status was actually below superior prefectures and above counties. Together, the two capitals and

13 provinces governed more than 20 direct prefectures (excluding native offices). The jurisdiction of direct prefectures was usually smaller than the prefecture. The number of prefectures governed by the superior prefectures varied from one to six. Many prefectures were not governed by superior prefectures. In addition, some superior prefectures were governed by Regional Military Commissions. For example, the Anle and Zizai prefectures where the Nüzhen people resided were governed by Liaodong Regional Military Commission. In the middle of the Ming Dynasty, there were 234 direct prefectures and sub-prefectures. During the Ming Dynasty, the chief official of a prefecture was called Zhizhou. He was also often respectfully referred to by ancient official titles such as regional inspector, regional commissioner, or prefecture magistrate.

Counties in the Ming were governed by superior prefectures, direct prefectures, or sub-prefectures. The Head of the office was called the District magistrate. Like superior prefectures, counties were categorized according to their revenue. For example, those that turned in 100,000 *dan* annually were of the first rank; those between 30,000 and 60,000 *dan* annually were of the second rank; and those under 30,000 *dan* were the third. According to historical records, there were 1,172 counties in the middle of the Ming Dynasty. Prefectures, sub-prefectural magistrates, and district magistrates were collectively regarded as "parent officials" of the local people.

Superior prefectures, prefectures, and counties were not only governed by provinces, but they were also controlled by organizations dispatched by Provincial Administration Commissions and Provincial Surveillance Commissions.

4. Grand Coordinators and Their Governing Areas

As previously mentioned, in the Ming Dynasty, in order to prevent local authorities from gaining too much power, the Province system from the Yuan Dynasty was abolished. Taking inspiration from the Song Dynasty's method of managing regions through separate inspectorate routes, the Ming established three distinct administrative bodies in each province: the Commandant, the Provincial Administration Commission, and the Inspectorate. While this tripartite system allowed these bodies to check and balance each other, the downsides of the system soon became apparent. Due to the dispersed power at the local level, the ability to defend against external threats and suppress internal rebellions was greatly diminished, especially in dealing with sudden or significant local events. In order to offset these deficiencies, the central government often sent two kinds of new officials, grand coordinators, and great inspectors, to the provinces for better communication between different branches of administration. These officials were responsible for the administration, military, and supervision, and they became the highest-ranked frontier officials. The grand coordinators and great inspectors at first were makeshift positions, but later became permanent and developed a new system. The jurisdiction area was also fixed. It gradually became a new set of the system of administrative division apart from "Du, Bu, and An": grand coordinator—supreme commander. In other words, the grand coordinator and supreme commander became a quasi-administrative division apart from two capitals and 13 Provincial Administration Commissions.

In AD 1391, Emperor Taizu sent his heir-apparent to inspect Shaanxi Province. The purpose was to broaden his horizons, research a potential new capital in future, and keep an eye on Prince Qin. As a result, the position of inspector came into being. In AD 1404, Emperor Chengzu sent Lei Tian, the Xunfu (inspector) in charge of supervision, to investigate Guangxi Province. In AD 1421, Emperor Chengzu asked 26 people, including Minister Jian Yi, to patrol the country and pacify the army and the people. However, it was only an ad hoc job at first, and there were no descriptions or formal responsibilities attached to the position. However, at this time, the Xunfu's role was only a temporary position for central officials without a fixed official title. Not only would the position be terminated once the task was completed, but there was also no clear stipulation regarding the specific powers and responsibilities of the governor.

In AD 1425, Emperor Renzong changed the status quo. He sent an inspector to Zhejiang as Grand Coordinator to punish gangsters in the area. In AD 1430, Emperor Xuanzong sent inspectors to the two capitals and other provinces. The position then became permanent with seats and distinct responsibilities. In AD 1453, inspector functions were finally legalized, allowing them to also inspect special delegates sent by Provincial Surveillance Commissions. Inspectors then became official and were called grand coordinators, reporting to the Chief Surveillance Bureau. In AD 1486, regulations on grand coordinators showed they were being localized. For example, they were no longer required to return to the capital to report and were allowed to take families with them to their posts.

Starting from AD 1457, officers in Regional Military Commissions, Provincial Administration Commissions, and Provincial Surveillance Commissions had to obey the orders of grand coordinators. Later, in the era between AD 1522–1619, grand coordinator posts became a matter of continuity, and the transition between predecessors and successors was systemized. Furthermore, most grand coordinators were given the post of Concurrent Superintendent of Military Affairs, meaning they had decision power in military matters too. In fact, Grand coordinators had transformed from being central government officers to powerful local officers.

Compared with grand coordinators, there were only a few supreme commander posts in the country. The latter focused more on military affairs in provinces. Therefore, these positions were often ad hoc posts. In AD 1441, the Ming administration set up the Yunnan Supreme Commander post to quell minority group rebels in Yunnan. This was the beginning of the supreme commander posts. In AD 1474, the central government wanted supreme commanders to supervise grand coordinators. In this system, some supreme commanders not only controlled grand coordinators, but also had their own governing areas. For example, the Ming set up supreme commander posts in Yunnan, Guizhou, Sichuan, and Huguang provinces in AD 1548.

In summary, the main responsibilities of a grand coordinator were to supervise tax and revenue, officer performance, and military affairs. A supreme commander oversaw grand coordinators and deployed armies. Grand coordinators focused on civil affairs with military affairs as supplementary duties. For supreme commanders, it was the reverse.

As time went by, grand coordinators and supreme commanders became the real head officers in local administrations. In the final years of the Ming, the system of two capitals and 13 provinces had been entirely transformed; the country, in fact, was divided into dozens of regions governed by supreme commanders and grand coordinators. However, it was not until the Qing that these areas officially became local administrative divisions.

The governing areas of Grand Coordinators were complex. It also had three categories "Du, Bu, and An": one was roughly the same as Provincial Administration Commission / Regional Military Commission (Liaodong, Shandong, Henan, Gansu, Zhejiang, Fujian, Guangxi); one was smaller than Provincial Administration Commission / Regional Military Commission (Shuntian, Baoding,

Fengyang, Yingtian, Xuanfu, Datong, Shanxi, Yansui, Ningxia); one was crossing the governing area of more than one Provincial Administration Commission / Regional Military Commission. In AD 1582, there were four grand coordinators and 24 supreme commanders. The southern Jiangxi grand coordinator was the most special one, whose governing area crossed four Provincial Administration Commissions: Jiangxi, Fujian, Guangdong, and Huguang. In addition, some grand coordinators may have had overlapping governing areas; for example, Tingzhou was jointly governed by the Southern Jiangxi grand coordinator and Fujian grand coordinator.

5. Regional Military Commissions and Garrisons

(1) Regional Military Commissions without Governing Areas

The Ming Dynasty had two types of administrative division: one was based on provincial administration commissions, superior prefectures, prefectures, and counties; the other on regional military commissions. Between AD 1425 and AD 1435, the Ming military structure was finalized. There were 16 regional military commissions, five regional branch commissions, with two regencies altogether. The 13 provincial administration commissions each had a military commission. Its head was called the Regional Military Commissioner.

Regional military commissions were often called "Dusi" (都司). The 13 regional military commissions which stemmed from provincial administration are listed below.

Regional Military Commissions (Dusi)	Seat
Shandong	Jinanfu
Zhejiang	Hangzhoufu
Jiangxi	Nanchangfu
Fujian	Fuzhoufu
Huguang	Wuchangfu
Shanxi	Taiyuanfu
Henan	Kaifengfu

(Continued)

Regional Military Commissions (Dusi)	Seat
Guangdong	Guangzhoufu
Guangxi	Guilinfu
Shaanxi	Xi'anfu
Sichuan	Chengdufu
Guizhou	Guiyangfu
Yunnan	Yunnanfu

The other three *Dusi* on the frontiers were:

a. Liaodong Dusi: With its seat in the mid-Liao Garrison (present-day Liaoyang), it covered a large part of modern Liaoning Province;
b. Daning Dusi: With its seat in Daning Garrison (West Ningcheng, Liaoning), it covered an area to the north of the Great Wall in modern Hebei and to the south of Xilamulun River in Liaoning. In AD 1403, its seat moved to Baodingfu;
c. Wanquan Dusi: With its seat in the Xuanfuzuo Garrison (present-day Xuanhua, Hebei), it covered an area of Chicheng, west of Huailai, north of Xuanhua, and Yangyuan.

Regional branch military commissions were set up on the frontiers. Their function was to support regional military commissions and to govern local garrisons. Thus, their seats were not located in the provincial capitals. The five regional branch military commissions (Xing Dusi, 行都司) in the Ming Dynasty were:

Xing Dusi	Seat	Present-day
Shaanxi	Ganzhou Garrison	Zhangye, Gansu
Shanxi	Datongfu	Datong, Shanxi
Fujian	Jianningfu	Jian'ou, Fujian
Sichuan	Jianchang Garrison	Xichang, Sichuan
Huguang	Yunyangfu	Yun County, Hubei

The Ming government also set up two regencies to guard royal family tombs. Head of this office was the Regent. In AD 1381, the Zhongdu Regency was set up to guard royal tombs in Emperor Taizu's hometown, Fengyangfu, Anhui. In AD 1539, Xingdu Regency was set up in Chengtianfu (Zhongxiang, Hubei) in Huguang Province to guard the royal tomb of Emperor Jiajing's father.

Regional military commissions and branch regional military commissions used to belong to the Chief Military Command. However, the latter was abolished and divided into five Chief Military Commissions because Emperor Taizu feared it had too much power. Details of the five Chief Military Commissions are as below.

Name	Governing areas
Chief Military Commissions of the Left	Zhejiang, Shandong, and Liaodong Dusi
Chief Military Commissions of the Right	Shanxi, Sichuan, Guangxi, Yunnan, and Guizhou Dusi; Shaanxi and Sichuan Xing Dusi
Chief Military Commissions of the Centre	Zhongdu Regency and Henan Dusi
Chief Military Commissions of the Front	Hugguang, Fujian, Jiangxi, Guangdong Dusi, Huguang and Fujian Xing Dusi
Chief Military Commissions of the Rear	Daning, Wanquan, and Shanxi Dusi; Shanxi Xing Dusi

Garrisons were set up underneath the regional military commissions and branch regional military commissions. A basic garrison unit was called "Guard," headed by a Guard Commander. Ming Taizu gradually abolished military unit names used in Yuan.

In the first year of the Hongwu era (AD 1368), Liu Ji proposed the establishment of a military defense system, distributing troops across strategic locations. Consequently, many military posts were set up in the capital and throughout the country. Generally, significant military cities had their own posts, while several cities in a region would collectively have a defense post. By the seventh year of the Hongwu era (AD 1374), the system was formalized. Each defense post was divided into five sections: "front," "rear," "middle," "left," and "right." If there were more than five sections, they were named in sequences like "front-front," "rear-rear," "left-left," "right-right," "middle-front," "middle-rear," "middle-middle," "middle-left," and "middle-right." Typically, a defense post was composed of

5,600 personnel; a section (or "thousand households") had 1,120 personnel; and a sub-section (or "hundred households") comprised 112 personnel. A defense post oversaw ten "thousand household" units. Each "thousand household" unit was in charge of ten "hundred household" units. Every "hundred households" unit had two banners, with fifty individuals under each banner, and each banner further had five sub-banners, with ten individuals under each sub-banner. The leader of the defense post was referred to as the "Commander," while the chiefs of the sections were named "Thousand Households" or "Hundred Households." Additionally, there were units designed specifically for guarding certain areas, termed "Guard Thousand Households," situated individually. While a few were under the defense posts, most reported directly to the superior military authority. Moreover, there were also "thousand households" units focused on agriculture and herding tasks, known as "tuntian" (military, agricultural colonies) and "qunmu" (group pastoral).

Garrisons were divided into two categories: the imperial guard and the peripheral guard. The imperial guards, apart from those directly managed by the central government, were governed by the Wujun Government-General; the peripheral guards were governed by the Regional military commissions. Branch regional military commissions excluded two peripheral guards that were directly governed by Wujun Government-General. In addition, the guards guarding the palaces of princes and the Guarding Etiquette Commission had the same rank as battalions. Garrisons in the Ming Dynasty were easily established and abolished. According to historical records, in the early Ming Dynasty, there were 329 imperial and peripheral guards and 65 defense battalions. However, by the end of the Ming Dynasty, there were 493 guards, 2,593 battalions, and 315 defense battalions.

There were four major different sources as to how the soldiers were enlisted:

a. Enlisted soldiers: Those soldiers joined the uprising of Zhu Yuanzhang before Ming was established.
b. Surrendered soldiers: Those were armies of Yuan Dynasty that yielded themselves to Ming.
c. Criminals: Those people had committed criminal offence and were then enlisted into the army.
d. Recruitment of mercenaries: They constituted the majority of Ming's soldiers.

Military personnel were under the jurisdiction of the Government-General, while civilians were under the Ministry of Household Affairs. Soldiers from the military posts were not subject to the jurisdiction of ordinary administrative officials, and in terms of identity, legal status, and economic position, they differed from the general civilian populace. If an eligible male from an ordinary civilian household was recruited as a soldier, his entire family would be committed to military service indefinitely, unable to leave the military registry. This became hereditary, and they were also required to reside within the designated military post. In addition to the regular army, the children of these soldiers were referred to as "Yu Ding" (surplus men) or "Jun Yu" (army surplus). The children of military officers were known as "sheren." When a primary soldier died or became old and ill, they were replaced by the next eligible man or the "Yu Ding." If all members of a military post soldier's family had died, it was mandatory to retrieve a relative from their place of origin to fill the vacancy.

The main responsibilities of regional military commissions and garrisons were to defend the country from invaders, quell rebellions, and solidify the power of the central government. When needed, military leaders would be sent to lead the soldiers to fight. After the wars were over, the military leaders would return to their places in the capital, and the soldiers would go back to their garrisons.

When regional military commissions were first set up, they were purely military organizations and had nothing to do with local governments. Later, when superior prefectures and other administrative organizations were abolished on the frontiers, local administrations fell into the hands of military offices who took up civil affairs as well. They were known in history as "Garrisons With Real Governing Areas" and were at the same level as superior prefectures. Battalions and companies were more or less the same as prefectures and counties. Inland garrisons were located within superior prefectures and didn't have any specific governing areas of their own. Usually, those military families cohabited with civilian families in the same place and even their farms were mixed with each other. Therefore, those inland garrisons were known as "Garrisons Without Governing Areas."

Among 16 Regional Military Commissions and 5 Branch Regional Military Commissions, the "Regional Military Commissions With Real Governing Areas" included: the Liaodong Regional Military Commissions; most of the Wanquan Regional Military Commissions; Daning Regional Military Commissions (before relocating in Baodingfu). Most Regional Military Commissions and their garrisons in the mainland did not have governing areas. Only Regional Military Commissions in Shaanxi, Sichuan, Huguang, Yunnan, and Guizhou contained some Garrisons With Real Governing Areas. As for the 5 Branch Regional Military Commissions, Branch Regional Military Commissions in Shaanxi and Sichuan had Garrisons With Real Governing Areas; Shanxi Branch Regional Military Commission once had Garrisons With Real Governing Areas before it was relocated at Datongfu; and Branch Regional Military Commissions in Huguang and Fujian only had Garrisons Without Governing Areas.

At the end of Ming, its administrative divisions included two capitals, 13 provincial administration commissions and two garrisons with land (Liaodong and Wanquan). Neither branch regional military commissions nor garrisons without land were considered part of the administrative divisions. In the early years of Qing, some of the garrisons were abolished, and some were turned into superior prefectures, hence no more garrisons.

(2) Jimi (羁縻) Regional Military Commissions

Jimi regional military commissions were set up in the regions where minority groups clustered. They were directly ruled by the Ministry of War. These commissions enjoyed more freedom than other official regional military commissions. Jimi officers at all ranks were assumed by local chiefs or tribe leaders. They were given seals and certificates by the Ming central government and could rule according to local customs and traditions. This was very similar to the situation of Jimi prefectures in the Tang Dynasty.

Geographically, these Jimi commissions were mostly located in the northeastern and northwestern parts of China, western Sichuan, Qinghai, and Tibet. They were considered local administrative organizations along with aboriginal offices and aboriginal superior prefectures, prefectures, and counties in southwest China.

In the Ming, the Nüzhen tribe inhabited the Heilongjiang River area in northwest China. The central government set up several Jimi commissions to control local tribes. In AD 1403, Ming Chengzu sent armies to the Nurgan area. The following year, Nurgan Garrison was set up and its assistant commissioner was Ladaha (剌答哈), a local tribe leader. This was a milestone indicating that administrative divisions had been set up in the lower reaches of Heilongjiang River.

In AD 1409, the Ming government renamed Nurgan Garrison to Nurgan Regional Military Commission. Nurgan Regional Military Commission was the highest rank amongst local administrative organizations in the Heilongjiang Estuary and Wusuli River region. At first, the officers were all circulating officers and only served for limited terms. Later, the positions became hereditary. The commission covered a vast area, stretching from Wonan River (present-day E'nen River) in the northwest, reaching north to the Beishan (present-day Outer Khingan Range), the boundary in the southwest connected to the jurisdiction of the Liaodong Command, and to the east it encompassed Kuhu (today's Kuye Island). The southeast extended to the Xu Jing Sea (present-day Sea of Japan), and southward it met the Yalu River and the Aye Ku River (present-day Tumen River). This roughly encompasses today's regions of the Heilongjiang, Ussuri River, and Songhua River basins, as well as areas to the north of the Outer Khingan Range. In AD 1411, the Ming conquered Kuwu and expanded its territories to Sakhalin Island. According to historical records, when the commission was at its peak, it had 384 garrisons, 24 posts, 7 regions, 7 stations, and 1 fortress. During the Ming Dynasty, the government appointed local leaders to serve as the commanders-in-chief, commanders, chiefs, leaders of thousands, leaders of hundreds, and garrisons of various Jimi forts, and granted them seals, allowing them to manage according to their original customs and pay tribute on a regular basis. Generally, these forts did not have jurisdiction over each other (see *Nurgan Regional Military Commission*).

Apart from assigning officials to govern the Nurgan area, the Ming sent officers to inspect the commission once in a while. From AD 1409 to AD 1432, Eunuch Yishiha and others visited the Nurgan Regional Military Commission and its surrounding areas many times. In the tenth year of the Yongle era (AD 1412), Yishiha, Kang Wang, and others toured various regions of the Nuergan as well as the tribes of Kuyi (Kuye Island). Kang Wang established the Yongning Temple near the administrative center of the Nurgan Regional Military Commission in Tielin, which venerates Guanyin. In the following year, a stone tablet titled *Officially Commissioned Record of the Yongning Temple* was inscribed. The inscription on the tablet was written in Chinese, while the shadow (or side) of the tablet was an abridged translation in Mongolian and Nüzhen scripts. In the eighth year of the Xuande era (AD 1433), another tablet was erected, titled *Reconstruction of the Yongning Temple*, which was solely in Chinese. The inscriptions on both tablets document the Ming Dynasty central government's establishment, management, and operation of the Nurgan Regional Military Commission. This not only robustly verifies that the Ming Dynasty had effectively administered the Nurgan region at that time, but also reflects the mutual exchanges and interactions among the various ethnic minorities in the area.

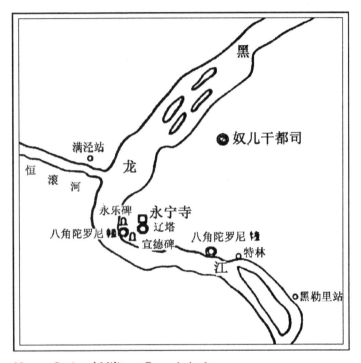

Nurgan Regional Military Commission[6]

The Ming administration restored Nurgan's postal services for transporting documents and tributes. The construction of Nurgan postal stations started in AD 1409 and finished in AD 1412. The route started from Manjing Station to the west of Telin, seat of Nurgan Regional Military Commission, and reached Dishibu (底失卜) Station in Haixi (海西). There were 45 post stations altogether with a total length of 2,500 kilometres. However, from the 17th century, Nurgan garrisons were gradually occupied by Later Jin, having been established by chieftain Nurhaci.

---

6. *Basic Facts in Chinese History (Ming and Qing Dynasties)* (Beijing: China Youth Press, 1980), 55.

The Uyghur tribes lived in the west of Jiayuguan and east of Hami. The Western Regions were of strategic importance to the Ming Empire's defense. In the early years of the Ming Dynasty, every time the government sent troops to Mongolia the army would march to the northwest. After the Ming army captured one place, it often set up Jimi Garrisons to strengthen its rule. The government would pacify the local chieftains of all ethnic groups and set armies to defend the areas.

Ming Taizu set up several garrisons there: Hezhou (present-day Linxia, Gansu), Xining, Minzhou (present-day Min County, Gansu), and Taozhou (present-day Lintao, Gansu). Later, Anding, Aduan, and Quxian garrisons were established in the northwestern part of modern Qinghai, followed by Handong (present-day east of Qinghai Lake, Qinghai) and Chijin Menggu garrisons (present-day northwest of Yumen, Gansu). Between AD 1403 and AD 1424, the Mongolian tribes in Shazhou (present-day Dunhuang) surrendered and Emperor Chengzu set up the Shazhou Garrison. And later the Hami Garrison was set up on the main route to the Western Regions. Seen from the map, Hami looked like a bottleneck, linking Gansu in the East and Turpan in the West.[7]

Consequently, the Ming government attached great importance to the area. In the era of Ming Taizu, the King of Hami tried to prevent western region states from paying tributes to the Ming, but he was defeated by their forces. Since then, the king had to pay tribute in return for his throne.

In AD 1406, Emperor Chengzu established Hami Garrison. Hami later became an important political, economic, and military center, serving as a base for the central government to strengthen its political control, as well as economic exchange in the Western Regions. However, almost 100 years later, Hami Garrison was occupied by Turpan tribes. Hence, the Ming lost all its garrisons in the Western Regions.

In areas of western Sichuan, Qinghai, and Tibet, the Ming administration adopted a similar system to the Yuan. In early years, Zhu Yuanzhang tried to rule these areas via local religious organizations, and Tibet in particular. In AD 1369, after Ming armies had conquered Shaanxi, Zhu Yuanzhang sent delegates to Tibet to try and win over local chieftains. The following year, the Ming armies conquered Hezhou—the seat of the Pacification Commission of the Yuan in Tubo. This shocked officials in Tibet, and they surrendered to the Ming administration.

---

7. Wang Shizhen, *Hami History*, in *Yanzhou Historical Records: Preliminary Collection*, vol. 8.

In AD 1373, former Tibetan leaders of Wusizang went to Nanjing to pay tribute to Zhu Yuanzhang, who granted them titles and positions. Afterward, Ming garrisons were set up in Ganduo, Wusizang, and Hezhou. Later Ganduo garrisons and Wusizang garrisons were upgraded to Ganduo Regional Military Commission and Wusizang Regional Military Commission. The governing area of Ganduo Regional Military Commission was the same as Ganduo Pacification Commission, and the governing area of Wusizang Regional Military Commission was the same as Wusizang Pacification Commission. Under these two Regional Military Commissions, there were structures such as the Commanding Officer's Office, the Pacification Commission, the Mobilization Commission, the Ten-Thousand Household Office, and the Thousand Household Office. For the Ali region in the western part of Wusizang, the Ming Dynasty also established the "Elisi Military and Civilian Marshal's Office" for administration. In the late Ming Dynasty, Ganduo Regional Military Commission and Wusizang Regional Military Commission was changed into Ganduo Pacification Commission and Wusizang Regional Military Commission respectively.

On the surface, the Regional Military Commissions set in Tibet by the Ming government was a way of military administration. However, it was those Lama chiefs of different schools who played significant roles in ruling Tibet. Therefore, the rulers of the Ming Dynasty would give these religious leaders the title of "Mentor of State" or "Buddha's son from the Western Paradise." The Ming administration let the Lamas manage Tibet according to local customs. However, they were required to attend respectively upon the Ming government. Thus, the area was largely peaceful during the entire Ming era.

6. Aboriginal Offices

Areas in Yunnan, Guizhou, Guangxi, Guangdong, and Huguang differed in natural conditions and economic development. And different ethnic groups, such as the Miao, Yao, Yi, and Dai people lived there.

In the early Ming years, Zhu Yuanzhang sent over 100,000 soldiers to appease riots in the southwestern provinces. He adopted the Aboriginal Office system of the Yuan to manage them. Ming Taizu ordered that whoever submitted themselves to the Ming could retain their positions in previous aboriginal offices.

Zhu Yuanzhang issued an order that any hereditary leaders of the southwestern minorities who came forward to submit were to be given their original official positions. To facilitate control, by the end of the Hongwu period, these aboriginal offices were divided into two systems: military aboriginal offices and civilian aboriginal offices, with the military aboriginal offices being the primary and the civilian aboriginal offices secondary. The military aboriginal offices had designations like the Xuanwei Commissioner, Xuanfu Commissioner, Anfu Commissioner, Zhaotao Commissioner, Provincial Commander, and Barbarian Commander, and they reported to the regional military command of each province, which in turn was under the jurisdiction of the central government's Ministry of War. On the other hand, the Civilian aboriginal offices had structures like the Army-Civilian Governor's Office, local state, and county offices, which reported to the regional civil administration of each province and further up to the central government's Ministry of Personnel. After the middle of the Ming Dynasty, the status of the civil aboriginal offices rose, and some could also manage the military aboriginal offices. At that time, the civil aboriginal offices of Yongchang were also responsible for several military institutions. In addition, although the distinction between military aboriginal offices and civilian aboriginal offices was clearly stipulated by the Ming government, in reality, the aboriginal officers did not follow Ming Taizu's method.

Most of the positions in aboriginal offices were hereditary, i.e., they went to local tribe chiefs. Only a few positions were available for candidates to be selected from other regions. Whoever wanted to inherit the position had to go to the capital for approval, no matter how far away it was. The responsibilities of the aboriginal officers included paying tribute to the central government, enlisting armies, and constructing new structures in the region. Whoever did not follow the laws of Ming would be punished. Management inside the region was carried out according to local customs, while the performance of local officers would first be evaluated by the aboriginal office and then reported to the Provincial Administration Commission and Provincial Surveillance Commission. Criteria of promotion was merit-based: if aboriginal officers helped Ming armies to win wars, they would be promoted, and consequently their offices would be upgraded too. In addition, the rank of the aboriginal office was also related to its geographical location and its relationship with the central government. The aboriginal offices located in the mainland relatively had a low status since they could be easily regulated by the central government; the original offices located around the border areas were rewarded with higher status. In order to effectively control local officials at all levels, the Ming government also appointed circulating officials to assist the aboriginal officers. Many jobs were held by circulating officials. A few aboriginal prefectures set up two chief governors to manage affairs of the aboriginal superior prefecture, prefecture, and county. Circulating officials were responsible for keeping the seal and managing government affairs; aboriginal offices were specialized in managing land and residents and patrolling and catching thieves.

According to the *Book of Ming · Geography*, there were chieftain-governor's offices, 47 chieftain-prefectures, and 6 chieftain-counties. Additionally, there were 11 Xuanwei Commissioner's offices, 10 Xuanfu Commissioner's offices, 22 Anfu Commissioner's offices, 1 Zhaotao Commissioner's office, 169 Provincial Commander's offices, and 5 Barbarian Commander's offices.

The aboriginal office system greatly helped to manage ethnic groups in a peaceful manner. However, there were also downsides. Since most positions were hereditary, aboriginal chiefs fought with each other for land and power. Sometimes, the feuds among them escalated to such an extent that the central government had to send armies to appease the conflicts. In areas where conflicts were extremely acute, the central government had to retrieve power from aboriginal officers. One method was to abolish the offices and replace them with the Ming's own prefecture system. The other method was to retain the aboriginal office system, but to replace its officers with. circulating officers These circulating officers were responsible for measuring the land, collecting revenue, setting up garrison and defense system, etc. Therefore, the area then became part of the local administrative division system. In AD 1413, Tian Chen, Pacification Commissioner of Sizhou (present-day Cengong, Guizhou), and Tian Zongding, Pacification Commissioner of Sinan (present-day Sinan, Guizhou), fought for land. Tian Chen declared himself "the Lord" and asked General Huang Xi to attack Zhenyuan, where the government office of Sinan Pacification Commission was located. Huang Xi killed Tian Zongding's brother and destroyed the ancestral grave of Tian Zongding's family. After Emperor Chengzu learned about it, he sent 50,000 troops to suppress the war. As a result, Tian Chen and Huang Xi were arrested in Jing (Nanjing), and Tian Zongding himself came to the capital to ask for pardon. Ming Chengzu killed them all. Later, Ming Chengzu abolished the two original offices in Sizhou and Sinan, divided them into eight superior prefectures and four prefectures, and established the Guizhou Provincial Administration Commission. In the early years of the Xuande period, Li Ying, the local chief of Yongcong, Guizhou, died without leaving an heir. The Ming government, therefore, transformed the original offices into circulating offices. During the Jiajing period, two aboriginal officers in Longzhou tried to kill each other. After the Ming Dynasty appeased the incident, the aboriginal offices in that place were also transformed into circulating offices. During the Wanli period, after the Ming Dynasty suppressed the rebellion of the Bozhou chieftain Yang Yinglong, they established two administrative units, Zunyi and Pingyue, which were subordinated to Sichuan and Guizhou provinces respectively.

However, it should be noted that the aboriginal officers had been inherited from generation to generation and had a deep-rooted influence in the local. Therefore, when the Ming Dynasty carried out this transforming policy, some aboriginal officers strongly resisted it. For example, during the reign of Emperor Xiaozong, circulating offices were set up in Mahu Prefecture in Sichuan Province. By the early years of the Jiajing period, there had been two attempts of transforming aboriginal offices into circulating offices in that place. However, the outcome was still "despite the appointment of official administrators, the native aboriginal offices continued to rebel, and the acts of killing and land seizure became even more severe than before."[8] As a result, the Ming government had to restore the Aboriginal office in that place. Therefore, the transformation of aboriginal offices was off to a shaky start. It was not until the middle of the Qing Dynasty that the government could implement it on a large scale. Some aboriginal offices even remained until the Republican Period.

7. Nine Frontiers of the Great Wall

The Nine Frontiers referred to the nine garrisons on the northern borders of the Ming Empire. After Ming was established, nomadic tribes often invaded its northern territory. Ming Taizu sent troops to the North several times. Even his

---

8. Gu Yanwu, "Sichuan," in *Book on the Strengths and Weaknesses of the Provinces and States of the World*, vol. 69.

sons, including Zhu Di and Zhu Quan, were given princedoms to guard these frontiers. When Zhu Di became Emperor Chengzu, he sent troops to Mobei five times and set up garrisons there.

At first, the Ming administration established four garrisons along its northern frontiers. Later five more garrisons were added. Collectively they were called the Nine Frontiers. Details are below:

Name of the frontier	Seat	Present-day
Liaodong	First Guangning, then Liaoyang	Liaoyang, Liaoning
Xuanfu	Xuanfu Garrison	Xuanhua, Hebei
Datong	Datong	Datong, Shanxi
Yansui	First Suidezhou, Yulin Garrison	Yulin, Shaanxi
Ningxia	Ningixa Garrison	Yinchuan, Ningxia
Gansu	Ganzhou Garrison	Zhangye, Gansu
Jizhou	Santun Garrison	Northwest of Qianxi, Hebei
Shanxi/Taiyuan	First Pianguan, then Ningwu	Shanxi
Guyuan	Guyuan Prefecture	Guyuan, Ningxia

The Nine Frontiers spread along the Great Wall, starting from Yalu River in the East to Jiayuguan in the West. Yansui, Gansu and Ningxia Garrisons were named the "Three Frontiers," with the seat in Guyuan, Ningxia.

Each of the Nine Frontiers had a chief commander, managing several auxiliary staff, such as the Deputy Commander-in-chief, Assistant General, Guerilla General, Garrison Commander, Leader of a Thousand, and Leader of a Group, etc. Those who guard a region are called "Zhen Shou" (Main Defender), those who independently guard a strategic passage are termed "Fen Shou" (Partitioned Defender), and those who guard a single city or fortress are referred to as "Shou Bei" (Garrison Commander). Those who co-guard a city with the main general are called "Xie Shou" (Co-Defender). In addition, there are also officials with titles like "Ti Du" (Commander overseeing multiple regions), "Ti Diao" (Senior Military Inspector), "Xun Shi" (Patrolling Inspector), and "Bei Yu" (Imperial Guard). A large number of troops were stationed in the garrisons in every place. According to historical records, around 600,000 soldiers were deployed in the nine garrisons during the era of Emperor Shenzong. In addition, there were also a great number of circulating troops. For example, there were 30,000 official soldiers in the Jizhou garrison during the Longqing period. However, there were more than 165,000 soldiers, including circulating troops, by the beginning of the Wanli period.

At first, food and other logistics were provided by state farms on the frontiers. Later, in the era of Emperor Yingzong, the Imperial Granaries became the major logistics provider. The following is a detailed description: 430,000 *liang* (AD 1488–1505; AD 1506–1521), 2,700,000 *liang* (AD 1522–1566), and 3,800,000 *liang* (AD 1573–1620). The annual provisions to the nine frontiers were almost the same as the annual revenue of the Ming administration. This was one of the major reasons why the central government's fiscal budget was tight.

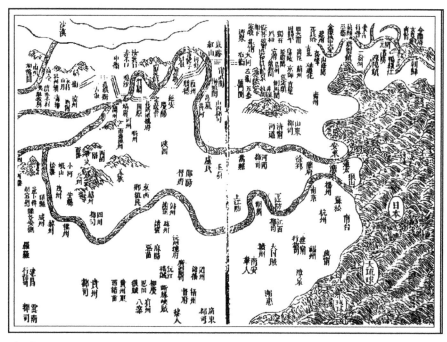

The "Nine Frontiers" of the Ming Dynasty

Year	Annual provisions/liang (兩)
AD 1488–1505	430,000
AD 1506–1521	430,000
AD 1522–1566	2,700,000
AD 1573–1620	3,800,000

The annual provisions to the nine frontiers were almost the same as the annual revenue of the Ming administration. This was one of the major reasons why the central government's fiscal budget was tight. The frontiers along the Great Wall strengthened the territorial security of the Ming Empire. However, its maintenance also cost a fortune and became a great burden on the Ming administration as well as its people. On the other hand, many officers exploited the provisions. As a result, soldiers at the bottom often received nothing or very little, leading to mutiny.

CHAPTER NINE

THE EMPIRE IN THE SHAPE OF A MULBERRY LEAF

—Territories and Administrative Divisions in the Qing Dynasty

1. Unification of Qing Territories

In AD 1583, Nurhaci, tribe chieftain of Nüzhen, rose to power and started conquering other neighboring tribes. He was previously Regional Military Commissioner of Zuo Garrison, governing an area of Shuzi River in Liaoning. After Nurhaci defeated the other tribes and conquered eastern Mongolia, he established the Kingdom of Jin and proclaimed himself as Khan, with his capital in Hetu Ala (east of Xinbin, Liaoning). It was known in history as Later Jin.

In AD 1617, Nurhaci turned against the Ming Dynasty. Two years later, his armies occupied the Liaodong area of Ming. In AD 1625, Nurhaci moved his capital to Shenyang and named it "Shengjing" (盛京). The following year, his son, Hong Taiji, became his successor. In AD 1635, Hong Taiji renamed Nüzhen as Manchu. In the next year, he proclaimed himself Emperor Taizong of Qing. In AD 1643, Qing expanded to the north of the Great Wall, covering an area of modern Inner Mongolia, Northwestern China, and the outer Khingan Range (from Lake Baikal in the East to Sakhalin Island in the West). After Hong Taiji died, his son became the Shunzhi Emperor with his uncle Dorgon as regent. They continued to invade the Ming.

In AD 1644, a rebel leader called Li Zicheng and his troops conquered Beijing. Emperor Sizong of Ming committed suicide, bringing an end to the Ming

Dynasty. The Shanhaiguan Regional Commander called in the Qing armies and defeated Li Zicheng. In May of the same year, Beijing was taken by the Qing. In September, the Shunzhi Emperor arrived in Beijing, and in October he became Emperor Shizu and named Beijing his capital. This marked the beginning of the Qing reign in China, which would go on to last for the next 260 years.

Afterward, Qing armies continued to wipe out the rest of Li Zicheng's forces. In AD 1659, they conquered Yunnan and the local chief fled to Myanmar. Until then, the Qing Empire had kept to "China Proper."

2. The 18 Provinces and Their Subordinate Administrative Divisions

Usually, a dynasty would change the administrative divisions of the previous regime. However, the Qing was an exception. It accepted the basic structures of the Ming and made few changes.

After being established, it renamed previous provincial commissions as provinces, which were the top level of local administrative divisions. The Qing administration kept the 13 provinces of the Ming Dynasty, but changed North Zhili (北直隸) to Zhili Province in AD 1644.

The following year, it changed South Zhili (南直隸) to Jiangnan Province. In the era of the Kangxi Emperor (reign: AD 1662–1722), some provinces were divided into smaller ones as Emperor thought some were too large to manage. For example, Jiangnan was divided into Jiangsu and Anhui, while Huguang Province was divided into Hubei and Hunan. In total there were 18 provinces in China Proper.

The structure of 18 provinces in China lasted for over 200 years, from the Kangxi Emperor until the Tongzhi Emperor (reign: AD 1861–1875). Details are as follows:

a. Zhili Province: Its seat was first in Zhendingfu. In AD 1669, the Kangxi Emperor moved it to Baoding. Its northern territory had expanded further than in the Ming Dynasty.
b. Jiangsu Province: In the early years of the Qing it was called Jiangnan Province, with its seat in Jiangningfu (present-day Nanjing). In AD 1667,

the Kangxi Emperor divided Jiangnan into two parts. The eastern half became Jiangsu, with its seat in Suzhoufu (present-day Suzhou).

c. Anhui Province: In AD 1667, when Jiangnan Province was divided, the western half became Anhui Province, with its first seat in Jiangningfu. In AD 1760, the seat was moved to Anqingfu.

d. Shanxi Province: Its seat was in Taiyuanfu.

e. Shandong Province: Its seat was in Jinanfu. Liaodong Dusi in the previous Ming Dynasty had been excluded from this province.

f. Henan Province: Its seat was in Kaifengfu.

g. Shaanxi Province: In AD 1663, the previous Shaanxi Province was divided into half. The eastern part was still called Shaanxi, with its seat in Xi'anfu.

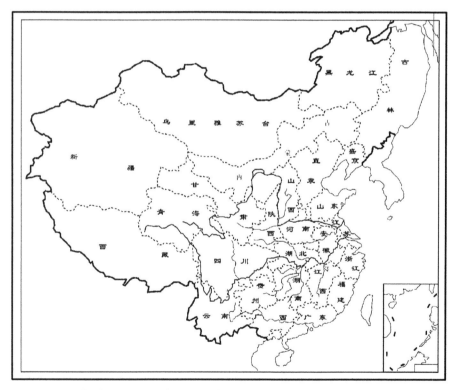

Territories and administrative divisions of China in AD 1820[1]

---

1. Sketchmap based on Tan Qixiang, *Atlas in Chinese History* (Beijing: SinoMaps Press, 1982).

h. Gansu Province: In AD 1663, when the previous Shaanxi was divided, its western part became Gongchang Province. Five years later, it was renamed as Gansu. Its seat was first at Lintao. In AD 1738, its seat moved to Lanzhoufu.
i. Zhejiang Province: Its seat was in Hangzhou.
j. Fujian Province: Its seat was in Fuzhoufu. In AD 1684, Taiwan and the Penghu Islands were merged into Fujian. In AD 1885, Taiwan was severed from Fujian and became Taiwan Province.
k. Jiangxi Province: Its seat was in Nanchangfu.
l. Hubei Province: In AD 1664, Huguang Province was divided into two parts. The northern part became Hubei. Its seat was in Wuchangfu (present-day Wuhan).
m. Hunan Province: In AD 1664, Huguang Province was divided into two parts. The southern part became Hunan. Its seat was in Changshafu.
n. Guangdong Province: Its seat was in Guangzhoufu.
o. Guangxi Province: Its seat was in Guilinfu.
p. Sichuan Province: Its seat was in Chengdufu. Compared to its previous size in the Ming Dynasty, its western part had expanded, while its southern part was diminished.
q. Yunnan Province: Its seat was in Yunnanfu (present-day Kunming). Compared to its previous size in Ming Dynasty, it had expanded its northeast part. In the era of Emperor Guangxu (AD 1871–1908), some counties in its western part, such as Chashan, Maliba, Tiebi, Huju, Tianma and Hanlong became part of Myanmar, then Burma. Two aboriginal offices in Yunnan's southern part, Wude and Mengwu, became part of Jiaozhi (present-day Vietnam).
r. Guizhou Province: Its seat was in Guiyangfu. Compared to its previous size in the Ming Dynasty, it had expanded its territory in the northwest.

The names and governing areas of the 18 provinces in the Qing Dynasty were not much different from China today. In modern China, we additionally have Taiwan, Ningxia, and Hainan provinces, and four direct metropolitan cities: Beijing, Tianjin, Shanghai, and Chongqing.

Not only did the Qing inherit the administrative divisions of the Ming, but they also copied the officialdom system. The Qing set supreme commanders and governors as the top-ranking local administrative officers and matched their governing areas with provisional territories. However, in the Ming Dynasty, the chief governor of a Province was the Provincial Administration Commissioner, not the Grand Coordinator or Supreme Commander. Therefore, Province was not the highest level of administrative division in the Qing Dynasty, but rather an informal or colloquial term.

Generally speaking, every supreme commander would govern two or three provinces. They were in charge of military affairs, civil affairs, and supervision over local officers. In the era of the Qianlong Emperor (reign: AD 1736–1796), the number of supreme commanders were finalized to eight, governing Zhili, Liangjiang, Minzhe, Shaangan, Huguang, Liangguang, Sichuan, and Yungui respectively. However, their governing areas did not cover the 18 provinces in China Proper. For example, there were no supreme commanders in Shandong, Shanxi, and Henan provinces. Instead, these provinces were ruled by governors. Usually, a governor was responsible for civil affairs in only one Province. However, there were also exceptions. For example, there were no governors in Zhili, Sichuan, and Gansu. Therefore, there were 15 governors seated in Shandong, Shanxi, Henan, Shaanxi, Jiangsu, Anhui, Zhejiang, Fujian, Jiangxi, Hubei, Hunan, Guangdong, Guangxi, Yunnan, and Guizhou.

Taking into account the fact that supreme commanders and governors had great power, the Qing administration saw to it that Manchu appointees took most positions. In the era of the Kangxi Emperor, the number of Han appointed to such posts would only account for 20 to 30 percent of the total. In the era of the Qianlong Emperor, Manchu and Han shared half the governor posts, but the Manchu still occupied most supreme commander positions. In the era of the Xianfeng Emperor (reign: AD 1850–1861), more and more Han Chinese were appointed in a bid to quell the Taiping Movement.

The Inspector and Grand Commander are assisted by officials in each province, namely the Provincial Administration Commission (also known as the Fan Office) and the Supervisory Commissioner (also known as the Niao Office). The original position of the Commander-in-chief set up by the Ming Dynasty at the local level was abolished due to the elimination of the military garrison system. Provincial Administration Commissions was responsible for civil affairs and finance; the Provincial Surveillance Commission was responsible for judicial administration. After the middle of the Qing Dynasty, the Provincial Administration Commission and the Provincial Surveillance Commission became a subordinate organization of the Grand Coordinator and Supreme Commander. In addition, every Province could only set up one Provincial Administration Commission. However, there were two Provincial Administration Commissions in Jiangsu Province. The Jiangsu Provincial Administration Commission was the first one set in Jiangsu Province with its seat in Suzhoufu. In AD 1760, Jiangning Provincial Surveillance Commission was set up with its seat in Jiangningfu. Therefore, Suzhoufu and Jiangningfu became the two provincial capitals of Jiangsu Province.

The officials of the Provincial Administration Commission and Provincial Surveillance Commission were called "Daoyuan" (magistrates of the circuit). The Daoyuan of the Provincial Administration Commission resided in a certain place with a fixed jurisdiction, and they were in charge of the financial affairs; Daoyuan of Provincial Surveillance Commission patrolled different places and were in charge of criminal cases. After the Qianlong period, even though the Circuit officers transitioned from temporary appointments to official local posts, the Circuit did not actually become a primary administrative division. Instead, it can only be termed as a quasi-administrative level. Besides the primary and inspection Circuits, the Qing Dynasty also established numerous specialized Circuit officers without specific territorial divisions in each province, such as the Grain-supply Circuit, Salt Regulation Circuit, River Circuit, Postal Circuit, and Customs Circuit.

The Qing administrative divisions went back to the three-layer hierarchy. Under the Province, there were Fu (Zhili Prefecture / Zhili Sub-Prefecture). Counties were at the bottom of the system.

The head of Fu was called Prefect. Shuntianfu was located in the capital and Fengtianfu was located in the auxiliary capital. The head officers of Shuntianfu and Fengtianfu were called Fuyin, meaning Prefect of a superior prefecture. A prefect was responsible for the government affairs of a superior prefecture. The prefect had to report government affairs to the grand coordinator and supreme commander before seeing that they were carried out. The supporting officials for the Prefect include the Associate Prefect, Assistant Prefect, and Prosecutor. In the middle period of Emperor Yongzheng's reign, there were 167 superior prefectures in China. During the reign of Emperor Qianlong, this number increased to 184. In AD 1899, it increased to 187. By the end of the Qing Dynasty, there were more than 200 superior prefectures across China.

In the early years of the Qing Dynasty, the notary of the administrative assistant and the military judge was appointed to supervise affairs in superior prefectures. After some time, Ting became a new genre of administrative divisions in the Qing Dynasty. It was not suitable to set up prefectures and counties in areas inhabited by ethnic minorities in the border areas. Instead, the Qing government set up Ting in these areas. Therefore, the notary of the administrative assistant or the military judge became the chief governor of Ting. Ting fell into two categories: one was called Zhili Ting (literally meaning directly attached), and the other was called San Ting. The former was under the supervision of the Provincial Administrative Commission. Its level was at the same rank as Fu or Zhili prefectures. At the end of Emperor Guangxu's reign (AD 1875–1908), there were over 100 Ting.

State also fell into two categories. One was called Zhili State, and the other San State. The former was under the supervision of the provincial administrative commission. It was at the same level as Fu, only smaller in size. San State was governed by a superior prefecture and had the same level as the county. The chief administrator of Zhili State and San State was called "Zhizhou" responsible for the affairs of a prefecture. The supporting officials include the Associate Magistrate and Assistant Magistrate, who are responsible for matters related to grain management, water conservancy, coastal defense, and river management. By the end of Guangxu, there were more than 200 Zhili State and San State in China.

Counties were at the bottom of all administrative organizations. The head of the county was called "Zhixian" (district magistrate), who was regarded as a "parent official" of the local people and directly governed people in his district. Anything concerned with tax, jurisdiction, and education were all within his responsibilities. By the end of the Qing, there were 1,358 counties.

3. Transforming Aboriginal Offices into Circulating Offices

In the early years of the Qing, the aboriginal officers did not pose a threat. After serious consideration, the central government decided to keep the status quo. Furthermore, the Qing administration also recruited some tribal leaders and appointed them as new aboriginal officers.

However, the central government still kept a wary eye on this. After the unification of China, some aboriginal office land had expanded to over hundreds of miles, with soldiers exceeding 10,000. And many aboriginal officers did not obey the laws. These were a bone of contention with the Qing government. Emperor Yongzheng was determined to resolve this. His solution was to transform aboriginal offices in southwest China into circulating offices—where officers were appointed by the central government and served for limited terms.

In the fourth year of the Yongzheng reign (AD 1726), E'ertai, the Governor-General of Yunnan and Guizhou, submitted several memorials to Emperor Yongzheng, emphatically arguing for the abolition of the aboriginal officer (local chieftain) system and the implementation of the "conversion of aboriginal officer territories to regular administrative regions" policy. He also provided specific methods on how to carry out this transition. Emperor Yongzheng adopted E'ertai's suggestions and entrusted him with the responsibility of overseeing the transition.

In May of the fourth year of the Yongzheng reign (AD 1726), E'ertai led the troops to first quell the rebellion of the aboriginal officer of Changzhai in Guizhou, establishing Changzhai Hall (present-day Changshun in Guizhou). This event marked the beginning of the policy implementation of "conversion of aboriginal officer territories to regular administrative regions" during the Yongzheng era. Soon after, E'ertai dispatched Ha Yuansheng with troops to crush the rebel forces of the aboriginal officer of Wumeng in Sichuan, Lu Wanzhong, and the aboriginal officer of Zhenxiong, Long Qinghou. These areas were subsequently reorganized into Wumeng Prefecture (present-day Zhaotong in Yunnan) and Zhenxiong County, placed under the jurisdiction of Yunnan, with officials appointed by the central government to administer them. The sweeping reforms in Yunnan and Guizhou quickly affected Guangxi. To facilitate a coordinated implementation of the reforms across Yunnan, Guizhou, and Guangxi, Emperor Yongzheng specially appointed E'ertai as the Governor-General of all three provinces in the sixth year of his reign. That same year, Zhang Guangsi, the provincial inspector of Guizhou, was ordered to carry out the reforms in southeastern Guizhou. Leading his troops, Zhang penetrated villages inhabited by the Miao and Dong ethnic groups, establishing administrative halls and assigning officials to handle local civil affairs. In Guangxi, a region densely populated by the Zhuang people, Cen Yingchen, the aboriginal officer of Sicity, was particularly overbearing. The Qing government forcibly confiscated his official seal and relocated him to Zhejiang.

The aboriginal officer of Simingzhou, Huang Guanzhu, unable to control various village leaders within his domain, voluntarily requested the Qing government to transfer the administration of fifty villages, including Donglang, to direct central governance. aboriginal officer from places like Liuzhou, Sien, and Qingyuan in Guangxi also succumbed to local pressures demanding reforms and surrendered their weapons to the Qing government. As a result, most of Guangxi's aboriginal officer regions underwent the conversion process. Under the circumstances, the aboriginal officer in neighboring provinces like Hunan, Hubei, and Sichuan, which bordered Yunnan, Guizhou, and Guangxi, also voluntarily ceded their hereditary territories and seals to the central government. By the ninth year of Yongzheng (AD 1731), most of the aboriginal officer regions in the southwestern areas had been transformed into jurisdictions governed by officials directly appointed by the central government. The Qing Dynasty, besides establishing new administrative regions, also introduced military establishments in these areas, conducted a census, surveyed the land, and levied taxes.

However, some high-ranking aboriginal officers were dissatisfied with the transformation and dreamt that the aboriginal officers would one day be restored. At that time, some Qing soldiers had lax military discipline, and the local people were deeply bothered by them. Meanwhile, some newly appointed circulating officers were inexperienced and were not good at management. Some officers even demanded bribes. Therefore, these discontented aboriginal officers thought that it was the right time to restore the aboriginal offices, and they rebelled against the government. In AD 1735, some nobles of the Miao tribes solicited locals in Guzhou and Taigong of Guizhou to rebel against the central government. Emperor Yongzheng sent troops but did not manage to quell the rebels. It wasn't until AD 1736 that they were defeated. Yongzheng's son, the Qianlong Emperor, learned a lesson. He decided not to collect taxes in newly annexed areas, and in the meantime adopted local customs in terms of judicial affairs. These efforts paid off.

Only aboriginal offices in southwest China became circulating offices during the Yongzheng era. Not only did it significantly strengthen the centralization of the Qing government, but also lessened the burden on locals and helped economic development in border minority areas to some extent.

4. THREE GENERALS IN SHENGJING (THREE PROVINCES IN NORTHEAST CHINA)

In the early years of the Qing, its northeastern part covered an area from the Outer Khingan Range in the North to Shanhaiguan. Its eastern border reached to the sea and Sakhalin Island. This region was where the Manchu tribe came to power. In AD 1644, the Shunzhi Emperor decided to relocate his capital from Sheng-Jing to Beijing. The following year, Sheng-Jing became the auxiliary capital.

In AD 1646, the title of internal affairs minister was renamed Angbang Zhangjing (Manchu language for Chief Secretary). The central government appointed Ye Keshu as the Chief Secretary. In AD 1650, Russians sent Cossack tribes to invade China's Heilongjiang area and occupied Jaxa Fortress. Two years later, the Russians asked the Qing government for land in Heilongjiang. At that time, the Qing's main focus was the fighting in South China. Some troops in the South were called back to fight against the Cossacks.

In AD 1653, Sarhuda was appointed as Angbang Zhangjing, with his seat in the Ningguta area to strengthen Qing's reign in the Heilongjiang and Ussuri River regions. Ningguta (Ning'an) was located on the upper reaches of Mudan River and was of strategic military importance. By then, there were two military secretaries in Northeast China. In AD 1654, Qing armies retrieved the Jaxa Fortress and in AD 1660 the Shunzhi Emperor drove out most of the Russian invaders.

In AD 1662, Shunzhi's son—the Kangxi Emperor—renamed Angbang Zhangjing in Sheng-Jing as general in the Liaodong region, and Ningguta Angbang Zhangjing as general in Ningguta. Russian invaders once again sent troops to the east of Lake Baikal and occupied Jaxa Fortress in AD 1665. When the Kangxi Emperor started to rule without a regent, he was faced with the task of retrieving Jaxa Fortress and driving out the Russian invaders. In AD 1681, when the Qing government had appeased the rebels in southwest China, it shifted its focus to the North. The following year, the Kangxi Emperor went in person to the Songhua River area and sent delegates to inspect Jaxa.

In AD 1683, the Kangxi Emperor added the post of Heilongjiang General. Former vice commander-in-chief Sabusu became the first appointee, with his seat in Aihui (瑷珲), governing an area from the West bank of the Songhua to the Outer Khingan Range. The East bank of the Songhua still belonged to the reign of the Ningguta General. Hence, there were altogether three generals in northeastern China—namely Heilongjiang, Ningguta, and Fengtian.

In addition, the Qing government set up 19 postal stations along the way from Aihui to Jilin, stretching 1340 *li*. Furthermore, officers were sent to build warships in Jilin. Waterways were repaired and maintained between the major rivers of the region. All these efforts guaranteed the smooth transportation of food and military supplies.

In the spring of AD 1685, the Kangxi Emperor decided it was time to fight back. Peng Chun was appointed Chief Commander and ordered troops to advance on Jaxa by land and water. Qing armies blocked the river with warships and fired cannons into the fortress, forcing the Russian armies to surrender. The Kangxi Emperor released some 600 captives back to Russia. Then the Qing armies burned the Jaxa Fortress and left for Aihui. However, the Russians came back despite promising not to.

In AD 1686, Qing armies surrounded Jaxa and the Russians in the fortress once more. The Russian Czar therefore sent delegates to Beijing to negotiate on the settlement of borders. On orders from the Kangxi Emperor, the Qing armies retreated. On August 22, AD 1689, the Qing and Russian governments began negotiations. After 16 days of debate, the Qing government made concessions and signed the Treaty of Nerchinsk, which settled the borders between the two countries. However, complications remained between who claimed exactly what territory.

The border lines ran through Honkirnaur, Shileka River, Ge'erbiqi River and Outer Khingan Range. The areas to the north of Heilongjiang River, to the south of Outer Khingan Range, and to the east of Ussuri River, including Sakhalin Island, were all part of Qing Empire. Hence, the Russians legally occupied the land stretching from Lake Baikal to Nerchinsk, which formerly belonged to China. The areas to the south of Ussuri River and to the north of Outer Khingan Range were left unclear, because by then Qing government had not appease the rebels in Outer Mongolia.

In AD 1712, the Qing government helped draw distinct borders with Korea. A stone monument was erected on the southern watershed of the Changbai Mountains, stating that the Yalu and Tumen Rivers formed the borders between Sheng-Jing and Korea.

In AD 1727, during the fifth year of the Yongzheng reign, the Qing Dynasty and Russia signed the Treaty of Kyakhta and the Treaty of Burinsk. These agreements delineated the border between Outer Mongolia and Siberia in Russia: starting from the confluence of the Argun River and its tributary, the Kherlen River (now the Hailar River), at Abagaitu, passing through Chakhtu (now within Russian territory as Chakhtu and within Mongolian territory as Altanbulag), and extending westward to the Sayan Mountains at Sharavinda Bahar (alternative name: Sharavenda Bahan) in present-day Western Sayan Mountains, Russia.

In AD 1757, the Qianlong Emperor renamed General Ningguta as the Jilinwula General—the General of Jilin.

In the era of Emperor Daoguang (AD 1821–1850), the Russians broke the Treaty of Nerchinsk and occupied the southern part of Wudi River. In AD 1858, during the Second Opium War, the Russians forced Yi Shan, then-Heilongjiang General, to sign the treaty of Aihui, which conceded a great portion of land to the west of Heilongjiang River. The Qing government refused to recognize the treaty at first, but was forced to two years later by signing the Treaty of Beijing. This treaty between Russia and China further confiscated Chinese land between the Khanka Lake and Tumen River. The following year, boundary tablets were erected on the borders. In AD 1886, several boundary tablets were relocated because of concessions made by the Qing government.

In AD 1900, eight allied forces invaded China. They were Japan, Russia, Britain, France, the United States, Germany, Italy, and Austria-Hungary. The Russians occupied the northeast of China and drove out Chinese inhabitants by force.

Strait of Tartary used to be governed by vice commanders-in-chief of three Banners in Jinlin Province. However, the Qing government did not manage the areas well, aside from collecting tributes. It didn't even know when the Russians and Japanese had invaded the island. In AD 1850, the Russians proclaimed the Sakhalin Islands to be its territory. When the Treaty of Beijing was signed, the Qing government did not make any objections, thus sort of recognizing Russian occupation of the island. In AD 1875, the island fell completely into Russian's hands. In AD 1875, Sakhalin was completely occupied by Russia. After the Japan-Russian War in AD 1905, Russia ceded the island areas south of latitude 50° N to Japan.

After the Russo-Japanese War, the situation in the Northeast region of China became increasingly complex. On April 20th, in the 33rd year of the Guangxu reign (AD 1907), the Qing government reorganized the jurisdictions previously under the three generals of Fengtian, Jilin, and Heilongjiang. They established three provinces, colloquially referred to as the "Three Eastern Provinces": Fengtian, Jilin, and Heilongjiang. Each province was overseen by a governor, and there was also a Governor-General appointed to oversee all three provinces. The Governor-General and the governor of Fengtian were based in Fengtian Prefecture (present-day Shenyang in Liaoning Province). The governor of Jilin was stationed in Jilin Prefecture (present-day Jilin City in Jilin Province), and the governor of Heilongjiang was based in Longjiang Prefecture (present-day Qiqihar in Heilongjiang Province). Due to some pasturelands from the Jirem Mengin Inner Mongolia being incorporated, there were some changes in the jurisdictions of the three provinces.

5. GENERAL OF ILI (XINJIANG PROVINCE)

At the end of the Ming Dynasty, Mongolia was divided into three parts: Monan Mongolia, Mobei Khalkha Mongols, and Moxi Olot Mongolia. In the early years of the Qing, Monan and Mobei Mongolia yielded to the central government and paid annual tributes. They were then called Inner Mongolia and Outer Mongolia.

The Moxi Mongolia was divided into four Weilate (tribes). Among them, the Dzungar was the strongest. In AD 1677, Khungtaidschi Galdan, Khan of Dzungar, occupied the northern part of what would be modern Xinjiang. Later he sent troops to southern Xinjiang, and controlled both the northern and southern regions of the Tianshan Mountains. In expanding his territory, Khungtaidschi Galdan invaded the Mobei Mongolia. Afterward, with support from the Russians, he continued to march into Monan Mongolia, and went as far as Wulanbutong (present-day Chifeng, Inner Mongolia).

The Kangxi Emperor decided to fight against Khungtaidschi Galdan. In AD 1690 and AD 1696, the Emperor himself led the Qing army and defeated Khungtaidschi Galdan in Wulanbutong and Zhaomoduo. In AD 1697, he led his armies to fight against Khungtaidschi Galdan for the third time. Galdan lost the battle in Ningxia and committed suicide by drinking poison. His tribe was also significantly weakened after an inner mutiny in AD 1745.

From AD 1755 to AD 1759, the Qianlong Emperor unified both northern and southern sides of the Tianshan mountains, and renamed the Western Regions as Xinjiang. The Qing government ruled Xinjiang by separating civil affairs from military affairs. In AD 1762, the position of Ili General was created. The general was the top officer in Xinjiang, governing all military affairs in the region. His seat was in Huiyuan (present-day Huocheng). In terms of civil affairs in the region, the Qing administration governed according to different local customs. For example, in the northern region of Mount Tianshan, two administrative divisions were set up, subordinate to Gansu Province.

In AD 1771, the Mongolian Hute tribe returned to the Ili district. The Qing administration copied the systems of Inner and Outer Mongolia and implemented the Zhasake (chiefs of different banners in Mongolia) system among the Hute.

After the Ili General was set up, the Qing administration moved thousands of immigrants to Ili for state farming. This was to strengthen its reign in the area. Many villages appeared, and the immigrants greatly developed agriculture and animal husbandry. The migration operations mainly included: 1,800 soldiers were relocated from Zhangjiakou to the Borotara River and Salim Lake in the northwest of Ili; 1,000 soldiers were relocated from Heilongjiang to the Xikuitun, Samaer, Horgos, and other river regions in Ili; 500 soldiers were relocated from Rehe (present-day Chengde, Hebei) to the Chalin and Tekes Rivers in the southwest of Ili; 1,000 soldiers were relocated from Shengjing (present-day Shenyang, Liaoning) to Chabuchaer in the south of Ili; 6,500 soldiers were relocated from Rehe area and other places in Xi'an to the Bayandai area of Ili; 3,000 soldiers were relocated from Shaanxi and Gansu to Talchi, Wuerlike, and Chahanwusu; 6,000 Uighur farmers were relocated from cities in southern Xinjiang to Guerzha and Hainuke region.

After these migrations, many villages were built in the north of the Ili River. Their tents were everywhere. Agriculture and husbandry in this area had been greatly developed. From AD 1761 to 1780, with Huiyuan City as the center, the Qing government established eight satellite states: Suiding (present-day Huocheng County), Taleqi (present-day Taerji in Huocheng), Zhande (present-day Qingshuihezi in Huocheng), Guangren (present-day Lucaogou in Huocheng), Gongchen (present-day Huocheng County in Huocheng), Huining (present-day Bayandai in Yining), Xichun (present-day northwest of Yining), and Ningyuan (present-day Yining). Each satellite state also set up officials and troops. These states were known as the "Nine States of Ili."

The Empire in the Shape of a Mulberry Leaf | 233

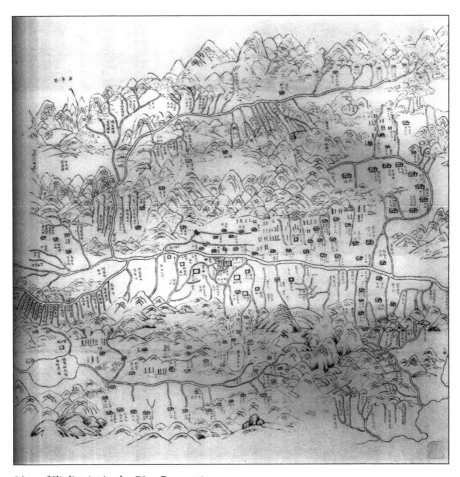

Map of Ili district in the Qing Dynasty[2]

---

2. Liu Zhenwei, *A Collection of Maps in Ancient China* (Beijing: China World Language Press, 1995).

In the mid-19th century, Russians took advantage of mutinies in Xinjiang and invaded Ili. In AD 1851, they obtained the right to set up consulates and do business in Ili and Tacheng. In AD 1860, the Treaty of Beijing stated that the western boundary between China and Russia in Xinjiang was established as follows: "Starting from Shabindaba, going to Zaisang Lake, then southwest to Temurtu Lake, and then south to Khovd as the boundary." In this way, the land that originally belonged to the Qing government, stretching from the southeast of Lake Balkhash to Temurtu Lake, was ceded to Russia. In AD 1864, the Treaty of Tacheng stated that the land east and south of Lake Balkhash was to be ceded to Russia too. People in Ili and Tacheng suffered greatly due to the invasion. However, just after this boundary was established, Russia took advantage of the situation in Central Asia, where the military leader of the Khanate of Khiva (located in present-day Uzbekistan), Agubat, established the "Yedisan" (meaning the "Seven City State"). In the 10th year of the Tongzhi reign (AD 1871), Russia occupied the Ili region in Xinjiang.

In AD 1877, Zuo Zongtang, Chief Commander of Shanxi and Gansu, was sent to Xinjiang to head military affairs in the region. Zuo's armies retrieved all the land in Xinjiang except Ili. Zuo requested that the Russians leave, but was refused. In AD 1881, the Qing government and Russia signed the Treaty of Ili. According to this treaty, the Russians would return Ili to the Qing government, but the Qing had to cede land to the west of the Horgos River to Russia in return and opened up the entire territory of Xinjiang. Ever since, the political center of Xinjiang was moved from Ili to the east of the region.

Before Zuo led his troops to Xinjiang, he proposed to set up a Province in Xinjiang which followed the same administration as China Proper. After Ili was retrieved, Zuo Zongtang, then-Chief Commander of Liangjiang, submitted a report titled "Urgent Proposal on the Establishment of Xinjiang as a Province and the Difficulties in Reducing the Defense Forces Outside the Pass" to the Eemperor on the importance of this. His proposals were accepted by the Qing government, and his efforts paid off. In AD 1883, Emperor Guangxu abolished the special border positions established in the early years and set up the Province with prefectures and counties. There were four Circuits, six Fus, two Zhili prefectures, eight Zhili sub-prefectures, one prefecture, and twenty-one counties. The provincial seat was located in Dihuafu (present-day Urumqi), and the General of Ili's seat was in Huiyuan. In 1913, Ili finally became a part of Xinjiang.

The set-up of Xinjiang Province unified the Western Regions of China. With bans on immigration lifted, and the administrative system integrated with the rest of China, communications between Xinjiang and China Proper were greatly enhanced. As a result, both economy and culture in the region developed further.

6. Tibet and Qinghai Territories

(1) Grand Minister Superintendent of Tibet

After the Qing Dynasty replaced the Ming Dynasty, it exercised more rigorous governance over the Tibet region, further institutionalizing and legalizing the exercise of sovereign jurisdiction by the central government in Tibet. In the early Qing Dynasty, Emperor Shunzhi invited the 5th Dalai Lama to Beijing several times. In the ninth year of Shunzhi (AD 1652), the Dalai Lama visited Beijing and was warmly received by Emperor Shunzhi. Considering the Dalai Lama's accommodation during his stay in Beijing, Shunzhi had a grand Yellow Temple constructed for him. The following year, Shunzhi Emperor granted a golden book and a golden seal, officially naming the Dalai Lama as "the great benevolent self-existing Buddha from the Western Heaven leading the worldly Buddhist teachings, universally known as Vajradhara Dalai Lama." This formally established the title of the Dalai Lama and his political and religious status in Tibet. In the 52nd year of Kangxi (AD 1713), Emperor Kangxi also conferred the title of "Banchan Erdeni" on the 5th Panchen Lama, Lobsang Yeshe, who was stationed in Shigatse, formally determining the title of the Panchen Lama. Thus, the theocratic governance system in Tibet was officially recognized by the Qing Dynasty, which also established the Qing Dynasty's ruling position in Tibet.

During the late Ming Dynasty, the power of the Mongolian leader Güshi Khan had already extended into Tibet. Therefore, after the death of the fifth Dalai Lama, Tibet was under the joint rule of Lha-bzang Khan, the grandson of Güshi Khan, and the Tibetan Regent Sanggye Gyatso. In this period, there was a contentious dispute within the Tibetan ruling class regarding the true identity of the sixth Dalai Lama. Two candidates emerged: Tsangyang Gyatso, supported by Sanggye Gyatso, and Yeshe Gyatso, backed by Lha-bzang Khan. This disagreement led to significant unrest in the Tibetan political landscape. In AD 1705, during the 44th year of Emperor Kangxi's reign, Sanggye Gyatso plotted to poison Lha-bzang

Khan and expel the Mongolian influence from Tibet. However, his scheme was exposed, and he was subsequently defeated and killed by Lha-bzang Khan. By AD 1717, during the 56th year of Kangxi's reign, subordinates of Sanggye Gyatso collaborated with the Dzungar tribe from Xinjiang, assassinating Lha-bzang Khan and plunging Tibet into chaos. To ensure the unity of the country and stabilize the situation in Tibet, Emperor Kangxi dispatched his 14th son, Yinxiang, as the General in Charge of Distant Lands, stationing him in Xining. He mobilized large armies from Yunnan, Sichuan, and Qinghai to march into Tibet. By AD 1720, in the 59th year of Kangxi's reign, the Qing forces expelled the Dzungar troops from Tibet. Simultaneously, the Qing government officially recognized Kelsang Gyatso, who resided in Ta'er Monastery in Xining, as the sixth Dalai Lama. Subsequently, Emperor Kangxi ordered General Yanxin to escort the sixth Dalai Lama from Xining in Qinghai to Tibet for his enthronement. Kang Jiding was conferred the title of "Beile" and was responsible for the administration of Ü-Tsang (Central Tibet). Meanwhile, Poluoding was given the title "Taiji" and assigned the task of managing the Tsang (Western Tibet) region.

In AD 1726, the Qing government formalized the borders among Tibet, Sichuan, and Yunnan provinces. A stone mark was established atop Mount Ningjing to the west of Jinshajiang River. A year later, rebellion broke out in Tibet and Kang Jiding was killed. After quelling the rebels, Poluoding was appointed as the Commandery Prince of Tibet, with full responsibility of Tibetan political affairs. Starting from this year, the Qing administration also sent two Grand Minister Residents of Tibet to the region, with their seats in Lhasa and Shigatse, respectively.

After Poluoding's death, his son Zhulmert Namuzhale inherited the title of Prince. He later rebelled, attempting to establish his own dominion over Tibet but was quelled by the Dalai Lama and the local Tibetan government. Taking lessons from this incident, the Qing government decided to reform the existing administrative system in Tibet. In the 15th year of Emperor Qianlong's reign (AD 1750), they abolished the system where Princes and Beiles held power. Instead, a new system was established where the Amban (officials dispatched to Tibet, who directly governed the northern Tibetan tribes and the Dam Mongol areas) and the Dalai Lama jointly handled Tibetan affairs. Underneath this structure, a local Tibetan government called the "Kashag" was set up. It consisted of four equal-ranking officials known as Kalons. Under the leadership of the Amban and the Dalai Lama, they managed the administrative affairs of the four Tibetan regions: Wei (Ü or Central Tibet), Tsang (Western Tibet), Kham, and Ngari. Furthermore, the Qing government dispatched troops to be stationed in Tibet long-term, strengthening their rule over the region.

After the death of the 6th Panchen Lama, a conflict arose between his brother Zhongba Hutuktu and younger brother Shemarba over the uneven distribution of property. Shemarba colluded with the Gorkha troops of Nepal to invade Tibet. Emperor Qianlong once again dispatched troops to Tibet, driving out the invading Gorkha forces. In order to consolidate its rule over Tibet, in the 58th year of Emperor Qianlong's reign (AD 1793), the Qing government promulgated the "29-Article Ordinance for the More Efficient Governing of Tibet." This ordinance explicitly specified that the Amban's status in Tibet was equal to that of the Dalai Lama and the Panchen Erdeni. The reincarnations of the Dalai Lama, Panchen Lama, and other high lamas were to be determined under the supervision of the Amban through a method called the "Golden Urn Lottery." This process involves placing the names of the final candidates into a golden urn and drawing lots to make the final decision. Additionally, the ordinance provided stipulations regarding border military defense, foreign affairs, fiscal taxation, and the upkeep and management of monasteries. This was a significant measure taken by the Qing central government to strengthen its control over the local Tibetan government. From then on, the political power of the Amban in Tibet was further consolidated, and the equal religious and political statuses of the Dalai Lama and the Panchen Erdeni were further established. For over a century after that, the principles set by this ordinance served as the blueprint for the administrative system and regulations in Tibet.

However, in AD 1840, during the era of the Daoguang Emperor, Kashmiri tribes invaded the region of Ladakh in Tibet's Ali District. In AD 1846, the British occupied Kashmir and Ladakh. In AD 1890, the British government forced its Qing counterpart to sign the Convention of Calcutta, which drew the border lines between Tibet and Sikkim. The Qing government had to cede land south of Chunpi in Tibet to Sikkim; the Qing also agreed that Sikkim was a protectorate of the Great Britain.

(2) Grand Minister Superintendent of Qinghai

In the early years of the Qing Dynasty, the Heshuote Mongol tribe from the western part of the desert, under the pressure of the Zhungar Mongol tribe, migrated from Xinjiang to the northern part of Qinghai. Subsequently, the Heshuote tribe accepted official titles from the Qing government. During the reign of Emperor Kangxi, the Qing government quelled the Galdan rebellion. Taking advantage of the situation, Galdan's nephew, Cewang Alabtan, annexed the Heshuote tribe in Qinghai and incited Prince Lobzang Danjin of the Heshuote to rise up against the Qing in the first year of Emperor Yongzheng (AD 1723), launching a rebellion.

In October of Yongzheng's first year (AD 1723), the rebel forces first launched attacks in areas surrounding Xining Prefecture. At the same time, monks from monasteries near Xining, under the instigation of Lobzang Danjin, also rebelled.

In response to the rebellion, the Qing government immediately ordered the Governor-General of Sichuan and Shaanxi, Nian Gengyao, to be the General of Fuyuan, and he mobilized troops from Sichuan and Shaanxi to station in Xining. Meanwhile, the Qing government appointed the Tidu of Sichuan, Yue Zhongqi, as the General of Fenwei to assist in military affairs. The Qing army deployed troops at multiple locations to prevent rebels from advancing and entering Tibet. Afterward, the Qing troops launched multi-pronged attacks on rebels in areas surrounding Xining. Lobzang Danjin was forced to lead his army to flee westward, and the rebellion was quickly quelled.

After the rebellion led by Lobzang Danjin was suppressed, the Qing government, taking advice from Nian Gengyao, implemented a series of remedial measures. First, in the third year of Emperor Yongzheng (AD 1725), administrative reforms were carried out in the Qinghai region: Xining Wei (military command post) was changed to Xining Prefecture, with two counties (Xining County and Nianbo County) and one Wei (Datong Wei) under its jurisdiction. Deputy General Da Nai was appointed as the first "Minister in Charge of Mongolian Affairs in Qinghai" (commonly referred to as the Qinghai Minister or Xining Minister), overseeing the administration of various Mongolian banners and Tibetan tribes in Qinghai. Then, in the sixth year of Emperor Yongzheng (AD 1728), following the Zasak system of Inner Mongolia, the Mongolian tribes in the northern part of Qinghai were organized into five divisions with twenty-nine banners. These included the Heshuote Division (with banners such as the Heshuo Front West Banner, Heshuo Front North Banner, Heshuo Upper East Banner, Heshuo Right

Central South Banner, and seventeen other banners), the Tuerhute Division (with banners like the Tuerhute Front South Banner, Tuerhute Rear South Banner, Tuerhute West Banner, and Tuerhute Central South Banner), the Choros Division (with two banners: Choros Central North Banner and Choros Right Head South Banner), the Huite Division with Huite South Banner, and the Khalkha Division with Khalkha Right South Banner. In addition, forty chieftaincies, including Yushu, were established in the southern part of Qinghai. From then on, the Qinghai region came entirely under the direct governance of the central government.

7. ULIASTAI GENERAL

In the eleventh year of Emperor Yongzheng (AD 1733), the Qing government established the Deputy General for Border Defense on the Left (also known as the Uliastai General), which oversaw the four divisions of the Khalkha Mongols in the north of the desert as well as the areas of Kobdo (present-day Jirgalangtu) and Dzungaria. It was stationed in Uliastai (now Zabkhan), commonly referred to as Outer Mongolia.

In the Mongolian nomadic areas, the Qing government adopted the method of ruling according to local customs. Modeling after the Manchu Eight Banners system and adapting it, they implemented the League and Banner system. The chief of a banner was called the Jasak, who managed military and civil affairs within the banner. Several banners combined to form a league. The league's chief was called the League Head, with both a principal and a deputy, responsible for overseeing the combined meetings of the banners and representing the emperor to supervise each banner.

The four Khalkha divisions consisted of the North Route Tüsheet Khan Division with twenty banners, the East Route Chakhar Khan Division with twenty-three banners, the West Route Zasagt Khan Division with nineteen banners, and the Middle Route Sain Noyan Khan Division with twenty-four banners. Kobdo had a ministerial counselor overseeing the Oirat and Dzungaria seventeen banners. Dzungaria, located in the northwest of the Khalkha Mongols, was divided into five banners (Kusugur, Tojin, Sarajig, Dzungaria, and Kemuqik banners) and forty-six subordinates, respectively under the Uliastai General, Zasagt Khan Division, and Sain Noyan Khan Division.

After the Second Opium War, in the third year of Emperor Tongzhi (AD 1864), Russia, through the Sino-Russian Treaty for the Delimitation of the Northwestern Frontier, annexed the northwest ten sub-regions of Dzungaria and two banners of Altai Naoer under Kobdo. Subsequent treaties, the Kobdo Boundary Treaty and the Uliastai Boundary Treaty signed in the eighth year of Emperor Tongzhi (AD 1869), further facilitated Russia's encroachments in these regions. In the ninth year of Emperor Guangxu (AD 1883), the border of Kobdo was redefined based on the Sino-Russian Beijing Treaty.

In the thirty-second year of Emperor Guangxu (AD 1906), the Qing government established the Altai Affairs Minister, stationed in Chenghua Temple, overseeing the southwestern Altai, New Tuerhute, and New Heshuote regions of Kobdo.

In AD 1911, the central 27 subordinate regions of Tannu Uriankhai were forcibly occupied by Russia, while the eastern nine subordinate regions were taken over by the Khalkha feudal lords who had declared "independence" at the time.

8. The Two Districts in Monan Mongolia

Monan Mongolia was composed of Inner Mongolia and Taoxi (套西) Mongolia (literally meaning west of the Yellow River loops). Inner Mongolia covered an area stretching from Horqin in the East to Erdos in the West. Before the Qing overthrew the Ming, the Inner Mongolian tribes had already submitted to the Qing Empire. The latter grouped them into six leagues, subordinate to the Court of Colonial Affairs. There were no leagues for the two banners in Taoxi Mongolia, who were mostly nomadic people in the region to the west of Helan Mountain.

9. Taiwan Province

As early as the Yuan Dynasty, a Military Inspectorate was established in Taiwan—responsible for the security defense of Taiwan and the Penghu Islands. By the early years of the Ming Dynasty, due to the rampant activities of Japanese pirates (often referred to as "Wokou") at sea, the Ming government abolished the Penghu

Patrol Inspectorate and evacuated the residents of the Penghu Archipelago to the mainland. Instead of curtailing the activities of the Japanese pirates, this move by the Ming government allowed the Penghu Archipelago to gradually become a stronghold for these pirates.

During the Ming Dynasty, the connection between Taiwan and the mainland was already very close, with many mainlanders crossing the sea to settle in Taiwan. Although the Ming Dynasty did not establish administrative institutions on the island, the Ming army had entered Taiwan several times while chasing "sea pirates" and designated the waters around Taiwan as a military defense area. In the second year of Tianqi (AD 1622), after the Dutch were expelled from Penghu by the Ming army for the second time, they turned their attention to Taiwan and occupied the area around Tainan. In the sixth year of Tianqi (AD 1626), the Spaniards followed in the footsteps of the Dutch and occupied the area around Taipei.

By the end of the Ming Dynasty, taking advantage of the opportunity when Zheng Zhilong (the father of Zheng Chenggong) who had established a regime around the Beigang area in central Taiwan shifted his activities from Taiwan to the mainland, the Dutch took sole control of Taiwan. In the eighteenth year of the Qing's Shunzhi reign (AD 1661), Zheng Chenggong, facing difficulties in resisting the Qing on the mainland, decided to use Taiwan as his base. Therefore, he launched an expedition from Xiamen to attack Taiwan. By the beginning of the following year, the Dutch invaders surrendered and left Taiwan. Subsequently, Zheng Chenggong and his son, Zheng Jing, established three appeasement offices in Taiwan and Penghu, along with subordinate Fu and prefecture, and founded the Zheng regime, which paid allegiance to the Southern Ming's Yongli emperor.

In the early years of the Qing, the central government was split by two opposing opinions regarding General Zheng. One was pro-pacification, and the other was pro-war. The pro-pacification side achieved a dominant position in the debate. However, after the Kangxi Emperor had quelled the rebellion of "Three Fan" (Wu Sangui, King of Pingxi; Shang Kexi, King of Pingnan; Geng Jingzhong, King of Jingnan) in Southwest China, his attitude towards the Zheng regime changed.

In AD 1681, Zheng Jing died in Taiwan, and the Zheng regime became chaotic. The Kangxi Emperor grabbed the opportunity presented. In AD 1683, he sent troops, led by General Shi Lang, to attack the island, and the grandson of General Zheng, Zheng Keshuang, surrendered.

After the destruction of the Zheng regime, two different opinions emerged on how to deal with Taiwan. Some people held that Taiwan was isolated and was beyond the reach of the Qing government, saying that it would be a waste of money and resources to send troops guarding there. Therefore, it would be better to simply abandon Taiwan Island and move its residents back to the mainland. Some people even suggested ceding Taiwan Island to the Dutch. General Shi proposed to the Emperor that Taiwan was of strategic importance. It would affect the security of Fujian, Guangdong, Jiangsu, and Zhejiang. Therefore, Taiwan must be guarded for the sake of the whole country. The Kangxi Emperor agreed to General Shi's proposal and decided to set up a garrison in Taiwan, putting it under the control of the central government. In AD 1684, the Taiwan Prefecture was established, as a subordinate to Fujian Province. The seat was located in what would be modern Tainan. Since then, Taiwan island, which had long been autonomous and managed by the local people, became an official administrative division of China.

However, since the mid-19th century, the Japanese had dedicated themselves to territorial expansion. Unfortunately, Taiwan was on their list. Their first step was to occupy Liuqiu Island to the north. In AD 1872, the Japanese forced the King of Liuqiu to accept the tittle of Regional Prince. Previously the kingdom had been a dependent country to China proper. In the following year, Japan sent officials to Beijing to make representations to the Qing government, requiring them to settle an incident that happened in AD 1874, where dozens of Liuqiu shippers were killed in a shipwreck at Langqiao, Taiwan. In AD 1874, the Japanese established a military base in Nagasaki and in the next year over 3,000 Japanese land and navy soldiers attacked Taiwan. The Japanese soldiers landed on Taiwan Island from Langqiao. The Gaoshan people, an aboriginal Taiwan tribe, fought back hard. They killed some 600 Japanese soldiers and forced them to retreat to Guishan Mountain.

Upon learning of the invasion of Taiwan by the Japanese army, the Qing government lodged a formal protest with the Japanese government. At the same time, it dispatched Shen Baozhen, the Fujian naval commissioner, as the special envoy, leading ships and troops to Taiwan under the guise of an inspection tour. The Qing also ordered Pan Wei, the Fujian governor, to assist in the matter. Facing resistance from the indigenous Taiwanese, the Japanese forces suffered significant casualties. With the reinforcement of Qing troops arriving in Taiwan, the Japanese realized that military occupation of Taiwan would be challenging. As a result, Japan shifted its strategy to diplomatic deception. With the assistance of British and American ambassadors to China, Japan eventually forced the Qing government to sign the Sino-Japanese Taiwan Special Agreement (also known as the Beijing Special Agreement). It stipulated that China would pay Japan 500,000 taels of silver as a condition for the Japanese withdrawal from Taiwan. The agreement also recognized that the indigenous Taiwanese people had "wrongly harmed Japanese citizens," and Japan's invasion was a "righteous act to protect its citizens." Later, using this as justification, Japan claimed that China had recognized the Ryukyu Islands as a Japanese vassal state. In 1879 (the fifth year of the Guangxu era), Japan formally annexed the Ryukyu Islands, abolished its kingship, and renamed it Okinawa County.

In AD 1885 (the 11th year of the Guangxu era), to strengthen its control over Taiwan, the Qing government separated Taiwan from Fujian and established it as a province. Subsequently, three prefectures were established: Taiwan, Taipei, and Tainan. Taitung remained under the jurisdiction of a direct-controlled county, and there were three administrative offices and eleven counties in total. The Governor-General of Taiwan was based in Taipei Prefecture. In AD 1895 (the 21th year of the Guangxu era), after the Qing government's defeat in the First Sino-Japanese War, it was forced to sign the unequal Treaty of Shimonoseki. Taiwan was ceded to Japan, becoming its colony. It wasn't until 1945, after the end of World War II, that Taiwan was returned to China.

BIBLIOGRAPHY

Ge, Jianxiong. *The Changes of Boundaries and Administrative Divisions in China.* Beijing: The Commercial Press, 1997.

———. *A Perspective of Chinese History: Unification and Separation.* Beijing: Sanlian Publishing House, 1994.

Gu, Jigang, and Shi Nianhai. *Change of Territories in Chinese History.* Beijing: The Commercial Press, 1938.

Guo, Hong, and Jin Runcheng. *History of Administrative Divisions in China, Vol. Ming Dynasty.* Shanghai: Fudan University Press, 2007.

Hu, Axiang. *Territories and Administrative Divisions of Six Dynasties.* Xi'an: Xi'an Map Press, 2001.

Jin, Runcheng. *Studies on Governing Divisions of Supreme Commander and Grand Coordinator in Ming Dynasty.* Tianjin: Tianjin Ancient Works Publishing House, 1996.

Li, Dalong. *Politics and Offices on the Frontiers in Western and Eastern Han Dynasties.* Harbin: Heilongjiang Education Press, 1998.

Li, Xiaojie. *General History of the Administrative Divisions in China: Pre-Qin Period.* Shanghai: Fudan University Press, 2009.

———. *Geography in the Eastern Han Dynasty.* Jinan: Shandong Education Press, 1999.

Liu, Tong. *Studies on Jimi Prefectures and Commanderies in the Tang Dynasty.* Xi'an: Northwest University Press, 1998.

Ma, Ruyan, and Ma Dazheng. *Frontier Policies in the Qing Dynasty.* Beijing: China Social Sciences Press, 1994.

Tan, Qixiang. *Atlas in Chinese History.* Beijing: SinoMaps Press, 1982–1988.

———. *Concise Atlas in Chinese History.* Beijing: SinoMaps Press, 1991.

———. *Changshui Ji (Selected Theses on Historical Geography, Part One and Two).* Beijing: People's Publishing House, 1987.

———. *Changshui Ji (Sequel).* Beijing: People's Publishing House, 1994.

Wang, Hui. *Chinese Historical Geography.* Taipei: Taiwan Student Book Press, 1984.

Yang, Yuliu. *Local Administrative Divisions in Chinese History.* Taipei: China Culture Press Committee, 1957.

Zhou, Zhenhe. *Historical Geography in Western Han Dynasty.* Beijing: People's Publishing House, 1987.

———. *General History of Chinese Culture · Local Administration Systems in China.* Shanghai: Shanghai People Publishing House, 1998.

Zhou, Yilin. *Summary of Chinese Historical Geography.* Shanghai: Shanghai Education Press, 2005.

———. *Chinese Historical Human Geography.* Beijing: China Science Publishing House, 2001.

A BRIEF CHRONOLOGY OF CHINESE HISTORY

Xia Dynasty		2070–1600 BC
Shang Dynasty		1600–1046 BC
Zhou Dynasty	Western Zhou Dynasty	1046–771 BC
	Eastern Zhou Dynasty	770–256 BC
Qin Dynasty		221–207 BC
Han Dynasty	Western Han Dynasty	206 BC–AD 25
	Eastern Han Dynasty	AD 25–220
Three Kingdoms	Kingdom of Wei	AD 220–265
	Kingdom of Shu	AD 221–263
	Kingdom of Wu	AD 222–280
Jin Dynasty	Western Jin Dynasty	AD 265–317
	Eastern Jin Dynasty	AD 317–420

Southern and Northern Dynasties	Southern Dynasties	Song Dynasty	AD 420–479
		Qi Dynasty	AD 479–502
		Liang Dynasty	AD 502–557
		Chen Dynasty	AD 557–589
	Northern Dynasties	Northern Wei Dynasty	AD 386–534
		Eastern Wei Dynasty	AD 534–550
		Northern Qi Dynasty	AD 550–577
		Western Wei Dynasty	AD 535–556
		Northern Zhou Dynasty	AD 557–581
Sui Dynasty			AD 581–618
Tang Dynasty			AD 618–907
Five Dynasties		Later Liang Dynasty	AD 907–923
		Later Tang Dynasty	AD 923–936
		Later Jin Dynasty	AD 936–947
		Later Han Dynasty	AD 947–950
		Later Zhou Dynasty	AD 951–960
Song Dynasty		Northern Song Dynasty	AD 960–1127
		Southern Song Dynasty	AD 1127–1279
Liao Dynasty			AD 907–1125
Jin Dynasty			AD 1115–1234
Yuan Dynasty			AD 1206–1368
Ming Dynasty			AD 1368–1644
Qing Dynasty			AD 1616–1912
Republic of China			1912–1949
People's Republic of China			Founded on October 1, 1949

INDEX

A

Aboriginal Office system, 181, 211
administrative division(s), 1, 4, 6, 7, 9, 10, 27, 32, 37, 48, 53–58, 62, 66, 68, 70, 71, 73, 75, 76, 77, 80, 89, 90, 91, 93, 95–97, 102, 106, 107, 111, 119, 121, 133, 140, 141, 142, 143, 145, 146, 148, 149, 154, 155, 159, 168, 169, 175, 176, 177, 179–82, 184, 191, 194, 195, 196, 200, 201, 202, 207, 213, 220, 222–25, 232, 242
Agriculture Commandery, 70
Aihui, 228, 229, 230
Ailao, 40, 51, 52
Altai Mountains, 105, 117, 185
Anhui Province, 3, 15, 28, 67, 70, 90, 91, 95, 109, 110, 133, 135, 145, 165, 171, 172, 192, 193, 194, 195, 196, 204, 220, 221, 223
An Lushan, 125, 126, 127, 129
An-Shi Rebellion, 120, 127, 128, 129, 149
Anxi Protectorate-General, 113, 116, 117, 118, 123
Ariq Böke, 185

B

Bai Juyi, 128
Ban Chao, 61, 62
Ban Yong, 62
Bechbaliq Pacification Commission, 185
Beijing, 15, 81, 121, 125, 127, 133, 150, 153, 154, 158, 159, 167, 177, 192, 193, 219, 220, 222, 228, 229, 230, 234, 235, 240, 242, 243
Bianjing (present-day Kaifeng, Henan), 132, 158, 159
Bingzhou, 56, 58, 65, 67, 72, 93, 112
Bohai Bay, 1
Bohai Sea, 3, 114
Bohai State, 127
Branch Secretariat System, 168–69

C

Cao Cao, 58, 66, 67
Cao Pi, 58, 66
Central Asia, 185, 234
Central Plains, 19, 93, 103, 104, 118, 136, 160, 169, 179, 184
Central Secretariat, 176, 179, 193
Chang'an, 59, 66, 79, 80, 83, 84, 107, 111, 112, 115, 117, 119, 122, 124, 129, 131, 142
Chengdu, 27, 66, 69, 72, 75, 80, 82, 89, 112, 120, 126, 131, 145, 152, 165, 172

Chieftain Zhizhi, 60, 61
Ci Shi, 56, 155
Colony Prefectures, Commanderies, and Counties, 89, 91, 92, 93, 94
Commandery-County system, 10, 11, 13, 15, 16, 19, 20, 25, 26, 28, 31, 32, 39, 40, 56, 57, 58, 76, 102
Commandery Governor, 26
Commandery Prince of Tibet, 236
Commission for Buddhism and Tibetan Affairs, 182

D
Dadu River, 27, 69, 127
Daifang Prefecture, 68
Dalai Lama, 235–37
Dali Kingdom, 171
Daner Prefecture, 43
Danyang Prefecture, 70
Darughachi, 178–79
Dihuafu (present-day Urumqi), 234
Dongting Lake, 76, 173
Dong Zhuo, 65
Dou Gu, 61
Dunhuang, 4, 44, 58, 87, 128, 161, 210
Dutch, 241–42

E
Eastern Han Dynasty, 47, 48, 49, 51, 53, 55, 57, 61, 65, 66, 68, 82
Eastern Jin Dynasty, 83, 84, 85, 91, 92, 93, 94, 103
East Sea, 3
Eergu'na River, 167
Emperor An of Han, 53, 54, 62, 94
Emperor Chengzu of Ming, 192, 193, 200, 210, 213, 215
Emperor Daoguang, 230
Emperor Guangwu, 46, 48–51, 61
Emperor Guangxu, 222, 225, 234, 240
Emperor He of Han, 62
Emperor Huai of Jin, 76, 80
Emperor Hui of Jin, 76, 82
Emperor Jing of Han, 35

Emperor Ling of Han, 55
Emperor Ming of Han, 50–51, 61
Emperor Ping of Han, 46
Emperor Shizu of Yuan, 181
Emperor Shun of Han, 55
Emperor Shun of Yuan, 187, 189
Emperor Taizong of Tang, 107, 108
Emperor Taizu of Ming, 195
Emperor Tongzhi, 240
Emperor Wen of Han, 33
Emperor Wen of Sui, 101, 102, 104
Emperor Wen of Wei, 68
Emperor Wu of Jin, 73–76
Emperor Wu of the Han Dynasty, 37, 39, 42, 43, 44, 56, 58, 60
Emperor Xian of Han, 58, 65, 66
Emperor Xuan of Han, 60
Emperor Xuanzong of Tang, 111, 112
Emperor Yang of Sui, 103, 104, 106
Emperor Yongzheng, 224, 226, 227, 238, 239
Empress Lü, 33

F
Fanzhen, 124, 126, 128, 129, 130, 133
Ferghana Basin, 60
fiefdom, 13, 56, 74
First Sino-Japanese War, 243
Five Capitals of the Liao Dynasty, 152
Five Dynasties, 101, 131, 132, 137, 140, 141, 149
  Later Han, 132, 134, 136
  Later Jin, 132, 133, 134, 136, 149, 152, 153, 190, 209, 219
  Later Liang, 83, 86, 131, 132, 133, 135, 136
  Later Tang, 132, 133, 134, 135, 136
  Later Zhou, 132, 134, 135, 139, 150
Five "Fu," 1, 4–6
Fu system, 111

G
Gansu Plateau, 43
Gansu Province, 4, 7, 33, 54, 66, 80, 82, 86, 87, 89, 128, 172, 222, 232
garrisons, 61, 97, 98, 99, 100, 101, 117, 126, 127, 156, 157, 203–11, 214, 215, 216

General Huo Qubing, 44
General Shi Lang, 241
General Wei Qing, 43–44
General Yue Fei, 161–63
Genghis Khan, 167, 185, 186
Goguryeo, 46, 85, 114, 122, 123
Goryeo, 107, 113, 114, 175
government-general, 112, 113, 121
Great Wall, 27, 109, 133, 150, 203, 214, 215, 217, 219
Great Wen River, 3
Guangdong Province, 26, 27, 70, 91, 104, 109, 126, 135, 145, 165, 167, 170, 172, 173, 180, 192, 193, 197, 198, 202, 203, 204, 211, 222, 223, 242
Guanghan Prefecture, 40
Guangxi Province, 26, 42, 70, 109, 110, 127, 135, 145, 165, 170, 172, 173, 180, 192, 193, 197, 198, 200, 201, 203, 204, 211, 222, 223, 226, 227
Guizhou Province, 27, 39, 40, 69, 70, 109, 110, 121, 123, 127, 135, 145, 172, 173, 181, 193, 194, 196, 201, 203, 204, 207, 211, 213, 214, 222, 223, 226, 227
Guizhou Provincial Administration Commission, 194, 214
Gu Yanwu, 195, 196

H

Hainan Island, 43, 104, 193, 198
Hami Garrison, 210
Han Dynasty, 28, 29, 32, 33, 37, 39, 40, 42, 43, 44, 46–58, 60, 61, 62, 65, 66, 68, 71, 74–76, 82, 103, 104, 107–9, 112, 113, 119, 141, 157
  Eastern Han Dynasty, 18, 46–49, 51–55, 57, 58, 61–63, 65, 66, 68, 70, 79, 82, 94, 96, 119
  Western Han Dynasty, 28, 37, 44, 46–51, 53, 54, 56, 57, 61, 68, 73–76, 104, 119, 141
Han people, 55, 70, 79, 156, 160, 187
Han River, 173
Hebei Province, 1, 65, 66, 81, 87, 114

Heilongjiang, 114, 154, 157, 158, 171, 207, 208, 228–32
Heilongjiang General, 228, 230
Henan Province, 33, 66, 84, 85, 95, 146, 193, 196, 197, 221
Hetao District, 26, 43, 106, 109
Hexi Corridor, 44, 58, 82, 86, 87, 127, 128
hierarchy, 4, 6, 9, 37, 99, 102, 113, 119, 143, 148, 166, 175, 190, 191, 198, 224
Hong Taiji (Emperor Taizong of Qing), 219
Horgos River, 234
Huai River, 3, 80, 82, 83, 90, 95, 103, 109, 135, 146, 163, 173, 194
Huan Wen, 83
Hubei Province, 3, 15, 33, 66, 67, 69, 70, 109, 110, 127, 130, 133, 135, 136, 144, 145, 147, 163, 165, 170–73, 203, 204, 220, 222, 223, 227
Huguang Province, 172, 181, 198, 204, 220, 222
Huguang Regional Military Commission, 192
Hunan Province, 3, 6, 15, 26, 42, 66, 70, 76, 109, 110, 127, 135, 145, 146, 147, 165, 170, 172, 173, 180, 194, 195, 220, 222, 223, 227

I

Ili, 105, 116, 186, 231, 232, 233, 234
Ili General, 232
Imperial Supervision Branch Office, 191
Inner Mongolia, 15, 43, 61, 81, 82, 87, 98, 99, 105, 115, 116, 152, 153, 154, 158, 167, 171, 172, 219, 231, 238, 240
Irtysh River, 117, 185

J

Japanese pirates ("Wokou"), 240, 241
Jiangnan Province, 220, 221
Jiangsu Province, 3, 15, 66, 67, 70, 71, 85, 93, 95, 109, 110, 133, 135, 145, 165, 171, 172, 193, 194, 195, 196, 220, 221, 223, 224, 242
Jiangxi Province, 3, 6, 15, 29, 42, 70, 109, 110, 135, 145, 146, 165, 170, 173, 192, 193, 198, 202, 204, 222, 223

Jiaozhi Provincial Administration Commission, 189
Jimi prefectures, 122–24, 207
Jimi protectorate-generals, 121
Jimi regional military commissions, 207
Jimi system, 52, 120, 182, 190
Jincheng Prefecture, 49, 54, 55
Ji River, 2
Jiuyuan Commandery, 27

K

Kangxi Emperor, 220, 221, 223, 228, 229, 231, 235, 236, 238, 241, 242
Khanka Lake, 230
Khungtaidschi Galdan, 231
Kingdom of Dayuan, 59, 60
Kingdom of Dian, 40
Kingdom of Linyi, 103
Kingdom of Mongolia, 167
Kingdom of Nanzhao, 127
King of Changsha, 29, 31, 33
King of Liang, 33, 35
King Ping of Zhou, 10
King Wen of Zhou, 25
King Wu of Zhou, 7, 8, 12, 25
King You of Zhou, 9
King Zhou of Shang, 7
Kobdo Boundary Treaty, 240
Kobdo (present-day Jirgalangtu), 239–40
Korean Peninsula, 27, 44–46, 68, 113, 122
Kublai Khan, 167, 169, 171, 182, 185, 186
Kyrgyzstan, 59

L

Lake Baikal, 116, 219, 228, 229
Lake Balkhash, 60, 116, 117, 234
Later Jin Dynasty, 136
Lelang Prefecture, 46, 68
Liaodong Peninsula, 46, 81, 83
Liaodong Prefecture, 44, 68
Liaodong Regional Military Commission, 192, 199
Liao Dynasty, 150–58, 176, 177

Liaoning Province, 3, 6, 15, 44, 46, 67, 81, 85, 113, 114, 121, 127, 154, 158, 171, 203, 215, 219, 231, 232
Liao River, 79, 85
Lin'an (present-day Hangzhou), 167
Lingnan region, 42, 43, 70, 109, 126, 132, 135
Li Si, 24, 25
Liu Bang (Emperor Gaozu of Han), 28–33, 43, 53
Liu Bei, 66, 69
Liu Che, 37, 39
Liupan Mountain, 55, 127
Liuqiu, 186, 187, 242
Liu Xiu, 46, 48, 61
Li Zicheng, 219, 220
Lobzang Danjin, 238
Longxi Prefecture, 49, 54, 55
Longxi Region, 43, 85
Lüliang Mountain, 55
Luoyang, 7, 10, 46, 65, 66, 80, 84, 89, 99, 111, 112, 119, 132, 142, 144, 148, 163

M

Manchu, 219, 223, 228, 239
Manchu Eight Banners system, 239
Meng'an Mouke, 160
Meng Huo, 69
Metropolitan Prefecture, 112
Ming Dynasty, 175, 187, 189, 192, 193, 194, 196–99, 202, 203, 205, 208–12, 214, 216, 219–23, 231, 235, 240, 241
Monan Mongolia, 231, 240
Mongke Qayan Khan, 167, 185
Mount Hua, 3
Mount Tai, 3
Mudan River, 228

N

Nanjing, 66, 89, 145, 165, 189, 192–96, 211, 213, 220
Nanling Mountains, 1, 26, 173
Nanyi area, 40
Nanyue Kingdom, 26, 40, 42, 43

Nerchinsk, 229, 230
Nian Gengyao, 238
Nine Frontiers, 214–16
Nine Provinces, 1, 2, 4, 6
   Jingzhou, 1, 3, 58, 66, 67, 69, 70, 76, 83, 91, 112
   Jizhou, 1, 2, 58, 67, 72, 93, 95, 215, 216
   Liangzhou, 1, 3, 56, 58, 66, 67, 68, 72, 80, 82, 83, 86, 91, 96, 104, 112, 124, 125
   Qingzhou, 1, 3, 56, 67, 72, 85, 93, 95, 144, 146
   Xuzhou, 1, 3, 56, 66, 67, 72, 85, 93
   Yangzhou, 1, 3, 56, 66, 67, 70, 76, 91, 93, 134, 145, 165, 170, 180
   Yanzhou, 1, 2, 56, 67, 72, 93
   Yongzhou, 1, 4, 58, 76, 80, 112
   Yuzhou, 1, 3, 15, 56, 58, 67, 72, 95
Nine States of Ili, 232
Ningguta General, 228
Ningguta (Ning'an), 228, 229, 230
Ningxia Hui Autonomous Region, 33
Northeast China, 228
Northern Qi Dynasty, 89, 101, 168
Northern Song Dynasty, 128, 133, 139, 144, 147, 148, 149, 151, 154, 158–62, 165, 166, 168, 176, 186
Northern Wei Dynasty, 79, 80, 84, 85, 87, 88, 89, 91, 95–100, 103, 168
Northern Zhou Dynasty, 89, 101, 102, 104, 105
North Korea, 27, 44, 114, 154
North Zhili, 220
Nurgan Garrison, 207–8
Nurgan Regional Military Commission, 190, 193, 208, 209
Nurhaci, 209, 219
Nüzhen, 133, 156–58, 160, 199, 207, 208, 219

P
Pacification Commissions, 179, 180, 181, 183–85, 210, 211, 213
Pamir Plateau, 60
Panchen Erdeni, 237

Penghu Islands, 186–88, 222, 240
Penghu Military Inspectorate, 186–88
People's Republic of China, 196, 198
Persia, 117, 124
Piling Prefecture, 70
Poyang Lake, 3
prefectural ministers, 113, 124, 126, 129–32, 141, 155
   Anxi Prefectural Minister, 125
   Beiting Prefectural Minister, 125
   Chengde Prefectural Minister, 129
   Fanyang Prefectural Minister, 125
   Hedong Prefectural Minister, 125, 134, 136
   Hexi Prefectural Minister, 124, 125
   Huainan Prefectural Minister, 134
   Huaixi Prefectural Minister, 130
   Jiannan Prefectural Minister, 126
   Lingnan Prefectural Minister, 126, 135
   Longyou Prefectural Minister, 126
   Lulong Prefectural Minister, 129
   Pinglu Prefectural Minister, 125
   Shuofang Prefectural Minister, 125
   Weibo Prefectural Minister, 129
   Xiangwei Prefectural Minister, 130
Prefecture-Commandery-County system, 66, 73, 89
protectorate-generals, 113, 116, 118, 119, 121, 122, 124
Provincial Administration Commissions, 190–94, 199–202, 223, 224
Provincial Surveillance Commissions, 190, 191, 199, 200, 201
Pyongyang, 27, 114

Q
Qiang, 49, 53, 54, 55, 79, 84, 128
Qianlong Emperor, 223, 227, 230, 231
Qianwei Prefecture, 39, 40
Qin Dynasty, 23, 24, 27–29, 31, 32, 42–44, 84, 86
Qing Dynasty, 173, 187, 195, 196, 214, 219, 222–25, 227, 229, 233, 235, 238
Qinghai Lake, 86, 106, 109, 210

Qinghai Province, 86, 183
Qin Shi Huang, 23, 25, 26, 28
Qiong Kingdom, 40
Qionglai Mountain, 39
Qiuci, 53, 62, 83, 117

R

rebellions, 8, 31, 39, 40, 42, 55, 65, 69, 79, 80, 97, 100, 107, 127, 128, 130, 131, 144, 148, 174, 189, 200, 206, 214, 226, 236, 238, 241
Regional Inspector, 56, 57, 103, 159, 160
Regional Military Commissions, 190, 191, 199, 201, 202, 206, 207, 211
Russian invaders, 228
Russo-Japanese War, 230
Ryukyu Islands, 243

S

Sanggan River, 55, 80, 81
Second Opium War, 230, 240
Secretariat, 168–72, 176, 179, 182, 191–93
"Seizing Power through a Banquet," 140
Shaanxi Province, 1, 2, 3, 4, 6, 7, 11, 15, 28, 33, 55, 67, 69, 80, 84, 87, 90, 93, 95, 109, 111, 129, 133, 136, 137, 143, 145, 146, 159, 163, 165, 170, 172, 173, 192, 193, 200, 203, 204, 207, 210, 215, 221, 222, 223, 232, 238
Shandong Peninsula, 44
Shandong Province, 1, 3, 66, 85, 175, 192, 221
Shang Dynasty, 6, 12
Shanxi Province, 11, 12, 33, 66, 80, 221
Shanxi Regional Military Commission, 192
Shaoxing Agreement, 163
Shen Baozhen, 242
Shengjing (present-day Shenyang, Liaoning), 219, 232
Shenli Prefecture, 40, 42
Shi Jingtang, 133, 136, 149, 152
Shu-Guo, 53–54
Shu-Han, 67, 69, 72
Shu Kingdom, 72
Shunzhi Emperor, 219, 220, 228, 235
Shuofang Commandery, 43, 55

Shu Prefecture, 39, 40, 42
Shuzi River, 219
Sichuan Province, 3, 6, 15, 27, 28, 33, 39, 40, 66, 69, 82, 83, 90, 95, 109, 110, 121, 126, 127, 129, 136, 145, 165, 170, 172, 173, 180, 181, 183, 184, 189, 192, 193, 194, 196, 201, 203, 204, 207, 210, 214, 222, 223, 226, 227, 236, 238
Sikkim, 237
Sima Qian, 23
Sima Rui, 75, 89, 90
Sima Xiangru, 39
Sima Yan, 72, 73, 76
Sima Yi, 73, 75
Sino-Japanese Taiwan Special Agreement (Beijing Special Agreement), 243
Sino-Russian Beijing Treaty, 240
Sixteen Kingdoms, 79, 80, 83, 88, 89, 92
Song Dynasty, 59, 93, 95, 128, 136, 139–44, 146, 147, 148, 149, 151, 153, 158, 159, 162, 165, 166–68, 172, 176, 190, 197, 199
Songhua River, 114, 157, 208, 228
South China, 69, 89, 123, 150, 162, 228
Southern and Northern Dynasties, 72, 89, 102
Southern Song Dynasty, 2, 139, 144, 149, 161–67, 169, 170, 185, 186
South Zhili, 220
Spring and Autumn Period, 9, 10, 11, 157
state farming, 232
Sui Dynasty, 76, 94, 95, 101–7, 118, 121, 168, 186
Sun Quan, 58, 66, 69, 70, 186

T

Tacheng, 234
Taihu Lake, 3, 195, 196
Taipei Prefecture, 243
Taiping Movement, 223
Taishou, 40, 53, 55, 60, 69, 71, 87, 94, 97, 103, 104, 108, 198
Taiwan, 186, 187, 222, 240–43
Tajikistan, 59

Tang Dynasty, 93, 107–14, 115, 117–24, 127, 128, 131, 133, 134, 135, 137, 140, 148, 149, 168, 174, 207
Taoxi Mongolia, 240
Temurtu Lake, 234
Ten Kingdoms, 101, 131, 132, 137, 140
  Chu, 135
  Former Shu, 132, 136
  Jingnan, 132, 136
  Later Shu, 89, 132, 134, 136, 139
  Min, 135
  Northern Han, 132, 133, 136, 137, 139, 140, 150
  Southern Han, 132, 136, 139
  Southern Tang, 132, 134, 135, 136, 139
  Wu, 134
  Wuyue, 135
"Three Fan," 241
Three Kingdoms, 65–68, 71, 72, 73, 77, 104, 168, 186
Tianshan Mountains, 60, 61, 117, 185, 231
Tibet, 168, 182, 183, 184, 207, 210, 211, 235, 236, 237, 238
Tiemuzhen, 167
"Tongpan," 141
Touxia Garrison system, 155–56
Transport Commissioner, 142, 143, 155, 159
Treaty of Beijing, 230, 234
Treaty of Burinsk, 229
Treaty of Ili, 234
Treaty of Kyakhta, 229
Treaty of Nerchinsk, 229, 230
Treaty of Shimonoseki, 243
Treaty of Tacheng, 234
Treaty of Tanyuan, 152, 156
Tubo, 118, 125, 126, 127, 128, 137, 182, 183, 210
"Tui En," 37, 39
Tujue, 104–7, 113, 115, 116, 117, 121–23, 125
  Eastern Tujue, 105, 106, 113, 115, 121, 122
  Western Tujue, 105–7, 116
Tumen River, 208, 230
Turkic Khanates, 104
Turpan, 60, 62, 83, 128, 184, 190, 210
Tuyuhun, 86, 88, 106, 128

21 Regions of the Yongjia Period, 72, 76, 77

U
Uliastai Boundary Treaty, 240
Uliastai General, 239
Uliastai (now Zabkhan), 239–40
Ussuri River, 154, 208, 228, 229
Uzbekistan, 59, 234

V
vassal kings, 25, 29, 31, 32, 33, 37, 48–51, 72, 75
Vietnam, 26, 27, 42, 43, 70, 103, 109, 118, 168, 173, 189, 222

W
Wang Mang, 46, 47, 61
Wanyan Aguda, 158, 160
Warring States Period, 4, 10, 14–17, 19, 20, 21, 29, 43, 44, 53
Wei Kingdom, 72, 76
Wei River Alluvial Plain, 27
Wenshan Prefecture, 40, 42
Western Jin Dynasty, 55, 71–76, 81, 89, 96
Western Regions, 44, 58–63, 68, 82, 86, 87, 106, 113, 115, 116, 122, 125, 210, 231, 235
Western Xia, 128, 145, 152, 158, 160, 161, 167, 169, 170, 172
Woluduo system, 155, 157
World War II, 243
Wudi River, 230
Wudu Prefecture, 40
Wu Kingdom, 72, 76, 104
Wulanbutong (present-day Chifeng, Inner Mongolia), 231
Wuling Mountains, 76
Wusun, 59, 60, 68

X
Xia Dynasty, 7
Xianbei, 54, 55, 79, 81, 85, 86, 89, 97, 98, 99
Xianfeng Emperor, 223
Xiang Prefecture, 42
Xiang Yu, 28, 29, 43

Xin Dynasty, 46, 47
Xingsheng, 169
Xingtai system, 168
Xinjiang, 59–62, 68, 83, 106, 107, 109, 116, 125, 128, 168, 171, 184, 185, 186, 231, 232, 234, 235, 236, 238
Xiongnu, 26, 27, 39, 40, 43, 44, 49, 53, 55, 58–63, 79, 80, 87, 100, 104, 160

Y

Yalu River, 208, 215
Yang Shangxi, 102
Yangtze River, 66, 70, 76, 83, 93, 103, 109, 110, 134, 173, 194
Yellow River, 1–4, 6, 11, 26, 27, 43, 55, 79, 80, 82, 84, 85, 99, 109, 127, 146, 151, 161, 162, 163, 171, 172, 173, 184, 196, 240
Yellow Sea, 3, 68
Yellow Turban Rebellion, 55, 57, 65
Yelü Abaoji, 152, 153
Yelü Deguang, 133, 152
Ying Zheng (King of Qin), 21, 23, 24
Yin Mountains, 27, 80, 107, 115
Yizhou, 40, 51, 52, 56, 58, 66, 69, 72, 76, 80, 82, 83, 91, 112, 126, 151, 152, 186
Yizhou Commandery, 40, 51
Yongchang Commandery, 51, 53
Yuan Dynasty, 167, 169, 170, 171, 173–79, 182, 184, 185, 186, 187, 189, 190, 193, 197, 198, 199, 205, 240
Yuexi Prefecture, 40

Yuezhi Kingdom, 59
Yu Gong, 1, 2, 4, 58, 77
Yunnan Province, 27, 39, 40, 52, 69, 83, 109, 118, 121, 123, 127, 168, 170, 171, 173, 180, 181, 189, 190, 192, 193, 194, 201, 203, 204, 207, 211, 220, 222, 223, 226, 227, 236
Yu the Great, 1, 4, 6

Z

Zhang Qian, 58, 59
Zhao Kuangyin, 139, 140, 141, 150
Zhao Tuo, 42, 43
Zhejiang Provincial Administration Commission, 193
Zheng Chenggong, 241
Zheng Jing, 241
Zheng regime, 241–42
Zheng Zhilong, 241
Zhili Province, 220
"Zhixian," 141, 225
"Zhizhou," 141, 148, 199, 225
"Zhou Bang," 7
Zhou Dynasty, 7–10, 102, 104, 134
    Eastern Zhou Dynasty, 10
    Western Zhou Dynasty, 6, 7, 9, 32
Zhuge Liang, 69
Zhulmert Namuzhale, 236
Zhuya Prefecture, 43, 104
Zhu Yuanzhang, 189, 195, 196, 205, 210, 211, 212
Zuo Zongtang, 234

ABOUT THE CHIEF EDITOR

GE JIANXIONG, PhD, born in 1945, is a professor at the Center for Historical Geographical Studies of Fudan University in Shanghai, China. He is also a doctoral supervisor and Director of Fudan University Library. His research focuses on historical geography, population history, migration history, and cultural history.

Selected publications of Professor Ge include:

- *History of the Population in China*, editor-in-chief and author of Vol. I
- *History of Migrations in China*, editor-in-chief and author of Vol. I & II
- *History of the Development of Population in China*
- *A Perspective of Chinese History: Unification and Separation*
- *A Short History of Cartography in Ancient China*
- *The Changes of Boundaries and Administrative Divisions in China*
- *The Natural Environment for Human Being in the Future*
- *Biography of Tan Qixiang*, Vol. I & II

ABOUT THE AUTHOR

LI XIAOJIE, PhD, born in 1965, is a professor and doctoral supervisor at the Center for Historical Geographical Studies of Fudan University in Shanghai, China. Li received his PhD in History from Fudan University in 1996. From 1988 to 1991, he worked as an assistant research fellow in the Palace Museum in Beijing. From 2001 to 2002, he was a visiting scholar at the Harvard-Yenching Institute in Boston, U.S.A.

Selected publications of Professor Li include:

- *Political Geography in the Eastern Han Dynasty*,
- *General History of the Administrative Divisions in China: Pre-Qin Period*,
- *General History of the Administrative Divisions of China: Qin and Han Dynasties (co-author)*,
- *General History of the Administrative Divisions of China: Five Dynasties and Ten Kingdoms*,
- *Administrative Divisions in Dynastic China*,
- *Explanatory Notes on Maps for Records of Rivers (Chief Editor)*.